HARVEST AT RANDOM

HARVEST AT RANDOM

Bill de Havilland

ATHENA PRESS
LONDON

HARVEST AT RANDOM
Copyright © Bill de Havilland 2004

ISBN 1 84401 279 4

First Published in 2004 by
ATHENA PRESS
Queen's House, 2 Holly Road
Twickenham TW1 4EG
United Kingdom

Printed for Athena Press

CONTENTS

CHAPTER I

In the Beginning

It all began on the Friday before Armistice Sunday in 1935 when I was born; although, so I am told, only just, as I needed a hefty slug of brandy to get me breathing. I weighed in at eight pounds and was breast-fed for a bare two months, after which Mother left me with her parents and returned to Egypt. My father was a regular soldier with the Royal Horse Artillery stationed in Cairo and, as was the norm in those days, was allowed his wife with him. A weekend away in Shepherd's Hotel was the excuse for bringing me into the world some nine months later!

I had always wondered why I enjoyed such an exceptionally close and loving relationship with my grandmother. Clearly she had an even greater influence over my pre-memory days than I realised. Her house, the Hall, was to be my spiritual home for the next half-century. Horkesley Hall, in Little Horkesley, was acquired by my great-grandfather at the turn of the century and in it my grandfather and his four siblings grew up, only two of whom I was to know.

'Uncle Hugh', as we all called him, became Bishop of Mauritius, a post he held for nearly thirty years. Quite why he was sent to Mauritius, history never related. A kindly man who never married, he eventually returned to England, leaving his beloved Mauritius behind; I don't think he was ever really happy afterwards, as not only did he find no particular motivation for ministering in England but I suspect the loss of his colonial lifestyle was a major factor. His brother, Uncle Malcolm, who died at a relatively young age having been dropped on his head in childhood, I never knew. The only record of him at the Hall was a couple of sties where he kept his pigs!

Uncle Franco was killed in the Boer War but left behind fascinating relics which I found one day in the coke store; an interesting collection of Zulu War memorabilia. There was one sister, who went by the unusual name of Mouffa, I never knew her real name, but she had two sons, Barry and Sandy. Uncles Malcolm and Franco, as far as I know, died childless. As in most families, there were numerous cousins – some close, some very distant – who appeared or were referred to from time to time. By the time I came on the scene, the Hall was occupied by my grandfather and grandmother only, although it was also the UK base for my own parents. Grandpa, as we all called him, was General Manager of the Sun Insurance Office and was reasonably well off, as was my grandmother's family. Granny came from Charlton, near Banbury, and when courting, used to come in a horse-drawn carriage all the way to Horkesley. I have inherited the front hooves of one of the carriage horses, mounted as brass doorstops, which today cause much amusement to visitors. She used to stay for at least a week at a time. Indeed, most of the early entries in the visitors' book were hers. Her family owned a herd of Jersey cows which eventually ended up at Horkesley and were destined to have considerable influence on my life. I truthfully remember almost nothing of my early years there – although much anecdotal evidence has been passed down – until the arrival of my brother John, some two and a half years after my own birth.

I clearly remember being introduced to him whilst he was lying on a pair of scales within the wicker basket; I grabbed a poker from the fireplace and was about to do him in when the poker was wrenched from my hand! From that moment on my recollections of life become clearer.

The Hall was a medium-sized country house, constructed, as many of them were, over a number of years, but mostly in the late eighteenth and early nineteenth centuries. The small estate which went with it consisted of twenty-five acres of parkland, five acres of formal garden, including two large ponds, and two acres of walled garden.

During the trough of the agricultural depression, my grandfather, being a City of London man, purchased a parcel of adjoining land amounting to some two hundred and twenty acres. Seventy-five years on, what has changed? This farm was run as an independent 'tax loss' operation with its own labour force. Additionally, some 2,500 acres of land were hired from neighbouring farmers for the shooting rights.

The house was run by five live-in domestic staff, four full-time gardeners, one chauffeur – who had earlier been a coachman but subsequently learned to drive a car – two gamekeepers and about half a dozen part-time staff. There was also an assortment of nannies and minders, usually two at anyone time. I can still remember all the staff names and all their faces, but the two who had the greatest influence on my life were Agnes, officially the parlour maid, unofficially assistant nanny, but who all her life took my side in any argument involving John, the treasured younger brother; and Bert Thurgood, officially head gardener, unofficially outside minder and tutor.

For the first five years of my life the two-acre walled garden and greenhouses were to be my playpen. This unquestionably was where my love of horticulture came from.

There were others too who influenced my life: Agnes' mother, Mrs Patrick, head housemaid, who like my wife today, would complain that I only had to stand still to make a mess; and Williams, the footman/butler who always wore a green baize apron for duties such as cleaning silver and other pantry occupations. He only ever took it off to come into the 'private' part of the house; Wick, alongside whom I would walk for hours as he pulled the roller across the lawn, or whom I would 'help' sweep up the leaves; and Ted Brown, now chauffeur but formerly coachman, whose very bowed legs intrigued me.

It was from them as much as anyone that I learned of my

mother's and her two brothers' younger days. All three of my grandfather's children were born in the first ten years of the century. My two uncles, Francis and David, both went to Marlborough College and then to Cambridge University, where their father had preceded them. My mother was never formally educated at all! She had a governess shared with a friend, Christian Stirling. Such education as she had took place at the Hall until she was old enough to go down the traditional route of the Paris finishing school. This seems extraordinary in the twenty-first century but was absolutely normal in those days. Even more extraordinarily, in the previous generation my grandfather had a friend at Cambridge who had been 'up' for seven years and never read anything at all; he was just there to enjoy university life. Whilst not approving of this educational bias, I feel at least 'Old Watty', as my grandfather called him, was honest enough to admit he was reading nothing, and did pay for himself to be there. My father's family, related to the aircraft company founders, whilst not being hard up could hardly be described as wealthy. The origin of the family was in Normandy, and the earliest de Havillands arrived in England at the Norman Conquest.

Over the years it has split into many branches, but its most famous 'sons' have to be Sir Geoffrey de Havilland, pioneer aviator and founder of the aircraft company bearing his name, and Olivia de Havilland, currently the only surviving member of the cast of the pre-war blockbuster film *Gone with the Wind*.

My paternal grandfather was a retired Eton housemaster, whose brother, my great-uncle Reggie, was Eton's famous rowing coach in the early 1900s, and also a housemaster there. My paternal grandmother came from northern stock; I believe her father was a senior manager at Cammell Lairds, the well-known shipbuilders. She was a hard woman, reflecting no doubt her upbringing in the harsh industrial climate of the North. They lived at the Manor House in Great Horkesley, to which was attached a small farm of about sixty acres.

I suppose there was almost a certain inevitability in that era about the ensuing courtship of the son of the Manor House and the daughter of the Hall in adjoining villages. However, the path of true love was not a smooth one; Mother always told me that as a girl she was none too keen, but Father was nothing if not persistent, and by the age of nineteen she had succumbed. However, her father forbad the marriage until she was twenty-one. This eventually took place a month after her twenty-first birthday.

Father had followed in his father's footsteps and was educated at Eton College. Although living there at the time were both his father and uncle, who were housemasters, his own tutor and housemaster was C H K Martin, who also happened to be his godfather. He always told me his Eton career was relatively undistinguished and he had frequent quarrels with authority. There must be a rogue gene in the family, as both he and I were always quarrelling with authority – not just at school, either. However, neither he nor I had any problem at all accepting military authority. After he left Eton he went to 'The Shop' at Woolwich, where he eventually passed out and became a junior officer in the Royal Horse Artillery (RHA).

We were all brought up on tales of how harsh life was there. By the time Father was in his eighties, I took him on a trip down memory lane, including a return to 'The Shop' some sixty years later. I could not begin to square talk of hardship and deprivation with what I saw. The silver collection alone was breathtaking and the whole ambience was, to say the least, very different to my naval experiences. Reluctantly, he agreed that perhaps it hadn't been too bad in retrospect. The only real difference he could detect was that in his day you rang a bell if you needed a drink in the mess; nowadays you got your own!

I know that from there he went to the cavalry school at Weedon, where his instructor was one Arthur Baillie, who I was to meet up with, together with his wife, Rosemary, some forty years later when I moved to Norfolk. She was a remarkable lady, who while well into her seventies was still competing in the show jumping arena. She was also an official British Show Jumping Association course builder, and could be seen puffing on her pipe (one of only two pipe-smoking women I was to encounter), accompanied always by her black Labrador, in Norfolk's arenas prior to the Agricultural Shows widely held at that time.

Father returned from Egypt in 1938 and was posted to the Royal Horse Artillery barracks in Norwich, from which the modern Barrack Street gets its name. We lived at Bowthorpe Hall, now the Bell School of Languages, but still spent a lot of time at Horkesley. The only vivid memory of Bowthorpe was being shut in the tennis court with my cousin Sally to keep us out of mischief. Half a century later that tennis court still remained unchanged.

The summers of 1938 and '39 were spent at Frinton, where my grandparents, in common with many other families, rented a house, usually for about a month. I used to get so excited driving down Connaught Avenue as the sea came into view and would jump up and down on the back seat of the car to the annoyance of both my mother and grandmother. The luggage would be unloaded and Nanny and I would immediately find our beach hut, get out the shrimping nets and spend what seemed for ever in those sunny days, trolling for shrimps. As far as I can recall, what we caught we ate. Shrimps, rather than prawns, are still my preference.

Our last visit in 1939 was memorable for the construction of the anti-invasion defences which were taking place. I remember being told what they were for, but the concept of war to a four-year-old was impossible to grasp in the days before mass media communication, *Star Wars* games and so on.

However, the message of impending doom came through loud and clear, and even at that tender age I think I was conscious of a golden age coming to an end.

Within two months of our admittedly somewhat restricted seaside paddles, I was in a room full of people at the Hall listening to Neville Chamberlain's broadcast of the declaration of war with Germany. The construction of an elaborate air raid shelter in the garden heightened awareness of all not being well.

Throughout that autumn I vaguely remember talk of a 'phoney war', not of course knowing what it meant. Father no longer being around did not really register, as I rarely saw him anyway.

The winter brought heavy snowfalls and a vivid memory is of the garden staff armed with large wooden grain shovels getting the snow off the flat roof, and these huge dollops of snow crashing to earth. I learned subsequently that snowfalls on flat roofs are potentially bad news, and have managed to avoid flat-roofed property ever since.

In retrospect it seems that that autumn and winter were a sort of settling-in period, not just militarily, but for the whole population. By the springtime, change was in the air and the talk was of evacuation, especially out of London, and away from the part of the east coast which would be over flown by the *Luftwaffe* en route to London and the Midlands, and which were at greatest risk of invasion by the Germans.

The offices of the Sun Insurance Company were moved out of Threadneedle Street in the City to Wrest Park in Bedfordshire, now home to the National Institute of Agricultural Engineering. My grandparents, Mother, and us two boys moved out of the Hall, with a skeleton domestic staff, to Fielden House near to Wrest Park. The war was now hotting up, with Hitler's invasion of the Low Countries and the downfall of France. Father, who was with the BEF, was evacuated from Dunkirk, but whilst waiting to be taken off the beaches was shot in the leg. During the time he was in hospital we lived at Edgebarrow Lodge at Crowthorne, very near to Wellington College, the boys' public school. A forest fire broke out in the woods behind the house; never ever shall I forget the smell and fear associated with this phenomenon. I cried and cried as these tall trees were consumed in this frightening, crackling inferno.

After Father's recovery in hospital he was posted to the Staff College, and Mother and we two moved into a house in Camberley. At this stage food shortages were not taking too serious a hold, although rationing was in force.

Whilst at Camberley I underwent the then obligatory removal of tonsils and adenoids. A very vivid recollection of this remains. The operation was to be performed on the kitchen table – as seemingly it always was – and on the appointed day I was deprived of my breakfast, which even in those days was my most important meal of the day. I was chloroformed by way of an anaesthetic, and a most unpleasant experience it was! It's interesting to reflect on 'fashionable' medical treatment and how it has changed. In those days circumcision, and removal of tonsils and adenoids, were almost obligatory. Later the fashion changed to braces on teeth, and nowadays many children are made to wear glasses. The cynic might think that this is simply a money-making issue for the predominantly private sector…

However, after a couple of days I could eat again and life improved. All this time, although still under six years old, I was becoming increasingly conscious of all the talk of invasion. Food shortages were suddenly beginning to pinch, and I remember especially the queues at the bakery and the triumph of coming away with penny loaves of Hovis bread. These were not like the rolls we know today but were mini-loaves. At about this time we acquired a full-time nanny, Nanny Forty, who remained with us until we both went to boarding school. My mother joined the Red Cross and drove an ambulance for the entire time we were in Camberley.

CHAPTER II

A Wartime Childhood

At the same time that we moved to Camberley the war in the air was increasing, and although it was not realised at the time, the period became known as the Battle of Britain. I certainly was aware of aerial combat and would watch the air battles between the RAF and *Luftwaffe* on a daily basis. Cheers rose as a plane with the black cross of the *Luftwaffe* came spiralling downwards, usually to explode in the distance, where we could see the columns of black smoke. But we felt sadness when a plane wearing the red, white and blue roundels of the RAF met the same fate. Of course, as children we had no appreciation of the human suffering, the horrific burns and blindness, not even of the death that came with each 'victory'. I suppose most of my generation in Southern and Eastern England were used to the unmistakeable noise of the Rolls-Royce Merlin engines and the rattle of cannon and machine-gun fire. When the Battle of Britain memorial flight takes to the air today, most of us, almost to a man, will leave whatever we are doing to gaze upwards with nostalgic memories.

We would listen to the regular news bulletins when the day's 'score' would be read out by such luminaries as Alvar Liddell and Frank Phillips, much as today's football scores are. History tells us these were wildly exaggerated by both sides but they served to boost a sagging morale.

By the end of September the Battle of Britain had been won by the RAF, and the Germans, having failed to destroy the RAF and their airfields, called off their invasion plans. Almost the last act of the defeated (though not for long) *Luftwaffe* was to drop a parachute mine right on top of our little church at Horkesley. The church of Saints Peter and Paul, in which I had been christened, was no more.

The blast destroyed the Beehive pub and large sections of the Priory as well as blowing out all the windows in the Hall. Visiting it shortly afterwards and seeing the shredded curtains in 'my' room, I thought, I am glad I wasn't here then, as I wouldn't be here now. This was my first direct contact with the reality of war.

The Blitz of London followed, where the German bombers would fly up the Thames Estuary, over the docks and the East End and carpet-bomb the area. Although Camberley was well away from the main target area we got used to the wailing sirens heralding another raid, and could hear the distant *crump* of bombs falling on London. Eventually the 'all clear' would bring a brief respite before the next raid. There were identification drawings of the various enemy aircraft, presumably published for the use of the Royal Observer Corps, which somehow came into our possession, and we became adept at identifying the various types, including Dorniers, Heinkels, Junkers and Messerschmitts, as well as our own Spitfires and Hurricanes.

Occasionally we ventured up to London's West End by train in the morning, when there were fewer raids, and returned in the evening. We once got caught in a raid and headed for the nearest tube station for shelter. Many of these were fitted out with bunks, but in the main, the platforms were covered in blankets and personal belongings, as for some people this was 'home'. If the homeward train was delayed or non-existent, we could get caught in one of these early evening raids.

Once Clapham Junction was being bombed, and we spent what seemed like all night marooned in total darkness in the train, with the *crump* of exploding bombs all around us. By this time I was developing a consciousness of bombs equating with death and destruction, and during our enforced delay on the train I was frantically worried whether my little girlfriend,

Biddy, was alright. I was so relieved to see her the next day, but never dared confess my concern, as I was sure she would laugh at me!

When my mother had told me earlier that I had to start going to school, the idea did not appeal to me at all. I was physically dragged downstairs, kicking and screaming, for my first day at the PNEU school. I was not a model pupil. So awful was I that for a time I was on a one-to-one teacher ratio. Nanny, John and I would walk through the woods to school, and one morning to our great excitement we came across an Me109 which had been shot down. From it I retrieved a small piece of wreckage as a souvenir, which the other two took home for me.

We had heard a plane crash in these woods during the previous evening, and as the wreckage was still smoking this must have been it. We didn't stop to look to see if the pilot was still in the cockpit; Nanny ushered us away. We learned subsequently that he wasn't, and were rather relieved that we hadn't left an injured man, even if he was only a German.

Food – and above all petrol – was becoming very scarce now, as the Battle of Britain was followed by the equally significant Battle of the Atlantic. The German submarine fleet was sinking our merchant ships faster than they could be replaced, and the island of Great Britain was gradually being starved into submission. This battle was to take another four years to win, this time by the Royal Navy. Strangely, although this was a far more titanic struggle, with far more lives risked and lost over a far longer period of time, it never had the acclaim and reputation it so deserved.

Unsurprisingly, in Camberley there was a considerable camaraderie within the service families, which most of the time was enjoyable. One side effect, however, was not: the garrison children's tea party, held each Tuesday at The Pantiles near Bagshot. This could only be described as a horror event; I was always sick, and even today when I pass The Pantiles I feel slightly queasy. Was this the starting point for my hearty dislike of parties? Unfortunately it was also the venue for dancing classes, at which I was so inept my mother was asked not to bring me any more.

After eighteen months I left Miss Webb and her PNEU school and was put in the charge of Mr Love at Cheswyk House School, where I remained for another two years. I have no real memories of either of these seats of learning except that I loathed them both.

The Camberley area is wonderful for its rhododendrons and azaleas, and in the late spring and early summer I spent every available hour with Nanny in the woods. By the late summer and autumn, though, the flies and mosquitoes were unbearable, unless you were smothered in fly repellent. The one Nanny used on us had the most heavenly scent, which in later life I learned to be citronella. I can never smell it even today without my memory going straight back to Frimley where it was first applied. The association of smell and places is very strong for me, and even the Embassy Darts Competition at the Lakeside Country Club at Frimley brings the scent of citronella to my nostrils.

I couldn't wait for the holidays, which were usually spent at Fielden House with my grandparents, and when possible my mother came too. During these holidays I learnt to fish in the lakes at Wrest Park, saw my first Chinese pheasant there and was fascinated by the orangery in the gardens.

Around this time I began to acquire the work ethic and my interest in the countryside, nature in general and farming in particular, began to develop. I 'helped' in the construction of the Anderson air raid shelter and once it was constructed, lived in it day and night, not out of necessity but out of a spirit of adventure. My specialist pastime was heating severely rationed chocolate up on a candle and mixing relatively plentiful cornflakes in with it; as delicious then as they are today – or at least to me.

I tried to be generally useful most of the time and 'helped' my grandmother on the other end of a bow saw, cutting up firewood, and assisted in the war effort by 'pulling' flax. The latter task was very hard on young hands. My grandmother was a passionate knitter and would make balaclava helmets, which seemed to be her speciality, by the hundred for our forces. I was always called upon to hold the skein of new wool, which was then wound off into balls for the knitting process. It was she who taught me to knit, a skill of somewhat dubious merit which I still have today!

By late Summer of 1942 Father had left the Staff College and been posted to North Africa with the Eighth Army to serve with General – later Field Marshal – Montgomery. Two incidents remain indelibly printed on my mind. The first was a letter home from Father enclosing an Eighth Army badge, and the second was after news of the victory at El Alamein came through, and Father safely with it; Mother invited us to share a glass of sherry with her to celebrate. I was just coming up to my seventh birthday and my brother was not yet five. He took the sherry but I opted for one of Father's cigarettes. He always smoked Chesterfields or Camels; from then on I was hooked, and to my shame I have smoked American cigarettes ever since. There is even a letter from school before I could do joined-up writing asking my mother to send some cigarettes! She declined but I always managed to get enough throughout my schooldays. I am not proud of this weakness at all, but to this day I still love my tobacco. However, I hate alcohol in any shape or form. My brother has the opposite taste. Coincidence – or are our habits formed so early?

The local farmer at Fielden House, Mr Marriot, started to teach me something about farming. I remember asking him one morning about a peculiar smell, to which he replied it was 'artificial' fertiliser as opposed to 'natural' animal and human waste. Harvest time was great fun, chasing rabbits from the corn fields as they were being cut, hiding in the stooks of sheaves made by the land girls, and in the winter watching the horses ploughing the fields for the next crop.

By the spring of 1944 invasion forces were amassing all over Southern England, and a company of tanks took up position in the lanes all around Fielden House. As soon as we were up and fed we used to go to see the soldiers and we were always allowed into one of the tanks. After one visit I jumped down off the tank and landed on one knee in the road, cutting my kneecap open to the bone. The soldiers placed a field dressing on the knee, and I returned to the house a very proud wounded soldier! I still have the scar of four lines looking like tank tracks. One morning without warning they had all gone.

The invasion of Europe had been successful and allied troops were fighting their way into Germany. The *Luftwaffe* were considered a spent force and there was no longer any likelihood of the Germans invading England.

Consequently, very shortly afterwards Mother and us two boys moved back to King's Farm, a beautiful beamed cottage near the Hall, which was originally given to my mother by her father as a wedding present. The house itself was listed in the original Doomsday Book, and once again we had a permanent home. My grandparents did not move back to the Hall yet as the Sun Insurance office was still at Wrest Park, and there was also considerable blast damage to repair in the house. Soon after our return, the V-1s – or doodlebugs, as they were called – started raining down on London, and we had our fair share over us. The noise of their flight remains as an unforgettable and deeply sinister memory.

One night we heard the noise of hundreds of large aeroplanes overhead. We were quite used to hearing the Americans by day, and the RAF by night, flying bombing missions into Germany, but this was a very exceptional air armada. We couldn't see anything but Mother decided we should take refuge under the sideboard. Quite what protection that would have given us I am not sure, but by daylight we were able to identify them as our own, and emerged from our funk-hole feeling slightly sheepish. It turned out that these aircraft were heading for the ill-fated Arnhem landings.

Around this time a mysterious Max – Uncle Max to us – appeared at regular intervals, usually bearing gifts. It transpired he was a Canadian fighter pilot stationed nearby!

One day, just as mysteriously, he disappeared.

As far as education went, John was to go to a day school near Sudbury and I was to go away to school. I was not happy!

CHAPTER III

Abberley Hall

The improvement in life for the country at large coincided with a marked deterioration of my own well-being – I was sent away to boarding school. Mother took me to lunch at Peter Jones and then delivered me to Paddington Station to catch the school train to Abberley Hall in Worcester. I was totally traumatised. Not only had I never before left the bosom of my family for even one night, but when I realised I was to be locked up for thirteen weeks before seeing them again I adopted the same attitude as I subsequently learned was adopted by POWs arriving at prison camps – non cooperation.

Abberley Hall school can trace its roots back to the year my grandfather was born, 1878. However, it was not on the existing site, and neither was it under its existing name. It arrived at its present location by a series of moves and changes of ownership. Abberley Hall is on top of a long line of hills culminating in the Malvern Hills, giving a clear view from the magnificent clock tower, built by a previous owner of the estate as a memorial to himself and his wife, into six counties. Abberley Hall was by any standards a large country house, with extensive outbuildings able to accommodate eighty boys, plus a large proportion of the teaching and administrative staff. These outbuildings housed, in addition to the classrooms, a chapel, theatre, sanatorium, carpentry shop and many other facilities. To me, it was like a prison camp, and my days of freedom had come to an end. But of course I wasn't there to enjoy myself, I was there to learn. Teaching was something the school was excellent at, and I am the first to admit – albeit with hindsight – that I received a very good all-round education there. The

Headmaster and owner of the school, Gilbert Ashton, was an excellent mathematician, and he took it upon himself to teach us all at some stage. It was straightforward teaching, none of today's nonsense; there was only one answer to any question – the right one. Mental arithmetic was hammered into us until we could all do almost any sum in our heads, a skill which I am immensely pleased to have acquired. Gilbert Ashton was ably assisted in the teaching of mathematics by Gordon Neal, who had the less than endearing habit of taking you on a 'bicycle ride' if you stepped out of line. This treat consisted of grasping a wisp of hair above each ear and twiddling it round and round like a set of bicycle pedals. It was very painful, and a great deterrent. In the first year we also learned French, Latin and Greek as well as History, Geography, Religious Instruction, Drawing, Singing and Music. Games played were cricket in the summer and rugger in the winter. We may have played soccer as well, but I have no recollection of ever playing it at any school I went to.

The academic day was long; our first lesson was at seven-thirty in the morning and the last at six-forty-five in the evening. Invariably this last lesson didn't actually start until seven o'clock, which enabled us to listen to 'Dick Barton, special agent'. I never knew whether the masters were being kind or merely wanted to listen to it themselves; I suspect the latter.

As in POW camps, where there were often one or more guards with a human face, so it was at both the schools I went to.

I had not been at Abberley long before one of the masters, Nick Wood, told me that I had been found in possession of a lethal weapon. After a look of incomprehension from me, he added, 'To wit, one catapult.' I couldn't deny it; I kept it in my bedside cupboard. To the question 'Do you know how to use it?' I replied I was learning.

'Report to me on Saturdays, before or after games, and I will teach you how to be a good shot, but it remains confiscated until the end of term, and then don't bring it back!'

He taught me how to use a catapult, how to shoot with a rifle, and a huge amount of natural history. The added advantage was that he was a chain-smoker of Woodbines, and as I was already 'into' the weed I used to be allowed to share one.

Mike Carr, whose wife, Barbara, had been largely instrumental in persuading my parents to send me to Abberley, Mr Pinney, Aubrey Butler and of course Nick Wood were all part of the 'human face'. One particularly inhuman face, though, was RSM Worsley, the Physical Training Instructor. He was responsible for teaching swimming. Abberley had an outdoor pool, always cold, and frequently dirty, in which this task was undertaken.

I was not a natural water baby. RSM Worsley used to hold us with a lifebelt attached to a pole which enabled him to draw his pupil slowly through the water, which I presume was to encourage one that forward progress was happening if the arm and leg movement was coordinated. After a particularly fraught session he announced that I was staying on the end of the pole until either hell froze over or I swam... Just before darkness fell, I swam! I can still swim adequately but I loathe and detest it as a form of recreation. Any connection, I wonder?

I joined the Cubs, the junior Boy Scout movement, which I loved, and in my last year the Boy Scouts, which I also enjoyed. We played our 'wide games' in the hills and woods surrounding the school, lived in tents, cooked over campfires and studied the beauty of nature all around us. I developed a passion for moths and butterflies and built up a sizeable collection with the aid of a net and a killing bottle. The Wyre Forest nearby was a wonderful source of fresh catches. We collected birds' eggs from every available source, learning how to drill and blow even the smallest egg. My mother kindly made her childhood egg collection available and I was even able to add some which she didn't have.

Her pride and joy was an emu's egg – although how she came by it I never really knew. In those days there was an abundance of every conceivable bird. The farming pattern was unchanged; no hedges had been pulled out and there was not the slightest threat to wildlife from this activity. We learned how to set snares to catch rabbits for our camp supper, and above all became appreciative of the natural wonders in every hedgerow and around every corner.

We all had to take our turn in helping in the school fruit and vegetable garden to make the school largely self-sufficient. Outside the school buildings life was good; inside I found it was considerably less so. On reflection this was largely of my own making. I had enjoyed almost total freedom all my life and this was still largely true in the outside environment. The confines of classrooms and the mind-bending boredom of learning dead languages like Latin and Greek combined to make me a difficult pupil.

I was in constant conflict with authority and was once inexcusably rude to Celia, one of the dormitory maids; called before the Headmaster, I had my first of many tastes of the cane. Anticipation was far worse than realisation, I was to discover over the years, and it was definitely preferable to writing out hundreds of lines of Latin verse or loss of liberty. I apologised profusely to Celia and we became quite good friends afterwards.

In general, the food was utterly disgusting, but I suspect we made insufficient allowance for the constraints of rationing. One strange quirk of Abberley was a requirement to bring our own cutlery marked with our name. I still have the solid silver egg spoon with my name on it.

What we were all extremely unappreciative of, however, was the morning cold bath. This was a ritual practised all the year round, whereby we formed up by dormitory, stark naked, and submersed ourselves in a bath full of cold water. We had to take it in turns, so the last boy in had the benefit of warmed-up water. The very harsh winter of 1947 saw us excused this form of torture. By then news of the German experiments in hypothermia in the concentration camps had been published, and perhaps the school had second thoughts!

One of the school perks was a six-boy toboggan, with which we had great fun in the snow of that year. It used to be driven by a master with at least a senior boy at the rear to act as brakeman. For some reason best known to myself I hijacked it one day and took it out on my own. Eventually I lost control and crashed through an iron railing fence, finishing up in the school pond. Fortunately the extreme cold had made the iron fence very brittle and it broke easily, the pond was frozen solid and I came to no real harm, apart from a few bruises. So relieved were the authorities that they didn't have a fatality on their hands that I escaped with a tobogganing ban for the term.

Sadly, we did have one fatality when a boy, David Fleury, died of an asthma attack. This was a cause of great distress to all of us, and I think it was our first realisation of our own mortality.

The school had the usual epidemics of measles, whooping cough, mumps, flu and all the general nastiness associated with a number of small boys in confined quarters. I succumbed to measles but escaped everything else. On the only occasion Father came to visit he was unlucky enough to time it just before an epidemic of mumps broke out. I escaped, he did not, and needless to say we never saw him again at Abberley.

There was no telephone available and the only method of contact with home was the compulsory letter-writing sessions on Sundays. These were all censored, so we never had the chance to whinge.

The school put on lots of extra things to keep us amused. These ranged from plays, Gilbert and Sullivan operettas, lectures from interesting people and of course regular matches of cricket and rugger against other schools. There was no shortage of schools to play against in the area, and it was always a pleasure to compare the ghastliness of one school against another. Eating afterwards was an interesting diversion from the horror of one's own school food; theirs was never any better, just a different variation of awfulness.

Chapel 'in house' or a visit to the church in Abberley

village was compulsory every Sunday, with the school's RE teacher, Canon 'Popgun' Richardson, officiating. I used to sing in the choir, apparently having a reasonable treble voice, with the added responsibility of taking my turn pumping the bellows of the chapel organ.

Whilst I was at Abberley, two outstanding events took place. Firstly came the surrender of Germany and the ensuing celebrations; secondly was the election of a Labour government and, as could be expected at a private prep school, the ensuing wake!

I had already been entered for Eton, and provided I passed the Common Entrance exam would be going in September 1948. I did manage a credible pass, and at the end of the summer term said my goodbyes. I was the only one going to Eton that year, so I had to face being an even smaller fish in an even larger pond, and on my own once again.

The final act of our Headmaster, Gilbert Ashton, was to take us leavers for a walk in the school gardens to talk about the 'birds and the bees'. As I already had a very good working knowledge of biology from my time on the farm at home, I was able to save him further embarrassment.

I left with absolutely no regrets and had no further contact with the school or any of its inmates until exactly forty-five years later. A chance announcement in *The Times* said that the present incumbent, Michael Haggard, was retiring as Headmaster. As Michael had been a small boy there at the same time as me, I felt I would like to visit again. I am pleased that I did; he had obviously been a wonderful headmaster, had modernised and expanded the school, and was achieving considerable academic excellence. I saw quite a number of boys I had been there with, which was fun, but they did all seem rather eccentric, to say the least. My wife said I fitted in well!

CHAPTER IV
Horkesley Hall

H orkesley, where I was born and bred, was my spiritual
home for over half a century. An imposing medium-to-
large Victorian country house, the Hall was approached via a
driveway between the church and a ten-acre grass field, known
as Hall Green. Of a predominantly nondescript colour, it, like
many others, was positioned back to front, with vehicle access
only at the rear of the house. The house consisted of two parts;
the main living area and a separate but interconnected part
known as the laundry. By the early part of the twentieth
century the laundry function had ceased to exist and that
section became spare bedrooms and storerooms. Continuing
past the front door and the long portico brought one to the
stable block, where the carriage horses, the mowing pony and
the carriages were kept. There was sleeping accommodation
over the stables for the coachman and grooms, and at ground
level a separate harness and tack room and feed store. Beyond
were the walled kitchen gardens, with two gardeners' cottages
adjacent.

Inside the main house, there were eight bedrooms upstairs,
with eight more in the laundry. Downstairs was a large
entrance hall, with to the left my grandfather's office, known
as the 'Holy of Holies' where children were absolutely
forbidden under any pretext; the dining room, with a large bay
window catching the early morning sun overlooking Hall
Green; and next to that the smoking room, used as a sitting
room. Opposite was a large formal drawing room about
seventy-five feet long and forty wide. The view from both the
smoking room and the drawing room was over the gardens

down to the two lakes. Despite its size, the Hall always had a warm, cosy, lived-in feel, and I loved it like nowhere I have ever been in since. Brought up in such an environment, I can truthfully say it doesn't get better, but it did nothing towards equipping me to appreciate the real world in which I had ultimately to live. So privileged was I that I feel it incumbent upon me to describe life there in some detail, hopefully for the entertainment of anyone reading this, but also to serve as a warning to any parent of the pitfalls of over indulging their children.

My grandfather's office was, as I have already said, a total no-go area. The only time we were ever allowed in it was on Christmas Eve, when we queued up to receive our Christmas cheques. Grandfather was generous to a fault to all his family, but every Christmas we were subjected to the admonition that this was probably the last time he would be able to give us anything at all, as he was so hard up. As a teenager I got so worried that I asked Mother, 'Is Grandpa really going bankrupt?' She said that all her life she had heard this cry, and I shouldn't worry; but living as he was under a ninety-eight per cent tax regime, life was not that easy for him. Indeed, he went on working until well over eighty. I much later learned that his definition of imminent bankruptcy was when the balance in his current account fell below £10,000. In the 1940s this was a lot of money, to say the least – perhaps £150,000 in today's terms!

The drawing room was really only used for entertaining, and especially at Christmas. It was a magnificent and beautiful room, essentially in two halves. The division was marked by two large ornamental pillars, each with a large ten-foot kentia palm at the base. The far end was where my grandmother's desk was and where she used to write her letters. She was a prolific writer to all her many friends and also to me when I was away at school. They didn't entertain in large numbers, so guests rarely migrated to 'her' end. There were two large chandeliers, one at each end, which set the room off beautifully. There were many lovely possessions, but one especially is worthy of mention. A very large Ming bowl rested on gilt legs in one corner, in about four pieces which had been stapled together. My mother's nanny had fallen into it years ago and broken it. It was not until the family moved out of the house and the contents were valued, that we learned that had it been in mint condition it would have fetched a high six or even seven-figure sum.

The entrance hall also only really came to life at Christmas. We always had a twelve-foot home-grown Christmas tree covered in real candles which were lit each evening. Because of the obvious fire hazard, somebody stood almost permanent guard over it while the candles were alight. The carol singers would come into the house and the family would all sit on the stairs listening to their rendition of a selection of well-known carols. Hot mince pies, together with a suitable alcoholic drink, were served afterwards.

The 'back passage', as it was irreverently referred to, led off the hall to the kitchen, the butler's pantry, the gunroom and the servants' hall and down to the cellar. My grandparents were totally undomesticated and rarely ventured down there, except for the nightly visit my grandfather made to select a bottle of claret from the cellar. He allegedly had never been into the kitchen in his life.

The boiler room was at the far end and housed a pair of coke-burning boilers. These consumed up to two tons of fuel a week in cold weather, all of which was barrowed in from outside. They were clinkered out morning and evening; being in an enclosed area, the fumes were quite overpowering and I wondered how the men survived. I was to experience the same sulphur fumes some twenty-five years later when I had a large solid-fuel boiler on my own nursery. My thoughts on survival were soon answered: you just get used to it.

We generated our own electricity up until the early Fifties. The generator was only able to be run twice a week, largely because of the general shortage of petroleum products.

Constant energy conservation was practised lest the batteries ran flat and we were plunged into darkness. Woe betide anyone who left a light on unnecessarily! Even when the mains came these strictures continued; for although it was much more convenient it was also more expensive. The arrival of mains electricity made the acquisition of a television set possible. My grandfather was incensed by this and at first refused to watch it in case he was corrupted by it.

The dining room had a very large curved glass bay window with a beautiful view over Hall Green and beyond. Normally the young Jersey heifers lived in this field and they alone guaranteed a beautiful scene. All this curved glass was blown out when the church was destroyed, and it cost a fortune to replace. We always ate all our meals except afternoon tea there, and many of these were memorable in their own right. The servants were allowed Tuesday afternoon and evening off, and always left a cold meal out for us in the dining room. My grandmother always called it Black Tuesday, which seemed a bit dramatic to me, as we didn't even have to clear anything away, let alone wash it up.

With the ownership of the Hall went the 'Patronage of the Living', which at its most basic gave my grandfather the right to hire and fire the parson. After the church was destroyed, services were held in the village school. Frank Lawrence, the vicar, carried on nobly under very difficult conditions, until he retired. It took nearly sixteen years to rebuild the church and during the 'interregnum' a series of temporary parsons were engaged.

As churchwarden and patron of the living, my grandfather used to influence the choice of hymns and the length and content of the sermon. After early communion, the visiting parsons used to come back for breakfast. Sometimes the most ferocious arguments would ensue, since no hymns numbered higher than two hundred and no sermon longer than fifteen minutes was, in my grandfather's view, allowed at the main service which was to follow. One Sunday during a particularly stormy session I really thought that any minute now the boiled eggs were going to fly! They didn't, but that particular parson never came again.

The government had a war damage fund that could be applied to for any rebuilding project. However, generally speaking all that was available covered no more than the bare essentials, and it was my grandparents' wish – and most, but by no means all, of the parishioners shared their desire – to build an exact replica of the old church of Saints Peter and Paul. This was to cost a significant amount more than was available from the War Damage Commission, so my grandparents launched an additional church rebuilding appeal. They both worked tirelessly supported by many in the village to raise as much as possible. A fête was held in the garden with all the usual sideshows including a darts competition. Although barely eleven years old I entered the darts competition early in the day and fluked a more than respectable score. After that, the board was never empty as all the village dart players kept re-entering to try to beat my score. Nobody did, but that event took more money than any other. It was a complete fluke but it paid off. After ten years and many fund-raising events the target was reached and the new church was dedicated in 1956.

The most used room in the house was the so-called smoking room, which had a wonderful view over both Hall Green and the Jersey cows, the Upper Lake, and beyond that to the Park.

Grandmother sat to the right of the fireplace and Grandfather to the left. There was an ancient radio to feed us the news at one o'clock, six o'clock and nine o'clock. After lunch and dinner, Grandfather's coffee was brought in, and he promptly went to sleep, waking only when someone came to remove his cup – which was untouched. He then drank it stone cold with a skin on, listened to the nine o'clock news and promptly went to sleep again.

By the time ITV arrived with its adverts he was totally confused, and would constantly complain that he didn't understand what was being advertised; I used to think, Silly old fool he's past it... Today I have total sympathy; so obscure are today's adverts that I know just how he felt.

Grandfather was never to be seen without his pipe, and in the evening with a large Havana cigar. He defied all modern thinking as he both smoked and drank heavily, though never to the stage of being even slightly merry. He was to die in his bed at the age of ninety-six, never having had a day's illness in his life.

The kitchen had also been modernised earlier and the old kitchen range had been replaced with an Aga. This made the kitchen staff's job considerably less arduous. Mains electricity also enabled a Hoover vacuum cleaner to be purchased, but Agnes refused to use it, preferring her old Ewbank carpet brush. All the silver, brass and copper was cleaned each day. Water was carried up to the bedrooms every day and then the dirty water had to be carried down again. Life for the domestic staff was not easy at all, and I was acutely aware of how privileged I was. Writing this at the beginning of the twenty-first century it seems barely credible how much life has changed – unquestionably for the better, for most people.

CHAPTER V

The Gardens

The gardens at Horkesley were not the work of any famous designer, neither were they particularly grand or pretentious, but to me they were as near as you get to heaven on earth. The smell of freshly cut grass first got me into a whole new world as I walked alongside the mower for hours on end. Grandfather had got a new toy in the shape of a thirty-six-inch cut Atco motor mower. Dolly, the mowing pony who had previously pulled a set of gang mowers, had been retired, and soon I was to learn to ride on her. She was very docile, although not too sure what being ridden was all about; but we got on well together all the same and I learned the basics on her. The Atco was temperamental and the gardeners, like all countrymen, were sceptical of anything new. I learned at a very early age that stones from the pathways and twigs from the trees wrought havoc on the blades, and one of the first practical tasks I was given was to destone and detwig the lawns in front of the mower.

The lawns in front of the house sweeping down to the lake were lined with standard roses, each in a small circular bed, and the same was true for the other lawns. A special small-cut push mower was used to cut round these. There seemed to be never ending miles of edges to be cut, not only round the beds but also along the pathways. Specimen trees around the lawns were of particular interest to me. These included an acacia, which I was told was the tree giraffes lived on; an evergreen oak, the holm oak, which kept its leaves all through the winter; a cork tree, indigenous in Portugal, from which (I was told) cork for table mats and wine bottles came; a beautiful London plane which, as they all do, shed twigs and leaves all the year round. This one tree caused more damage to the mower blades than all the others put together, driving my poor grandmother mental as a result. I understand her better now, as we have in our own garden not one but two, and any tree less suitable for a garden I have yet to come across. There was a huge macrocarpa which my grandmother passed her hatred of on to me. This has not lessened over the years as I look out of my window today, at a group of three which are slowly poisoning the garden, but which I am unable to take down. Best of all was a huge cedar of Lebanon, a truly magnificent tree. However, my grandmother's favourite, for some obscure reason, was a gingko – which apparently had some strange medicinal qualities, although quite what I was never to find out. Then came a line of three sycamores, known as the three sisters, the middle one of which still had the fittings for my mother's childhood swing attached; and beyond them was the orchard. This orchard was full of every imaginable ancient variety of top fruit. There were medlars, the ugliest looking fruit of all, but which makes a delicious jelly; quinces; cooking apples and pears; plums and cherries; and two mulberry trees. I don't ever remember the orchard being very well maintained, although considerable quantities of fruit were picked and stored each autumn.

The choicest dessert fruit was all grown inside the walled garden. The walls were covered in peaches, nectarines and dessert cherries. Down each side of the two central pathways were espalier-trained apples, pears and plums. Additionally there were three large fig trees and a vinery. My special favourites were these last two, and as I grew older I was constantly trying to outwit 'Mr McGregor' – as we nicknamed Bert Thurgood, the head gardener. I could, and still can, gorge myself on ripe English figs, and can never get enough! The modern supermarket Turkish fig is not the same thing at all!

Poor Thurgood! What with me, the blackbirds and the wasps, he was often hard pressed to find enough figs for the house. We all swore he knew every individual fruit by name, whatever variety and type it was. The vinery, however, was his special domain. Nobody else was allowed in there, ever. He taught me the art of growing the two varieties, Black Hamburgh and White Muscat, especially pruning the individual bunches to give large, uniform and perfectly formed fruit. The essential skill was an ability to squint all day into the sun. When I later had my own rose nursery it was once again necessary to squint into the sun after midsummer to disbud the roses, once the growth was above head height. I still can't choose which was the most uncomfortable – squinting into the sun, or working with your arms above your head all day. With both crops, though, the gain was more than worth the pain.

The soft fruit was grown in a cage outside the main walled area. Once when we visited during the war I was shut in this cage with two tins of paraffin and left to pick off all the caterpillars from the gooseberry bushes and drop them into the tins. Within a few years I was to learn the benefits of DDT for this operation!

The gardens enabled the house to be totally self-sufficient in all fruit and vegetables. The largest areas were devoted to asparagus, potatoes and onions – the latter to my grandfather's great annoyance, as he hated this particular vegetable. Another function of the gardens was to enable my grandfather to enter and win virtually every class at the Great and Little Horkesley annual Horticultural Show. I once had the temerity to ask him, if, with a regiment of gardeners and acres of garden, he thought it quite fair to compete against cottage gardeners with none of these advantages. He looked at me uncomprehendingly and said, 'I don't know what you mean.' Strange life!

Apart from the vinery there were two other greenhouses. One was a large lean-to carnation house, with the sole purpose of producing a vase of fresh carnations for the house and a buttonhole every day for my grandfather. Although I never grew carnations myself, they were the first commercial crop which I studied. The other remaining greenhouse was a pit house, with the bulk of it below ground level but with a glass roof. There were two halves to this house, one kept at a higher temperature than the other. The warmest part grew melons, cucumbers and high-temperature requirement pot plants; while the other, cooler half housed the tomatoes and lower-temperature requirement pot plants. Little did I know it at the time but the seeds were being sown for my own glasshouse nursery career. I remember so vividly Thurgood teaching me about the 'feel' of the growing environment. 'When it feels right and you can smell things growing, it is right,' he used to say. I was eventually able to put his teaching to good use.

The two lakes – upper and lower – were also a source of wonderment and pleasure to me. I found it difficult to believe that my mother and her brothers used to swim in these as children. The remains of the landing stage were there, but by now the upper pond was silted up and almost totally overgrown with water lilies. However, it was full of fish, mostly tench and eels, both of which I became adept at catching. A line of nine hooks one night had seven eels on it in the morning. I soon learned where the expression 'as slippery as a basket of eels' came from. The tench were sometimes caught on a line but more often in a cage baited with a large sunflower. We did eat them, but they needed a good soak to get rid of the muddy flavour.

The rhododendrons and azaleas round the back of the ponds were beautiful but had got completely out of control by the time the war was over. It was to be another twenty years before the ponds were dug out and the rhodos brought back under control. I forget exactly when, but within five years of the end of the war, most of the old regime had retired. Bert Thurgood had gone to live at Bishop's Stortford, where I was occasionally able to visit him and acquire more of his knowledge. His successor, Mr Hull, was charged with the unenviable task of making the gardens pay for themselves. My grandfather was by now well into his seventies, and although still working full-time, was feeling the strain of tax rates up to ninety-eight per cent. The walled gardens were turned over to whatever vegetables could be sold to greengrocers in Colchester; but this was never going to be a truly viable proposition, and slowly but very surely the decline set in and the area maintained shrank every year.

The slow decline outside was reflected inside the house as the 'vocation' of domestic service in the post-war egalitarian age was socially unacceptable, especially at the minimal rates of pay which were the norm. Although Agnes remained in her post and accepted ever more responsibilities, she had now married and was living at West Bergholt, with understandably different priorities. The family advertised extensively for staff and we had a succession of East European refugees whose experience of, and ability to cope with, the demands of an English country house were non-existent. The best china was either broken or stolen, and the bed linen was either burnt with the iron or again went missing. Furthermore, their cooking abilities were to say the least minimal. East European cooking was not at all what my grandparents were used to. They really tried to get used to it but to no avail. The food served up was definitely well below the standard of boarding school food which I was used to, and that supposedly was as bad as it got! It was not until later that I fully understood just how bewildered and confused my ageing grandparents were by all this. By the late Fifties my grandmother was constantly ill with heart and associated problems, and she died in 1959. My grandfather was by now in his eighties, and although still working, was, like most men, unable to cope on his own, even though he now had a housekeeper. Father had meanwhile retired from his post-Army career and my parents were now living once again at King's Farm, about four hundred yards from the Hall. Mother assumed responsibility for her father and the domestic affairs of the Hall. Father decided he was going to take over the running of the farm, which by now had grown to some six hundred acres. This effectively shut the door on my hopes and ambitions of farming at home. I was just leaving the Royal Agricultural College then, and was incensed by his actions, especially as he barely knew a sugar beet from a turnip!

It was not long before the gardens were virtually shut down. The tennis court and front lawns had cows on them, and the walled garden was cleared and flattened to accommodate horses. A very small area around the perimeter of the house was maintained in some semblance of order, but even that proved increasingly difficult. It was a strange irony that as the gardens and the Hall were gently decaying, our little church had risen like a phoenix from the ashes, and the services filled it to a capacity far beyond the numbers resident in the parish.

CHAPTER VI

Postwar Germany

The Second World War ended formally on May 8th 1945 amid tumultuous celebrations nationwide, especially in London. I was at Abberley at the time, although I have no recollection of doing anything special beyond offering a prayer of thanks for the nation's deliverance from evil. My father had served with Field Marshal Montgomery ever since the battle of El Alamein, and finished the war with him at the surrender of the German forces at Lüneburg Heath. For the next four years we spent at least half our school holidays in Germany, with the rest being spent at Horkesley.

Our mother took us over the first time, but thereafter we used to make our own way. The standard route was Harwich to the Hook of Holland, across Holland and ending up in Osnabrück, where we would be met. The boat train left Liverpool Street Station in London and travelled non-stop to Harwich. There was little point in us going all the way from Colchester to London and then all the way back again, so when enough petrol was available we would be driven direct to Harwich. However, on at least a couple of occasions my family had enough influence to have the boat train stopped at Colchester to take us two boys straight to Harwich, thereby eliminating an unnecessary journey to London.

On one of these trips I somehow managed to travel on the footplate of a real live steam engine. This was quite an experience for anyone, let alone a small boy. The noise, heat and excitement were unbelievable, but even more unbelievable in retrospect is how it was ever arranged! On one occasion we sailed on the *Empire Parkeston,* a coal-burning troopship, and were shown all over her, from the engine room to the bridge. It was my first and only experience of a coal-burning ship's boiler room. I can never forget the rows of boilers being fed by sweat-stained stokers wielding the traditional 'stoker's slab', which held fourteen pounds of coal for each throw. I hope it is as near to Dante's *Inferno* as I ever get, although after the life I have led it may well not be!

We used to arrive at the Hook of Holland at about six o'clock in the morning and then catch the train across to Germany via Utrecht, Amersfoort, Appeldoorn and other unpronounceable names, little knowing that in later life I would become familiar with them all. Customs clearance was at Bentheim, where we were escorted off the train by the Military Police and into the station restaurant. There we would have the most superb breakfast of bacon and eggs. I revisited Bentheim Station fifty-three years later and found it still in its original condition except for an extra coat or two of paint.

Two trips were especially memorable. My parents had always been keen followers of hounds, and one of Father's first non-military acts was to establish a pack of English foxhounds. This was an unknown phenomena to the Germans, to whom hunting meant shooting. A bitch 'in pup' called 'Stealthy' was found, and my holiday task was to deliver her to Iserlohn, where she became the founder member of the Iserlohn Vale Foxhounds. As far as I know, 'The Vale' still exists today.

The other memorable visit was during the murderously cold beginning to the very harsh winter of 1946–'47. On this occasion we were met at the Hook of Holland by my father in his old Morris 12, which had been exported from England for the family's private use, and he drove us across Holland and Germany in the coldest conditions I can ever remember. The car had no heater to speak of and the roads were packed with snow and ice, but somehow Father got us there. His standard of driving was never as good again, I recall. At the end of the holiday we repeated the journey in reverse and I duly arrived back at Abberley, where I was volunteered to write an article for the school magazine which I reproduce here:

My Visit to Germany

It was pitch dark when we arrived at The Hook of Holland. When it got light we looked out of the porthole and found there was snow on the ground. We then went through Customs, where my father was waiting with our big car. When the luggage was all on we drove through The Hague, where we saw people skating on the canals. Then we drove over Arnhem and Nijmegen bridges, where the big air invasions took place and where troops were dropped by parachute in 1944. We stopped for lunch just before we crossed the border, and it was terribly cold.

When we crossed the border we had to stop to show our passports to the Dutch frontier guards. Then when they had checked them we were allowed to pass. Then we went to Cleves (where Henry VIII got his wife, Anne of Cleves) but it is only a mass of ruins now. Then we continued, for some time, along the Rhine, which was frozen (which is a very rare thing indeed). Next we went through Xanten, where Julius Caesar crossed the Rhine. When we got to Iserlohn there was not enough snow to make any use of, but on New Year's Day we had about six inches which very quickly went.

When it was not too cold we sometimes rode through the massive woods with their winding paths. Sometimes you saw German peasants collecting firewood with their little home-made trolleys; otherwise you did not see a sign of habitation anywhere. You often saw old wooden watchtowers, built out of not very strong sticks, and old German field telephone exchanges with all their mechanism scattered around. On the last day of the holidays we rode through an old ammunition dump which had been blown up by the Germans to prevent the British troops getting at it. Unless you kept to the paths you could get blown up by the mines the Germans had planted around it. Right the way through the dump were old food containers almost as big as bombs, and the old huts made of plaster had been completely blown to bits. Then we rode back through a farm as we had lost our way and could not find it again, but we eventually got home.

After several nights of hard frost the lake near to us was frozen and we were able to try to skate, but it soon thawed.

Every afternoon we used to take the hounds out on foot, but invariably tree stumps were being blasted and they all ran home.

On an old dump that was down by the stables, I found an old German machine-gun in perfect condition, some rifles, an old wireless set and a few helmets which we kept for souvenirs.

When we wanted to do any shopping we had to go to the NAAFI, where you could spend more on something than you ever could in England.

There is a little school in the town for English children, where they learn Maths, English, French, Russian and German. When you want to have your shoes mended you have them done at the Families Institute, where parties etc. are always held.

On Tuesday, 14th January, we set sail on a very rough sea for England.

W P de H (11yr 2mth)

We had first gone out to Germany in 1945 and lived in a requisitioned house in Tuckwinkel Strasse in Iserlohn. The house was memorable by virtue of being almost totally covered in Virginia creeper and having a highly productive peach tree growing on the wall, off which we never picked a peach; they all mysteriously disappeared overnight. We had a butler by the name of Fritz and a cook, Sybil. Fritz was the archetypal butler, who proclaimed that he never went to sleep, merely lay down. In his room he had a large painting of a nude woman, complete with pubic hair, which to a ten-year-old was of great interest! My brother, being suspected of having TB, was unable to drink cow's milk, so consequently we acquired a goat, thenceforth known as 'Frau Ziege' – literally interpreted as

'Mrs Goat', as goat's milk was apparently tuberculin-free. The unfortunate Sybil had to milk her twice a day. Now milking a goat is a far more complex operation than milking a cow. They only have two teats, both virtually touching the ground, so the goat had to be stood on a table and milked into a saucepan, as no bucket would fit under the udder. The main part of the process was difficult enough, but the final stripping out would invariably be accompanied by violent kicking, with frequently predictable results. Stripping out had to be done, otherwise, as with cows, the flow of milk will rapidly dry up. Eventually we had to get her in kid again, and a second goat appeared to keep up the milk supply while Frau Ziege was dry. She eventually had triplets, which we ate, partly because food of any kind was at a premium and partly to get our own back on her; undoubtedly the only edible part of a goat – the milk being, to me, undrinkable.

During the daytime we two boys went scavenging on the battlefields. We rummaged into old tanks, gun emplacements, foxholes and trenches and always brought home some ordnance, or at the very least an old helmet, preferably with a bullet hole in it. Machine-guns, rifles, field telephone sets, hand grenades, bayonets, daggers – you name it, we found it. How we managed to keep it all hidden I really don't know. All Mother said to us each day was, 'Don't blow yourselves up, darlings.' The fact that we didn't is more down to luck than judgement. We tried to ship some of our spoils of war back to England in two school trunks but were apprehended at Harwich by the Customs officials. Everything was confiscated except an SS ceremonial dagger, which I have since used to open my mail every day of my life.

My father was absolutely furious and always said he had had to use all his connections and negotiating skill to prevent us from being locked up!

As an ex-Royal Horse Artilleryman, Father now made riding compulsory for me. I was grateful for my early tuition on Dolly, the mowing pony, some five years earlier. Yes, riding a horse is like riding a bicycle – you don't forget; and without my early riding experience I should never have coped with 'the Ferret'. This inaptly named horse (ferrets are far nicer animals) did everything to make my life hell.

She came from the Army riding school in Iserlohn where they had an indoor arena with a peat base. I lost count of how many bales of peat I swallowed. Father was a keen polo player as well as an expert horseman, so I was clearly a great disappointment to him.

Whilst at Iserlohn, Father took us on the monorail system running from Wuppertal to Dortmund and also to the Mohne and Eider dams, scene of the *Dam Busters*' raid. I remember sitting eating a picnic with him on the bank of the Eider dam while he explained all about the raid to us. Again we were really too young to fully absorb what he was saying and had to wait until the film was made in order to fit the story together.

All our shopping was done at the NAAFI with tokens valued in BAPS, which I assume was some form of NAAFI currency. Apart from some of the grooms at the riding school and occasional encounters with German farmers whilst we were exploring, we had virtually no contact with the local population. There was in fact an official policy of 'no fraternisation' for the first eighteen months. In the unofficial economy, coffee and cigarettes would buy you anything – and I mean anything. I was aware of appalling poverty and deprivation as the local population went about their daily tasks, with prams, handcarts and the occasional wood-fired lorry. The wood-fired vehicles were presumably pre-war steam wagons brought out of retirement.

We never then, or at any stage of our life in Germany, experienced the smallest degree of hostility from the local population. Perhaps I was too naive or insensitive to notice it, but I don't think so. In retrospect there appeared to be almost a feeling of gratitude, presumably at their deliverance from the ghastly tyranny of National Socialism. To this day I cannot believe that had the boot been on the other foot, the British would have behaved towards the occupying powers with quite such equanimity. Perhaps this attitude was not found in cities like Cologne, Dresden and Hamburg, but we had no contact with the local population on our urban visits.

Father took us with him whenever it was practical, partly out of interest at the time and also, as I now realise, as part of our education: he was showing us that the real casualties of war are not amongst the politicians, who by their ineptitude end up waging it, but amongst the innocent civilians, women, children and the elderly. The levels of destruction and human misery we saw at first-hand were simply appalling to a young mind. I remember one day walking through a wood and coming across a body hanging from a tree, swinging gently in the wind. Suicide, reprisal... we never knew, but it was far from an unusual occurrence. The British forces, soon to be named officially as BAOR (British Army of the Rhine), not unsurprisingly formed a close-knit community in many ways similar to that at Camberley, but mercifully without The Pantiles.

At the Tuckwinkel, as the house was always known, Father's campaign caravan was parked in the garden. This we used as a sort of modern day playhouse. If the house was full of guests we used to sleep in it as well. One night when Father was having a dinner party for some senior army officers and their wives, we had been asleep for an hour or so in the caravan when all hell broke loose, and we were faced with Father cracking his hunting whip and threatening to flay us alive!

In whatever expressions one uses as a small boy, I enquired what we were supposed to have done. We were accused of putting explosives in the fireplace. We denied all knowledge and were rescued by Mother, who added her usual calming influence to the situation. It transpired that Father had taken the shot out of some cartridge cases in order to clean the port decanter and had thrown the empties into the waste paper basket.

Fritz had emptied the waste paper into the grate and when after dinner they decided to light the fire, the primers eventually went off, blowing the fire out of the grate! My mother thought the incident hilarious, with all these battle-hardened soldiers diving for cover behind the sofa, believing they were under attack.

My mother, always an animal lover, acquired a German short-haired pointer dog puppy for the princely sum of two hundred cigarettes. For reasons unknown he was christened 'Remus', but unfortunately he died after a few months. She so liked the breed that he was replaced with another who became 'Remus II'. He turned into a great and amusing character and also an excellent guard dog. On his eventual repatriation to England he became the founding member of the GSP (German Short-haired Pointer) Club and sired many a useful litter.

We eventually moved from Iserlohn to Bunde and were living in a house owned by the head of a margarine factory in the town. An Olympic-sized swimming pool went with the house, complete with rows of changing rooms and showers. I had by then learned to swim at Abberley, and in so far as it is possible to enjoy swimming we had great fun in this pool. The owner used to call quite often, and relationships between him and our family appeared to be cordial. Whatever his true feelings may have been he was extraordinarily kind to us boys, and took us on more than one occasion to look round his factory. We brought horses with us from Iserlohn, together with two German grooms, Hamke and Skeba, both of whom were alleged to have been members of the SS. Whatever the truth of these allegation, they made good grooms and looked after the horses well. Fritz, Sybil and Frau Ziege also came with us, and life carried on much as before.

At this time a brother officer of my father 'found' a magnificent grey horse who had been towing a gun on the Russian front, and suggested he would make an excellent present for my mother. She was thrilled, and she rode and hunted him regularly for the next fifteen years. My mother always rode side-saddle, and the grey had the ideal build for that job. I used to ride with her almost every day, but my brother never learned to ride, being solely interested in shooting and, very sensibly, somewhat nervous of horses.

After my morning ride we would continue our explorations. Of special interest were some anti-aircraft gun emplacements, still intact. Also by now I was beginning to take a more active interest in the German farming scene, watching in detail various horse-drawn implements at work. I also had my first day on skis, and having mastered the art of standing up without falling over, I tried a pair of skates: impossible! Two weeks' holiday at the Army Ski School at Winterburg in the Bavarian Alps followed. I learned the old-fashioned telemark turn and how to stop. Compared to today the skis were at least half as long again, but from that time on, the use of ever shorter skis became standard practice. Certainly, parallel turns on short skis are a lot easier than telemark turns on long skis. Even so, skiing held little interest for me; but the bobsleigh track was a total fascination, although I never got to ride it.

Father earned promotion and became Deputy Regional Commissioner of the CCG (Control Commission for Germany) in Schleswig-Holstein. In simple terminology he became military head of the Control Commission under the Regional Commissioner; the latter being a purely political appointment. The CCG had been created to oversee the reconstruction of Germany, and the time spent in Schleswig was the most interesting of all for me, as not only was I that much older but also because it was a time of unprecedented privilege. My father lectured me on an almost daily basis that I was not to assume that this was 'normal' life and that I would find life very different in the harsh reality of post-war Britain. At that stage of my life I did not really understand what he was saying but I was soon to learn what he meant.

The house which we were to occupy had been built in 1940, using slave labour, for the Gauleiter of Schleswig-

Rolstein. On the edge of Eckenforde Bay overlooking the Baltic, with a large private beach and substantial gardens, decorated with swastikas and boars' heads in virtually every room, it was awesome, especially when thinking of its life thus far. Interestingly, the plot to evacuate senior Nazi leaders, including Goering, Himmler and Doenitz, involved a pickup by seaplane from Eckenforde. Possibly these villains would have assembled in this, the home of the local Gauleiter.

Attached to the house, but separately owned, was a large arable farm. I was in my element and got up each morning really not knowing what to choose to do next. We acquired extra staff in the form of a mother, her two sons and a daughter. The children were Gerhardt (twenty) Gunther (seventeen) and Giselle (fourteen). One of the grooms from Bunde had left, and Gerhardt was his replacement. Gunther appeared to be a general helper, but much of his time was spent with us doing all the things young boys do. Giselle was at school and helped her mother as and when needed in the house. In addition to my father's staff car we also had a Volkswagen and a civilian chauffeur, Max. The house was far more isolated than the previous two, and some form of additional transport was essential, the old Morris by now being back in England. The Control Commission had a single-car diesel train and an ex-Kriegsmarine Air Sea Rescue launch fitted with triple MAN diesels and a crew of seven. Periodically the Regional Commissioner would also invite his Deputy, my father, to join him on a weekend trip. We always went too, and I caught many mackerel on these trips, most of which we ate. Surely our launch was the most spectacular mackerel boat ever built! I later learned that the real reason for this apparent luxury was to provide a means of escape for CCG staff and families in the event of a Russian invasion.

There was considerable tension at this, the time of the Berlin Airlift, the Russians having sealed off the Allies' road access to Berlin, leading to the western half of the city having to be supplied by air. As part of the peace settlement, Germany had been divided in two, the border between East and West Germany becoming the front line of the Cold War. The eastern half was administered by the Russians and the western half by the Allies. Berlin, as the capital city, held special significance, but was of course well inside East Germany. Berlin itself was divided into four administrative zones – Russian, British, American and French – later of course to be divided by the Berlin Wall. The Western Allies' access to 'their' zone depended on the Russians allowing an access corridor through East Germany. After one of the regular spats between the powers had got out of control, the Russians sealed off road and rail access in an attempt to starve West Berlin into the Soviet camp. The only solution was to supply West Berlin by air. This was every bit as tense a time as the Cuban Missile Crisis fifteen years later, as had the Russians shot down an Allied plane this could have been the trigger for World War III.

At Lindhoft, the usual routine was to ride in the morning; the afternoon was often spent in an old windmill which became our 'den'. Frequent beachcombing expeditions were also made and one day we had a real find. In our innocence we thought it was a mine but in fact it was a paravane which had broken adrift from some minesweeping gear. The farm horses were recruited to pull it up to the house, where it joined our collection of militaria. By this time we had both learned to shoot and had our own shotguns. The basic quarry were starlings, but we honed our skills shooting butterflies by day and bats by dusk. The bird life was different to England and the farm supported a quantity of storks and also ravens and buzzards. We did not attempt to shoot these, not from any spirit of conservation but because our .410s were about as effective against them as pea-shooters on a battleship!

We also had air rifles with which we wreaked much havoc in the garden. We both became highly skilled at shooting lavender heads out of the bedroom window, and it was not until our mother's gladioli collapsed with what were diagnosed as caterpillars nipping the stems through that we felt we had better stop. I think this must have been the basic training which enabled my brother to win the sniping competition at Bisley as a schoolboy a few years later.

Gunther taught me the art of canoeing and he and I became more and more adventurous, until one afternoon we decided to paddle right across the bay. By the time we had gone as far as our weary arms could take us we realised we were beyond the point of no return. We stayed where we were, hoping to be rescued by one of the many fishing boats which sailed out to the fishing grounds; but none came, and there was nothing for it but to keep going. We eventually made landfall, and I said we must find the Daniels family who I knew lived somewhere on that side of the bay. We eventually found them and they telephoned to Lindhoft, only to discover that a full-scale alert had gone out for us. Max came to get us and I think Gunther was in severe trouble for putting our lives at risk. Another lesson learned: before you go anywhere make sure you can get back!

Father took us to the Kiel shipyards one day and this was another occasion when the devastation of war hit me hard. However, further down the basin Kiel Yacht Club was still more or less in one piece and there in all its glorious majesty was a J-class yacht. I don't know which one but it may have been *Endeavour*. A sail on her was arranged for a later date. What an experience! The mast really did reach to the sky. The J-class were surely the most beautiful yachts ever built.

During my last summer at Lindhoft I was allowed to help in the harvest field and was trusted to drive one of the tractors bringing in the sheaves of corn. The Lanz Bulldog I was in charge of was far bigger than anything I had driven in England. I don't know exactly what fuel it ran on, but the combustion chamber was heated with a giant blow lamp, the steering wheel was taken out and stuck into the centre of the flywheel in lieu of the more conventional starting handle, and with luck after a few turns the single cylinder engine would be fired up! The two ladies on top of the load were Frau Bindemann and Gräfin von Schwerin, and every time I let the clutch in I was required to call out, '*Halt fest, Frau Bindemann! Halt fest, Gräfin!*' I was aware that Gräfin von Schwerin was very definitely not your typical farm worker; she was treated with great deference by the others and something approaching reverence by me. She was a stunningly beautiful nineteen-year-old blonde, who seriously disturbed my twelve-year-old loins.

During this summer at Lindhoft two troubling items of news came through from Horkesley. The first was that the year's harvest at my grandfather's farm had all been gathered safely in when the stack yard caught fire and destroyed nearly all of it. It appeared that a spark from the engine driving the elevator was the cause. It was a hot summer and everything was tinder dry. Grandfather was devastated, not least because he was considered the leading light on fire insurance. I think his pride was hurt as much as his pocket. As if this was not enough, King's Farm had been let via our house agent to what turned out to be a criminal gang from London. They had developed in the garage the chemistry for not only removing the red colour from petrol but also the active ingredient of the dye. Red petrol was untaxed for farm use and using it in private cars was highly illegal, but very profitable. In our absence it caused much consternation in the village, as once the police had found one crime they started looking for another.

An East End car dealer, Stanley Setty, had been found headless and for some reason they assumed this gang might be behind that too. The surrounding area was searched for the missing head to no avail.

This summer of 1949 was our last in Germany and it was ironic that instead of helping with the harvest at home, where all the drama was, I was helping with it at Lindhoft. I was sad to leave such a beautiful house and to say goodbye to all our German friends. My parents made many friends amongst the local population during their four years there, many of whom they maintained contact with all their lives, exchanging Christmas cards every year. As I commented earlier, could this possibly have happened in England?

CHAPTER VII

A Budding Agriculturist

During the depths of the agricultural depression of the 1930s my grandfather had purchased a parcel of land of about two hundred and twenty acres including two farmhouses, Knowles Farm and Crabbes Farm, together with a number of cottages. Knowles Farm was given to his youngest son, my Uncle David, and after the war a further fifty acres from Crabbes Farm were also transferred to him, on the whole of which he established a fruit farm.

Crabbes Farm was the centre for the arable and dairy enterprise which my grandfather ran with the aid of a farm manager. The Jersey herd from Charlton also arrived and was accommodated at Crabbes.

The time I had spent in the gardens at the Hall and also at Wrest Park had excited my interest in growing things. Mr Marriot at Fielden House had widened my interest into farming and I now started to take an active interest in agriculture as well. Although only just coming up to twelve years old I was aware that the new Labour Government's 1947 Agriculture Act heralded in a new era for agriculture and I was beginning to see the possibility of a career in farming.

Being born a lark rather than an owl, I could always get up in the morning, and farming insisted on crack-of-dawn starts. I very soon learned how to milk and calve a cow and indeed all the other biological realities of live-stock farming.

I had had some experience of horses, originally with old Dolly who had by now disappeared, and also in Germany where I rode regularly with my mother. My next equine experience was with the Suffolk Punches on the farm. I used to be allowed to turn them out into the field, get them in and, the greatest excitement of all, lead one of them (Prince) in the harvest field. I used to lead him with his wagon between the 'stooks' of corn. On each side there was a pitcher who forked the individual sheaves of corn to the stacker or loader, who arranged them so that in spite of the rolling and pitching of the load it never fell off. When the wagon was full I then led Prince and his load back to the stack yard. If the stack yard was more than a short distance along the road, an older man would bring his empty wagon back to the field, where I would hand over mine and take his, which not only gave me experience of other horses, but more importantly prevented a twelve-year-old being on the public highway. I can't remember the names of the other horses involved, but Prince was 'mine'.

Eventually came the most exciting job of all – threshing. Now at last the farmer would know what he had really got to sell. A set of steam threshing tackle consisted of three basic pieces of equipment: the steam engine, the threshing 'drum', and the elevator to take the straw away.

The layout of the stack yard was for the convenience of the threshing tackle. Normally the 'drum' would be positioned between two stacks, usually of the same crop, and would be 'fed' from both sides.

The machine had to stand completely level, and setting it up with spirit levels and chocks was a painstaking operation. Next the elevator or baler to take the straw away would be positioned and the webbing drive belt fitted. Finally the steam traction engine would be positioned at the other end and the main drive belt fitted. This all sounds very easy in theory, but in practice the narrow steel wheels of the drum frequently caused it to get stuck in the mud, and extricating it would make deeper ruts, usually exactly where it needed to stand. All this operation was usually done the day before the real action. Around four a.m. the engine crew would arrive on site to light the fire in the boiler and get steam up for a seven a.m. start. Apart from the engine crew, who were the contractor's men, the rest of the gang were provided by the farmer. On a large farm they would consist of farm staff; on a small farm casual labour, often from a neighbouring farm, would be brought in. A minimum gang would be eight men excluding the engine crew.

The man on the stack had to drop each sheaf exactly to the hand of the 'feeder', who with one easy movement would pick them up, cut the string, retaining the knot end in his hand (saved to tie the sacks of corn, amongst other uses) and tease the sheaf out to give a steady flow through the drum. This steady flow through the drum was essential to extract every last grain of corn. The hum of this process was a never to be forgotten sound, which can still be recalled at steam rallies around the country. The feeder had arguably the most skilled job. The 'chaff', the outside husk of the grain which was used for bulking up animal feed (roughage, in today's parlance), was collected in large sacks. Removal of this, together with the 'cavings', as the unusable rubbish was called, was the dustiest, dirtiest, filthiest job of all and was always given to the junior hand. This, of course, was where I started. The grain was sacked off into four bushel sacks and weighed off eighteen stone for wheat, sixteen for barley, twelve for oats, twenty for peas and beans. These would be collected from the drum by other farm staff and taken to the granary. All had to be carried on a man's back up narrow four-inch steps, invariably wet and slippery. As most weighed well over a hundred kilos in today's measurements, the reader can see farm work was hard physically, and it is no wonder that men suffered permanent arthritis and back pain.

Whilst many of today's health and safety regulations are nitpickingly stupid, others are of manifest benefit to farm personnel. There were virtually no safety regulations then and we all had to pass under the driving belts, which because of the necessary slack in them would whip up and down alarmingly. The stack to be threshed was surrounded with wire netting to stop the rats, which always made their home in grain stacks, from escaping. An assortment of terriers had a field day with much squealing and shrieking. Presumably this activity today would be banned under the 'hunting with dogs' regulations!

During the next three or four years I did every job in the gang, and my proudest moment came with promotion to feeding the drum.

The Jersey breed of cow has very special characteristics compared to others. They are one of the smallest physically, but also one of the toughest; the females are the most docile of all breeds, whilst the bulls are unquestionably the least docile of any breed. They had the highest butterfat but produced one of the lowest gallonages. At the time they were of no value as beef animals, which rendered the unwanted male of the species valueless. Their milk was especially valued because of the high butterfat content, as every fraction of a percentage – point on the fat content earned an extra premium. The Horkesley herd at one stage averaged seven and a half per cent butterfat, making it one of the best in the country. How things have changed! Such milk would have a very limited sale today.

The main volume-producing breed was the Friesian, but their milk quality was very poor, with a butterfat content less than half that of the Jersey. The excellent pedigree of the Horkesley herd ensured there was a ready market for young stock to introduce into other Friesian herds to boost the quality of their milk.

The cows were very well trained, and as I used to walk up from the Hall at four thirty a.m. through the field in which they had been overnighted, they meekly followed me into the milking shed and went to their allotted places, where all I had to do was loop the tethering chain around their necks. I can still smell that wonderful scent of a warm cow on a winter's morning, as the act of looping the chain round the neck inevitably meant burying your nose in their skin!

There was an old bull and a young bull; the older one did all the work but I had no contact with him, being too young to handle him. The old boy was called Buscot Ajax and had a well developed paranoia about vets. Most animals have a strongly developed sixth sense, and he certainly knew when the vet was within a mile of the farm and would kick up an unholy racket until he had gone. The bulls had a large copper ring in their noses to which the bull pole was attached; indeed, at service time two poles were attached as the sight or smell of a cow 'in season' excited him so much that it took two men to control him. As a twelve-year-old, I was of course curious to see what happened. As this story has no pornographic aspirations, suffice it to say that the accuracy of the bull's aim was impressive.

I was allowed to exercise the young bull on my own, but once he reached the bovine equivalent of puberty he became too strong for me. The defining moment was when he mounted the foreman's wife when she was bending down weeding a flower bed in her garden; she was a very large woman, and no doubt an inviting target! I was able to get him off, but being a smutty youth I was not considered contrite enough over the incident; so when the next school holidays came round it was suggested I seek 'employment' elsewhere. This was not a one-off incident, as the next day the same bull pinned me against the cowshed wall; I was very lucky in that his horns went either side of my body. After that he became an adult's responsibility. Subsequently he turned out to be so vicious that he had to be put down.

As Buscot Ajax was getting old and the home-grown replacement had had to go, my grandmother bought a bull from the Ovaltine Dairy Farms herd near Cambridge, who turned out to be a great success. At this time there was no de-horning or artificial insemination (AI) practiced.

The natural consequence of putting bull to cow was, of course, calving. Just before the due date an examination of the pelvic bones would tell you fairly accurately when calving was going to occur. The birth process was messy; presentations were sometimes the wrong way round and occasionally the calf had to be pulled out by rope. The calves would spend a few days on the mother, basically until the milk was clear of colostrum, and then they would be weaned and the mother went back to the milking shed. Weaning was a noisy process with both mother and calf protesting vehemently.

In the spring, once there was reasonable growth in the grass all except newborn calves were turned out into the fields.

During the winter all the arable fields had been ploughed over, and those that were to grow root crops would have had the muck from the stockyards spread over them first and then ploughed in. But now in the spring the farming year began afresh. Horse-drawn rollers, cultivators and harrows were the basic seedbed preparation equipment. The Smythe drill would put the seed into the ground in rows, and a light set of harrows would cover it over.

Once the drilling was complete and the stock were all out to grass, the stockyards would be cleaned out and the muck stored in heaps to rot down before being carted out to the field where it would be needed in the autumn and winter. Again, with no machinery the procedure was digging out by hand with a special muck fork, loading onto two-wheel carts called tumbrils, and on arrival at the muck heap it was offloaded, again by hand. This particular activity always gave one a marvellous appetite, whether because of the physical energy expended or the smell of ammonia I never knew. Depending on the perceived workload on the farm, this task was sometimes left until the autumn when the muck could go straight onto the field, thus avoiding double handling.

The social life – or lack of it – at Crabbe's Farm was also about to undergo rapid change. Much romantic talk of the 'good old days' is just that – romanticism. A farmworker's lot was a tough one not just for the men but especially their families. They had at best a cottage of sorts, with no modern conveniences or even basic sanitation, from which they could be evicted at seven days' notice – and many were. The stockmen and foreman usually had a perk or two such as free firewood out of the hedgerows and a pint of milk a day, but that usually was all. Most villages had a grocery shop and a baker and butcher would come once or twice a week in a horse-drawn cart. Entertainment came from a battery-operated radio for the women and the pub for the men. In our village there was a weekly bus to Colchester which returned almost as soon as it had got there. Strangely enough, this totally inadequate public transport system is the one aspect of village life that seems to have remained intact to the present day.

The dustcart would come usually every two weeks and the 'honey cart' to empty the buckets from the EC (earth closet – to differentiate it from the WC or water closet) once a week. The EC was always at the bottom of the garden in a specially constructed brick 'privy'. Depending on the size of family and construction of the 'privy', a visitation was either a solitary or in large families a communal affair. The largest one I ever came across was an eight-in-a-family three holer. During the winter the contents of the bucket would be applied to the vegetable garden, especially the leek beds, as human waste was supposed to be especially beneficial for the growing of prize leeks for the annual horticultural show. However, this quaintly old-fashioned rural life was soon to change dramatically, and within five years the 'old order' was all gone.

The early Fifties saw the change from the old ways of agriculture to the new accelerating, rapidly. Indeed, by the end of the decade there was almost nothing left of the old way of life. I helped to stook the last traditional harvest of my lifetime at Crabbes Farm with Jim Martin. Jim had been a stoker on HMS *Ajax* during the Battle of the River Plate, and his continuous chatter about Navy life was beginning to push me in a Naval rather than an Army direction for National Service. At the other end of the naval hierarchy was my grandfather's neighbour, Admiral of the Fleet Sir George Creasy, ultimately to become First Sea Lord. I was totally in awe of him; both he and his wife were always pleased to see me and although he did nothing to try to persuade me to become a sailor, as he knew this would be against my father's wishes as a professional soldier, he did not dissuade me either.

This last traditional harvest was indeed a hard and hot one. A great deal of barley had been grown which was heavily infested with thistles. This combination reduced even covered arms to the state of raw meat. Much as we enjoyed the free beer, the greatest pleasure came from seeing the first combine in the area and the realisation that we should probably never have to harvest by hand again.

After this last harvest was safely in I did not go back to Crabbes in a working capacity again, although I obviously kept in touch.

My parents were now based in North Yorkshire and my holidays were again shared between Brandsby, where they lived, just at the edge of the Yorkshire Moors, and Horkesley. A friend of the family, Bruce Seton, farmed in Great Horkesley and he kindly continued to teach me some more about farming. I worked for him – still without pay – on a similarly casual basis to that which I had done at Crabbes Farm. His was a predominantly arable farm with but a few livestock, pigs, chickens, a few bullocks and just a couple of house cows. The main crops were wheat, barley and mixed vegetables, including cabbages, peas, beans and carrots. Strange crops like opium poppies and sugar beet for seed were also grown. The vegetable crops were all destined for Stratford or Spitalfields market and the 'funnies' to specialised outlets.

The horses had all gone and had been replaced by two Fordson Majors, one standard Fordson and one little Allis Chalmers. The old Smythe drill was now used only for sugar beet and vegetable seed drilling, but for corn drilling a new combine(d) drill, where the fertiliser and corn were applied simultaneously down separate pipes, had appeared. The theory was that fertiliser placement next to, but not touching the seed, led to faster take-up of nutrients. Nitrogen was still applied as a top dressing to autumn-drilled crops in early spring. The binder had been consigned to history and there were now two combine harvesters: a small Allis Chalmers, primarily for the seed crops, and a Claas for the cereal crops. Both were tractor-drawn machines driven from the power take-off (PTO) at the rear of the tractor.

The grain was collected in sacks at the top of the machine and slid down a metal chute which could hold three sacks at a time before the lever was pulled to deposit them on the ground. As the machine went round the crop, the operators would always try to have the drops reasonably close together to ease the task of collection. The straw thrown out of the back of the combine was baled up with a tractor-drawn baler, frequently operated by the old threshing contractors, whose livelihood was otherwise slipping away.

Not all corn was combined; in the early days crops of barley and oats were the first target for the combines as they were the most difficult and most unpleasant to harvest in the traditional way. For quite a few years after the introduction of the combine there was still a tendency on some farms to harvest wheat in the traditional way. Wheat straw suitable for thatching could only come from traditionally harvested crops, as opposed to combined crops. All grain crops had to be dead ripe for combining, and by then the straw was so brittle it would break up in the combine and was useless for thatching. Although the threshing of wheat stacks was still done by the old threshing drums, the power source had changed. Steam traction engines had been replaced by the ubiquitous 'Field Marshall' single-cylinder diesel tractor, whose distinctive engine noise soon became as much a part of the country scene as the sound and smell of the steam engine had previously been. Even so, there was not enough threshing to keep all the contractors in work, and many diversified into contract combining. They fought a gallant rearguard action for about ten years, but eventually the firms which had started life with steam tackle would see their entire lifestyle gradually disappear.

From this brief description it will be obvious that two men at harvest time were now doing the work of at least six under the old system. So began 'the drift from the land', about which so much has been written in economic and social history books.

Unlike corn which had been stacked and was completely dry, combined corn frequently needed drying to bring the moisture level down to around fifteen per cent, at which it could safely be stored. The driers were oil-fired, and there were several types and different ways of passing the heat source through the grain, although the end result was the same. It also had to be 'dressed' to get out the weed seeds and other extraneous matter, which the new combines admittedly could not do as well as the old threshing drums.

The opium poppy crop was the hardest to deal with as the stems could not be left until they were ripe or the seed would all shatter onto the ground. We cut them by hand with a pair of sheep-shearing scissors and then they were spread out on the barn floor until ripe. Once ripe they were fed into the little Allis combine in stationary mode. It was an immensely time-consuming job and could only be done on a small scale, as the poppy heads needed nearly as much room to dry as they did to grow. However, there was a hugely valuable end product. Not much seems to change over the years with this crop, as the Afghan growers can testify. I assume it was legal to grow in those days, but I never asked!

A year-round job on Laurel's Farm was harvesting cabbages. A strong knife which looked like a cut-down version of a 'panga' was used for cutting; the cut heads were thrown into heaps, before being bagged into hessian sacks which were then sewn up with baler twine. The bagging was a job entrusted to experienced men who had to recognise when forty-pound weight was a bagful. The bags were then loaded onto carts and then offloaded in the yard onto the market lorry. Trade was then, as now, very volatile and prices equally so. Frosty bright weather was good for trade; warm wet weather was bad. Pigeons were a constant enemy and provided good sport for those with a gun.

Peas and beans were also picked for the fresh market, and

again were packed in forty-pound sacks. Another important crop was sugar beet. I can hardly believe how this crop was managed compared with today. For me, learning the hard way, the crop was a nightmare from start to finish. Sugar beet seed is a cluster with many seeds within the cluster; the Smythe drill was used to drill this with a cup size equivalent to one cluster. When the seed germinated, at least six seedlings would appear from each cluster, which would themselves be about three inches apart. To say that they looked like hair on a cat's back is an understatement, but these had to be thinned down with a hoe to one seedling every eight or nine inches. At this stage the men would go onto piecework rates and would hoe all the hours of daylight. First the seedlings had to be gapped, leaving about two or three every four to five inches. Depending on the weather, a second thinning was done about two weeks later, with the eventual aim of leaving one strong seedling every eight or nine inches.

This was much easier said than done. Attempting to disentangle tiny seedlings with a hoe, especially in wet or windy weather, would try the patience of a saint. Having done this, the crop had to be continuously hoed to keep the weeds at bay and to remove any bolters. Without a doubt, hoeing sugar beet is the worst job I have ever had to do in my life. Even today I get backache if I even see a hoe. At lifting time you tied a sack round your waist, took hold of a beet by its leaves, one in each hand – they had already been 'squeezed' out of the rows with a special device – and knocked them together to remove as much soil as possible. Then you laid them down again. Another man came behind and, picking one up at a time, chopped the top off at exactly the right place – hopefully without cutting his hand off – and threw it onto a heap, as with the cabbages. The topping called for considerable accuracy, as too much top removed would be a waste of valuable beet and too little would be penalised by the beet factory as too much 'top tare'. Both these jobs were done at the stoop, all day, every day in all weathers.

The beet was then taken to somewhere readily accessible by lorry and heaped up, again all by hand. When the lorry arrived it was a case of all available hands to man the forks and throw the beet on. The lorries were always high-sided, so the beet had to be thrown up some six to eight feet off the ground. From my student viewpoint, I hated everything to do with the crop at every single stage of its production. However, to the farmer it was a very valuable cash crop, providing not only the root break so necessary for cereal production, but also stock feed in the form of pulp from the factory and the tops themselves.

I had by this stage learned to 'go solo' on a tractor and undertook all the basic cultivations. My mentor on this farm was Hans, a German POW with whom I had an excellent relationship, extending to going with him to see the wrestling every Tuesday night at the Colchester Corn Exchange. It was there that I became acquainted with Dale Martin Promotions and their stars such as Mick McManus and the Royal Brothers, to name but a few. I maintained this interest in wrestling as a form of entertainment until the TV broadcasts finished some quarter of a century later. The new wrestling bouts from the US were no substitute, having an entertainment value somewhat less than zero.

It was Hans who really taught me how to plough with both trailed and hydraulic lift implements. Some of my early attempts were laughable and Hans took a fair bit of stick from the village, who thought he was responsible for the mess. The farm had very mixed soil types, varying from light sand to very heavy clay, and I learned an enormous amount about the way these different soil types affected not only cropping but the soil preparation process. Tractor driving was for me the most pleasurable activity of all, ploughing in good weather being my favourite. To look back on a straight furrow, with all the rubbish buried and thousands of seagulls following behind looking for worms, was a wonderful sight.

Ploughing in cold, wet weather was a far less enjoyable

experience, particularly on a 'high' Major. The metal seats were covered by the inevitable corn sack, and an ex-Army greatcoat for protection against the elements was all that was available. By lunchtime your crotch was wet and cold, the rain had run down the neck, and even a youngster like me was bent almost double when I got off. For winter ploughing one of the tractors would be fitted up with spade-lug rear wheels, and being unable to travel on the road 'lived out' all winter. At the end of the day's work, if there was any likelihood of frost the radiator was drained down, a tin was put over the exhaust pipe and the tractor was rugged up against the weather in rather the same way as a horse would be.

The following morning, water was carried out, the radiator refilled, the tractor unrugged and away we went. Starting on the handle was not easy on a very cold morning, but by this time I was strong enough to do it. Only one of the tractors had a hydraulic lift plough, and as this was a much more versatile combination it stayed on rubber tyres and did not live out. The very heavy land in the various counties which used to be ploughed with steam engines was not suitable for wheeled tractors and steam was replaced by 'crawlers', as tracked tractors were always called. These also 'lived out' and the routine was much the same as I have just described.

The plant breeders were now also beginning to make an impact and a lot of the old-fashioned varieties of wheat, such as Little Joss and Squareheads Master, were going out of fashion. Both were long–strawed varieties suitable for yielding thatching straw, with the former having a beautiful red chaff so attractive at harvest time. Thatching straw was no longer in such need as the relentless advance of the combine continued. Instead the requirement was for high-yielding short-strawed varieties.

The same progress was being made in all crop varieties, but it was to be quite a few years before the old-fashioned varieties of potato, King Edward and Majestic, were to see any serious rivals.

By now I was determined to follow an agricultural career and had applied to go to the Royal Agricultural College at Cirencester. Quite how I was going to pay for it I wasn't sure, as father was adamant that he wasn't, as he saw no future at all in farming, especially as we had no money with which to buy a farm. I always had in the back of my mind, but never said so publicly, that my grandfather would see me right with Crabbes Farm – eventually. I knew that one of the conditions for entry to Cirencester was to have completed a twelve-month cycle of practical farming. Bruce was kind enough to agree to take me as an official pupil once I had completed my National Service, and was happy to certify that I had had at least a full year's practical experience, even if it was spread over more than one year. The College were satisfied with this, and I felt that this was as far as I could go for the time being.

CHAPTER VIII

Eton College

I n 1948 I took my Common Entrance exam at Abberley and gained the requisite pass mark to allow me to go to Eton in September of that year. I did not appreciate at the time how immensely privileged I was, to be following in my father's and his father's footsteps to what was unquestionably the best educational establishment in the world. It has been a matter of bitter regret all my life that I neither enjoyed myself there nor made full use of an education most parents would sacrifice almost anything to give their children. However, the Eton experience has stood me in good stead, and has in large part allowed me to 'get away' with things and enjoy experiences which would probably not have been possible to the same extent had I gone anywhere else.

At the end of the summer holidays, most of which had been spent in Germany, I had the hell of school to face up to, made even worse by being a new boy again. Having somehow contracted a huge 'boil', something I have never had before or since, on my arm, I was convinced I would be regarded as some sort of freak to be made fun of. Even today I wonder whether this wasn't a rather drastic manifestation of self-induced affliction. I pleaded not to be sent to a new school in this condition, but to no avail. The drive there was the longest I have ever endured and I was affected by a deep sense of foreboding. The so-called 'welcome' tea party was a nightmare, made particularly memorable by my father buttonholing another parent and giving him a lecture on the evils of socialism. It transpired that he was a peer of the realm who sat on the Labour benches in the House of Lords. This sort of embarrassment, however unintentional, from one's father did not get a small and apprehensive boy off to a good start. It did, however, trigger a friendship between myself and the peer's son which was to last throughout my five years at Eton. Being 'publicly' embarrassed by our two fathers established that initial new-boy bond that helped to settle us in. Two decisions had to be made on the very first day: who were you going to pair off with for the ritual of afternoon tea, cooked on a communal stove and served and eaten in the room, and were you going to become a 'dry bob' and play cricket, or a 'wet bob' and row? Julian and I decided we could do worse than pair off together for tea, an arrangement which lasted most of the time we were there. He decided to be a 'dry bob' and I decided to be a 'wet bob', not because I knew anything about rowing but I had had enough experience of cricket at Abberley to know that if I could get out of that, I would. In our first years we only had the two choices for summer sport, although a category defined as 'slack bob' was later introduced, which included such esoteric sports (then) as tennis, golf and eventually shooting.

The system of 'fagging' still existed at Eton, as did corporal punishment. My 'fagmaster' was, quite fortuitously, House Captain, and we quickly established an amicable working relationship. I don't remember which 'fagmaster' Julian drew.

First we had to find what classes we were in for what subject, and where and when we had to turn up. There seemed to be literally hundreds of class lists which we had to fight our way through hordes of boys to see, but we got there eventually. Julian was more clever academically than I was and we were not in any of the same classes.

This was the initial Eton experience, being chucked in at the deep end without any guidance at all and told to 'sort yourself out'. Of all the benefits I gained from Eton, this requirement to stand on your own feet from day one was the most valuable, and has stood me in the greatest stead all my life. It, and everything that followed, gave me enough self-confidence to cope with anything. Abberley had also taught me the same, as in both cases I was a small fish arriving in a big pond entirely alone.

The other matter which had to be addressed urgently was the Eton equivalent of the London cabbies' 'The Knowledge'. We had three weeks in which to learn everything, and I mean everything, before being examined.

The first few weeks were quite traumatic. There was just so much to learn, to do and to cope with. As was normal at that period there was no home or parental contact at all beyond the occasional letter. Letter writing, though, was not compulsory as it had been at Abberley.

The school was divided into a Lower and Upper School, which roughly meant the first two years being spent in Lower School and the rest of one's time in Upper School. Each half of the school had its own chapel, attendance at which was compulsory once every weekday and twice on Sundays, with a third compulsory visit on Sunday after confirmation. I enjoyed the services, especially in College Chapel, where the singing of six hundred boys and masters of 'proper' hymns with 'proper' tunes was very awe-inspiring.

The boys' houses and classrooms were spread all over the town, and switching between lessons often entailed a miniature route march from one classroom to the next. Our academic day started at seven thirty and finished at nine in the evening. Games were compulsory three afternoons a week.

My housemaster, known colloquially as 'm'tutor', was Tom Brocklebank. He ran the house together with his wife, Jane. They were assisted by a 'dame', who was responsible for the health and welfare of the boys. One of Eton's unique features was that every boy had his own room, and consequently his privacy, from the very first day. We were allowed into other boys' rooms but definitely not after lights out at nine forty-five. Anyone found in another's room after lights out was automatically suspected of covert sexual activity and usually sent home without appeal.

Each house normally held about forty boys, usually on three floors. Our rooms were adequate in size and consisted of a fold-up bed, desk, wash-stand and the ubiquitous ottoman in which everything was stored, acting as the equivalent of 'under-the-bed' storage. There was no running water, the hot water being brought in by the boys' maids at a quarter to seven. Each floor had its own 'boys' maid' who also cleaned and tidied our rooms. This may explain why so many Old Etonians are untidy creatures; we never had to clear up behind ourselves. The boys' maids were always ancient crones but one housemaster did try to move with the times and recruited three young Italian girls to give a more modern image. He was clearly more than a little naive, as by the end of the first term all three were pregnant!

Carter House, which was Tom Brocklebank's, was structurally one of the oldest boys' houses, and we were only there for a year before he moved to The Timbralls, the last boys' house on the road to Slough. All housemasters were referred to by their initials, which in the case of Tom Brocklebank were TAB. He had been an outstanding athlete in his youth, rowing in the final of the Diamond Sculls at Henley and taking part in an expedition to Mount Everest. Such physical exertion took a terrible toll on his body and he never enjoyed good health during the time I was there.

TAB never taught me any academic subject. This was by accident rather than design, I think, but such a troublesome pupil was I to become that it may have been deliberate after all. My classical tutor, who took me and about ten other boys for evening prep, was Brian Whitfield (BGW), a lovely man, something of a cross between my mother's father and Rumpole of the Bailey. He was also a housemaster on the verge of giving up his house to DJ Graham-Campbel, to whom my brother was to be assigned in two years' time. Included in his evening classes were the late Charles Benson, whose academic expertise was to be found in the *Sporting Life* which appeared to be the only literature he ever studied. Charles was to join the *Daily Express* as racing correspondent under the pseudonym 'Bendex'. He ultimately aspired to the post of senior racing correspondent, succeeding Clive Graham as 'The Scout'. The late Robin Douglas-Home was also a fellow member, as was Colin Ingleby Mackenzie, one-time Captain of Hampshire County Cricket Club and latterly of Wentworth Golf Club; also the Eckersley brothers, both brilliant racquets players. The rest of us were and are somewhat less distinguished. During these sessions we seemed mostly to study the works of Shakespeare with a singular lack of seriousness. There were frequent opportunities in some of Shakespeare's works for vulgar jocularity, much to the irritation of B G W, who nonetheless took it all in good part.

The Eton academic year was divided into the usual three terms, perversely referred to as 'halfs'. For teaching we were all, from day one, 'streamed' for each and every subject. The classes, referred to in Eton speak as 'divisions', generally averaged about twenty boys. Life at Eton revolved around the twenty-six or so boys' houses, each of which had its individual house colours and whose occupants were collectively referred to as 'Oppidans', whereas the seventy or so scholars were referred to as 'Tugs' or 'Collegers'.

The average Eton house, as I said, accommodated roughly forty boys, with the housemaster in overall control. He lived with his family in the 'private' side of the house with the boys accommodated in the rest. Each house was run by a senior boy chosen by the housemaster as Captain of the House. He in turn was assisted by about four others, known collectively as 'the Library'. They were generally chosen from the house Captain of Games, senior 'wet bob', house head of the CCF, and others who had distinguished themselves either on the sporting field or academically. Each member of the Library had his personal fag who acted as valet and additionally were allowed to stand at the top of the stairs and yell 'Boooooy!' at the top of their voice to summon other juniors to run their errands. At this call all junior boys had to run to do their master's bidding, and the last one to arrive had the short straw.

All had to turn up, and absence from the house was the

only allowable excuse. Failing to answer the call was a punishable offence.

The Library members alone were allowed to enforce discipline, and although canings were frequent they could generally only be administered by the House Captain, and then only with the housemaster's permission. Lesser punishments, like being sent for a run round the school playing field, did not require the housemaster's permission. The next layer of authority was about six of the next most senior boys who formed 'the Debate'. It was from this group that next year's 'Library' was invariably elected. I managed to achieve the unenviable distinction of being elected to Debate one week and sacked the next. My nemesis was none other than the current 'Father' of the House of Commons, Tam Dalyell. I don't recall what crime I had committed but I was never reinstated and of course never made the Library either.

I nonetheless retained my position as both senior wet bob and senior member of the CCF, which in fact gave me authority in those spheres over members of the Library. An odd situation, which perhaps I abused, and so earned no friends in the hierarchy. Indeed I have been accused in later life of so abusing my position in the CCF that I was responsible for driving Tam into his apparent hostility towards our armed forces! Nowadays I have no political feelings either way, but I do have a huge respect for Tam's integrity and consistency, especially in his dislike of the way the House of Commons is sidelined on all important issues.

The school itself was organised along similar lines to the individual houses, with the Eton Society, known as 'Pop', as the enforcers. They, together with the Headmaster, maintained discipline for offences not coming under each individual house's procedures. The normal school dress was tailcoats, but short jackets known as 'bum freezers' were worn by those who nowadays would be described as 'vertically challenged'. However, once elected to Pop, the uniform was check trousers and garish waistcoats.

Much has been written about public schools' addiction to corporal punishment, and certainly there was a sizeable element of sadomasochistic abuse by both boys and masters. Punishment rituals were strictly observed and obviously enjoyed. Within the house the conventional bamboo cane with a crook handle was used, but the victim was fully clothed. Pop 'tannings', as they were called, were usually, but not always, carried out on 'the bare' with a vicious knobbly cane producing very painful and gruesome results. The ultimate sanction, one short of expulsion, was a birching from the Headmaster – always on 'the bare'.

Whilst none of these were 'public' there was always an audience of sympathetic sadists. Lesser punishments were writing out endless lines of Latin verse. In fact I found the latter far worse as they lasted much longer. Five hundred lines – a Georgic – of Latin verse was first cousin to a life sentence. The most heinous offences were theft, overt homosexual practices, being drunk on the river or being caught at Windsor Races, or simply going AWOL.

Winston Churchill once described life in the Royal Navy as consisting of rum, sodomy and the lash. The same description could apply to life at a public school, but without the rum. The house system gave rise to considerable tribal warfare, the houses competing against each other at everything, and it was a moot point whether one's primary sporting allegiance was to the house or the school. Apart from the summer sports of rowing and cricket there was relatively little inter-school competition, largely due to the archaic games we played.

In the autumn half we played the Field Game. This was peculiar to Eton and played by no other school anywhere. The ball was shaped halfway between a soccer and a rugger ball and first of all had to be manoeuvred over the goal line between your feet to score a 'rouge'. Then the rouge had to be converted, which required the formation of a four-man battering ram to charge through the opposition in the narrow goalmouth. This was fun, and as one of the bigger boys I found it was one of the rare occasions where one was justified in using brute strength. I believe the practice has now been banned on safety grounds!

The inter-house games were fiercely competitive, but the school team could only play against other Old Etonian teams.

The other even more archaic game was the Wall Game, which despite the players' protests to the contrary, was essentially a brawl in the mud. There were only two teams, the Oppidans and the Collegers, and of course other Old Etonian scratch teams. The last 'goal' was, I believe, scored in 1947, the year before I went!

In the Easter half we played soccer or rugger. Here we did play other schools, but invariably were well beaten as the opposition had been playing throughout the autumn and had got their act together, whereas we invariably had not, our efforts having gone into either the Field or Wall games.

As a 'wet bob' I was allocated my own single scull, clinker-built racing boat and thenceforth devoted as much of my life to the river as time and the authorities allowed. I fell in love with the Thames and spent every available spare minute on it. I am still in love with it today, and try to find time at least once a year to enjoy it. As we got older and worked our way up the rowing ladder we could be on the river from January to July. This made life not just tolerable but even enjoyable.

Academically, I did enough to get by and never failed an exam; I even passed my School Certificate, the forerunner of O levels, to everyone's amazement.

The school rightly prided itself on schooling boys for the professions, but as I had no wish to follow this path, preferring an agricultural or engineering career, I was the despair of both my parents and the school. In the end they gave up, and presumably to test whether I was serious about agriculture I had to write a paper on land reclamation. They were amazed at how much I knew and how well I could express myself, so my tutors reluctantly wrote to my father saying that I appeared to have the makings of Eton's first agriculturist. They added a sting to the tail when they doubted, however, whether I would make my mark as a useful social or public being!

We won the house Head of the River race every year I was in the crew, and TAB and I got along well with all things aquatic, less so with things academic. He once wrote on my end of term report that after four years he still had no idea what made me tick. What he did know, however, was that if there was any noise or disruption in the house I would be in the thick of it, but if ever he wanted anything done that same person was the one to get it done, come what may. At about this time I had been made senior member of the CCF at house level. The CCF was almost entirely Army and I don't remember any significant naval or air faction. I do however remember one of our big parades at which the Royal Marines provided the band and at some stage played 'Sunset'. I was so moved and emotional I began to think, Am I in the wrong uniform?

The death of King George VI saw the Eton Cadet Force providing a guard of honour outside St George's Chapel. We had endless practice at the 'slow march' and 'resting on our arms reversed'. This referred to the position of the rifle rather than our bodies. Come the appointed day, and whilst gathering in the assembly area, we were 'entertained' by Prince Monolulu. Those of my generation will remember him as a racing tipster dressed up as a Nigerian prince. What on earth he was doing there or how he was allowed in, history never related. Eventually we took up our position outside St George's Chapel, where we had a first-class view of the procession, although we were not allowed to look up and appear to be watching. Despite the bitter cold, biting hunger and thirst, we all survived.

Later that summer, with National Service looming on the horizon, I was interviewed for and accepted into the 9th Lancers, despite my misgivings. Call-up time was still nearly two years away, and that to a teenager is a long time.

For my sixteenth birthday Father took me on a surprise trip

to Pride & Clark in London, where he bought me a second-hand Triumph 350cc twin motorbike in good condition. I was absolutely thrilled, and any friction there may have been between us evaporated. It was loaded onto the train at Liverpool Street and I met it at Colchester Station. With Father following in the car, I rode it the six miles back to Horkesley.

He had equipped me with an RAF sheepskin flying jacket and goggles, I acquired some gloves – and we were away! Two or three days after delivery my mother watched in horror as I sped off, with my brother riding pillion. Both my parents put their foot down and I had to give an undertaking – I think on oath – that I would never, ever do such a thing again. My pedal bike had quickly become redundant.

Some four months after the late King's funeral came the Coronation of the new Queen. Time off was given to attend the Coronation ceremony in London, and John and I were lucky enough to be able to watch from premises rented for the day by the Sun Insurance Office near Admiralty Arch. Closed-circuit television was available so that we were able to watch the entire proceedings. Even more fortunate were my mother and father who were seated in Westminster Abbey. My mother, having a weak bladder, equipped herself with a device known as a 'Why-be-wet' to cope with the extreme length of time they had to be in the Abbey. This caused much vulgar amusement to all of us.

In the morning, news came through of the conquest of Everest by Edmund Hillary, which was additional cause for celebration. Tom Brocklebank was thrilled that 'his' mountain had finally been conquered, especially at such an auspicious time. It was a typical English June day – cold and wet – and I was grateful to be in the dry.

The Coronation was a very grand ceremonial occasion. I was particularly impressed by the Royal Navy contingent, and again I was wondering whether I was doing the right thing for my National Service. During the time in London I went to see the film *The Cruel Sea* and at the end I really fancied my chances as a Royal Navy officer. I made discreet enquiries about doing National Service in the Navy but learned that it was nigh on impossible unless one belonged to the RNVR first. In the following January, Father, who by then had returned from SHAPE headquarters in Paris where he had been senior liaison officer between British and American forces, had taken up a post as Chief of Staff, Northern Command, based in York. He took me to a parade at Catterick Camp where he was taking the salute and announced that this was where I would probably be coming for part of my Army service. Now Catterick Camp in mid-January is something else entirely, and the prospect of serving under Father was too much. At the end of the holidays I asked my mother to take me to York Station to catch an early train back to school. I spun some yarn as to why I needed to do this, and on my way to Waterloo Station I stopped at HMS *President* tied up on the Embankment, which was the RNVR headquarters, and signed on!

My rowing was going well, and I seemed to have secured my place in the Second Eight and also had two trials for the First Eight. I must have done something terribly wrong, as instead of promotion to the First Eight I was demoted to the Third. To my eternal shame, instead of redoubling my efforts I totally freaked out and never rowed in a school crew again. Once those whom I thought inferior replaced me that was it. I behaved like the spoilt brat I probably was. I was unsettled and depressed and a total pain in the ass to everybody, so much so that I was asked to leave two days before the official end of term.

So ended my school days. I collected probably the worst set of school reports that there have ever been, and I still have them all preserved for future generations. I am not remotely proud of this record and feel guilty even referring to it.

However, it was too late for regrets, as I had another hurdle to overcome – confessing to Father that in a month's time I was to start my naval career. As it turned out his reaction was not as violent as I had expected, although he hardly expressed approval.

CHAPTER IX

National Service

In spite of my father's latent hostility I spent the time between leaving Eton and my call-up at Brandsby. I had initially given the authorities my Horkesley address, not least because I did not want letters for me with 'Admiralty' stamped all over being intercepted by him at the Yorkshire address. With my official notice to attend 'Summer Camp' came my free travel warrant and joining instructions for boarding HMS *Indefatigable.* I was caught out now, as the warrant was from Colchester station. It was my grandmother who saw me off, and the photograph of me is taken on the terrace on the day of departure.

HMS Indefatigable was a large aircraft carrier assigned to training duties along with her sister ship, HMS *Implacable,* both at anchor in Weymouth Bay. I had already got an issue of kit, consisting of a hammock, basic necessities and a uniform, which I travelled down in, leaving my civilian clothes behind. On arrival on board I was assigned to a particular class with sleeping accommodation, viz. somewhere to sling a hammock on one of the mess decks.

First impressions were, What have I done? Whilst I had experience of a North Essex accent from life on the farm, all these other strange noises emanating from the mouths of Geordies, Scousers and Brummies were to me, otherwise used to hearing only Etonian accents, something of a culture shock – as well as being unintelligible! An admission of incomprehension gave rise to ridicule, to say the least, and frequently verbal abuse, of which 'Posh bastard' was one of the milder ripostes. Even so, I did not despair, as all this lot had

had to go through the same selection process as I did, and I consoled myself with the thought, If this is the pick of the crop, thank God I didn't go in the Army! Reveille too was far from the polite knock on the door of the boys' maid. At six a.m. the bugle sounded over the tannoy system, shortly followed by the senior petty officer on duty, who advanced, armed with a short stave, and beat any still occupied hammocks on the underside with the shouted refrain of 'Hands off cocks, on socks!'

We were quickly segregated into 'sheep and goats', and fortunately my new class consisted entirely of 'officer potential' recruits. We were able to distance ourselves from our coarser brethren. There was safety in numbers now, although of course segregation gave rise to even more snide remarks. However, the Abberley and Eton education came in handy, as I had had ten years of survival training, and was still big and powerful for my age and above all prepared to use it. Tom Brocklebank, my Eton tutor, lived at Blandford and came every Sunday of the three-week period to collect me, take me home, give me a hot bath and a Sunday lunch, and then took me back in time to catch the liberty boat back on board. This was an act of immense kindness by him and his wife, Jane, especially as I had led them such a dance at school.

We were all issued with *The Manual of Seamanship* and a copy of QRs & AIs *Queen's Regulations and Admiralty Instructions*. These were the sailors' bible. We had endless instruction in drill, knot-tying and the use and purpose behind each knot. Basic housekeeping included how to polish boots, mend clothes, washing and ironing, as well as naval traditions and terminology, and boat handling, both rowing and sailing.

In many ways this was not unlike the first term at Eton where we had to learn house colours, traditions and 'Eton Speak'. I also very quickly learned that rowing in a racing eight on the Thames was not at all the same thing as a naval whaler on the sea. The most rigorous medical ensued, especially regarding eyesight, and any propensity to colour blindness was soon spotted. Unfortunately an undescended testicle, which had earned me the nickname 'Cyclops' at school, had to be rectified before I could be taken in the RN proper. I undertook to have this done and was allowed to carry on with my training.

I quickly made some friends and runs ashore consisted of visits to the local cinema and pubs. I survived all these and gave the RN shore patrol no trouble. Strangely, my bolshiness, which had prevailed all through school, completely evaporated – not out of fear of the authorities but because this was something *I* wanted to do and had chosen of my own free will.

At the end of the so-called Summer Camp I returned home to Yorkshire to spend time with my parents before being called up. Whilst Father wasn't exactly thrilled at my defection to the Navy he was perfectly amenable throughout the time I was living with them.

He kindly arranged for my hernia to be rectified at the Military Hospital in York at either his or the Army's expense. This was my first ever visit to hospital and was more enjoyable than I anticipated. Having my pubic hair shaved off by a rather agreeable little nurse of my own age was quite exciting on its own, both literally and metaphorically. Maureen and I went out regularly until I was eventually called up for National Service proper. In the meantime, though, I was able to report to the Admiralty that all was now well, and sent them the surgeon's report as confirmation. I knew that I was liable to be called up in the spring, so with a school friend, Chris Davy, enjoyed a final fling of six weeks' skiing in Kitzbühel from January to February. Snow and I don't go together very well, and whilst I religiously attended ski school every morning, the afternoons were spent playing bridge with the old ladies who had chosen to overwinter in Kitzbühel. My parents had taught me to play when we were in Germany, and this final holiday before call-up was to be the last time I played for nearly forty years.

Call-up papers arrived shortly after I returned home telling me to report to Victory Barracks at Portsmouth on March 16th. The first act was to be assigned a service number – PJ/938690. Like all servicemen I was to remember this for the rest of my life. Nothing can happen without it, and above all you cannot get paid without it. The first six weeks of initial training were to some extent a repetition of the three weeks on the *Indefat*, as she was always called, but was both more extensive and at the same time intensive.

Two incidents especially stick in my mind. The first were the compulsory injections, or PULHEEMS as they were known. You placed a hand on each hip and marched between four SBAs (sick berth attendants), two on each side, who speared you with the appropriate needles. The same needle did the whole phial of whatever substance you were being injected with, so the ones furthest back in the queue had the bluntest needles. No problems with HIV in those days!

The second incident took place as I changed into my pyjamas. The leading seaman of the mess, a regular sailor probably no more than five years older than me, came up to me and advised that 'if I valued my arse I shouldn't wear pyjamas'. To my pained enquiry of, 'Why not?' he said, 'Think about it.' I did – and have never worn pyjamas since!

Our instructor was CPO Hull, a gunnery instructor (GI) from the Royal Naval gunnery school at Whale Island, and we seemed to square-bash all day every day. CPO Hull was a typical GI by day but a great father figure by night when he sometimes took the whole class greyhound racing at Fratton.

At the end of six weeks I got my joining instructions for HMS *Implacable,* again at Weymouth Bay. As this was the sister ship to the *Idefat*, I was not quite so lost and bewildered by the below decks layout as I had been nine months earlier. Once again, a lot of what followed was a rerun of what had gone before, except that I spent three months instead of three weeks on board, and the training was again both more extensive and intensive than before.

This time we had the opportunity to actually go to sea for

two days. I found it hard to imagine flying off this huge and seemingly unstable platform. It must have been a hairy experience for the Fleet Air Arm pilots with their Swordfish or 'Flying string bags', as they were known. To be aboard a large fleet carrier under full steam is a mighty impressive experience of raw power. The night we returned from our sea trip it was my turn to lower the White Ensign while the Royal Marines band played 'Sunset'. What a lot had happened since I first heard this haunting sound on the playing fields of Eton, and how thrilled I was to be here for real!

Our next sea trip was on a destroyer out of Portland. We were shown all round the ship and ate our midday meal with the ship's company. As we left harbour I was on the port side adjacent to the ship's rail. I heard the engine room telegraphs ring and a few seconds later she literally jumped forward as full power was put on, presumably at least partially for the visitors' benefit: a truly unforgettable experience. I was loving the life, and felt really happy except for one little fly in the ointment: the never-ending boat drills were not going well. The boat deck was one below the flight deck, and we were required to walk along a four-inch beam and then down a Jacob's ladder (rope) and into the whalers pitching on the sea below. This was just about alright, but reversing the process and climbing back up, pulling on a slender ratline and regaining balance on the beam, was not easy. It was gradually dawning on me that I had no real sense of balance. The possibility of having to climb masts and rigging was horrendous.

I had by then been segregated into the Upper Yardsmen's class as once again suitable for officer selection. In the first instance this meant more detailed navigation classes and lessons in leadership. I attended the initiative tests at Lee-on-Solent and did alright, if not spectacularly. After all the written exams had been done I was called before the selection committee and offered a commission in the 'Supply & Secretariat' Branch, as there were no vacancies in the Seaman Branch for national servicemen. Only myself and one other of our class were offered anything; some were failed and the rest were deferred and told to re-apply in six months' time. Having decided some time ago that whatever I did in life it was not going to be in an office shovelling paper, I declined the invitation to be an office wallah and elected to stay as I was. A couple of days later our instructor announced to the class, who he knew were disappointed by the lack of vacancies, that the Admiralty had taken two or three national service midshipmen into the Submarine Service, as they wanted to keep the service a volunteer one and were not getting enough regular sailors coming forward. They were now looking to take in non-commissioned ratings as a trial. Would any of us be interested? Myself and two others put their hands up. The option of joining as midshipmen was not available as we could not re-apply for another six months. So three of us said we would like to go to submarine school to serve on the lower deck.

About a week later we heard that we were to report to Fort Blockhouse at Gosport for training. Blockhouse consisted of HMS *Dolphin,* the submarine base, and Dolphin 2, the training school. Dolphin 2 adjoined the base of the other special arm of the Royal Navy; HM Coastal Forces, which operated the MTBs, MLs etc. As a youngster I was unbelievably excited by the whole atmosphere.

MTB crews shared the same distinction with submariners as the only two groups of warships' crews which, in peacetime, did not show their ships name on the cap 'tally'. They also shared the common distinction of referring to their craft as 'boats' not ships. The cap distinguishing marks were 'HM Submarines' and 'HM Coastal Forces'. Interestingly, submarines were one of the slowest warships and the MTBs were the fastest except for the *Manxman* and *Apollo,* two fast mine-laying cruisers of World War II fame.

At the submarine school the whole philosophy of submarine design and layout was gone into in the most intimate detail until we could locate every single part on board. Escape training was another major subject, and whilst the

DSEA (Davis Submarine Escape Apparatus) was the standard equipment, a new idea was coming into being, known as 'Free Ascent'. In essence, this was escape without breathing apparatus. We all had to go into a decompression chamber to ensure that our ears, sinuses and lungs were in good enough order to tolerate the pressures involved. Disaster struck and I found the pain unbearable at a simulated depth of only forty feet. Expecting that the cause was the remains of my hay fever at the end of the summer, I persuaded our instructor that I was getting over a cold and to let me have another go the next day, Friday. I failed again and was told that they (the authorities) would decide what to do with me on Monday, but I would probably be sent back to General Service. I really felt that being hung from the yardarm would be preferable. All Saturday I tramped round the chemists looking for a cure. At last I found one who could help; he sold me a small bottle of 'Vasylox', and as soon as I put two drops up my nose all the associated tubes began to pop and partially clear. By Monday morning I was totally clear. My mood of elation was soon dampened when I was presented with my 'draft chit' back to General Service.

I wheedled, I begged and I grovelled to be allowed a final chance 'as my cold had now totally cleared up'. I had to promise on oath that I would signal if the pain became too much, and was told that if I burst my eardrums out of sheer pig-headedness I would be court-martialled for disobeying an order. As I sat in the decompression chamber watching the simulated depth gauge I couldn't believe it wasn't hurting, but I made it down to three hundred feet. The instructors couldn't believe it either, but they swallowed the cold theory and I was allowed to stay. I still don't know what really caused the problem but can only assume my tubes had been blocked since birth. Certainly I'd always had ear, nose and throat problems up until that time, but have never suffered since.

A new one hundred-foot escape tower had been built at *Dolphin* and we were the second class to go through it. The technique was to go into an airlock, take a deep breath, duck under the canvas 'elephant's trunk' as it was known and float up the hundred-foot column of water, breathing out all the way up. Learning to breathe out underwater is not a natural process, as most people try to keep their mouth shut in this situation. Failure to breathe out resulted in burst lungs – not a nice way to go! There were instructors in airlocks to the side of the tower who watched each individual making his ascent and any lack of bubbles would cause an instructor to swim out and grab the offender until he was breathing out properly. I was certainly apprehensive on the first ascent but thereafter it was quite fun. I learned that everybody has either negative, neutral or positive buoyancy.

Fortunately I had positive buoyancy, and during the next few days made several 'escapes'. Once over the initial fear it was good fun, but done for real it would clearly be a very different story. We also had a number of day trips round the Isle of Wight in the submarine *Alaric* to experience life at sea in a submarine. Descending via the fore hatch into the forward torpedo compartment was a totally new experience and I immediately realised that I had taken the correct decision to join this select branch of the service. As we slipped our moorings and the Captain manoeuvred us away from the jetty using the main motors, I had crazy visions of going out on a war patrol to sink Germans; all that I had read in the book *Unbroken* by Alistair Mars appeared vividly in my head.

I was brought back to the real world as the main engines spluttered into life to take us on an unknown journey of experiences in the English Channel. I was certainly conscious that we were close to the area where the *Affray* had gone down with the loss of all hands some eighteen months earlier, but contented myself with the knowledge that lightning rarely strikes in the same place twice.

We trainees then all gathered into the control room as the boat went to diving stations, and as I write these words the hairs on the back of my neck still react to the excitement I felt at the sound of the diving klaxon, the rush of men taking up their individual diving station, the sudden silence as the main engines were stopped, the sound of air escaping through the vents in the top of the ballast tanks as they were flooded and all the reports coming into the control room. I watched the depth gauges showing how deep we were, and then at periscope depth (thirty-two feet) we levelled out and all was silent. A very gentle hum of ventilating fans, quietly spoken orders and well-ordered calm prevailed. We were in our own private world, which I think was one of the attractions for all submariners: no telephone, no post, no relatives, no newspapers, no hassle. In the forty-eight years since I left the service I have many, many times longed for this escapism. We were shown over the entire workings of the boat, and my impressions of my first day would fill a book on their own.

Returning to harbour on the surface I confess to having felt slightly seasick; the stench of diesel oil which pervades every boat doesn't help queasy stomachs. However, I requested a visit to the bridge, which was granted, and the fresh air settled my stomach okay.

On subsequent trips I got progressively more used to it and eventually found what to any normal person would be a disgusting smell becoming more and more evocative.

After this first trip, for the first and only time in my life, I worked and studied like a man possessed for the exams which were to come. I knew that I had used up a 'life' with my ear problems, and that I owed a considerable debt to those who had given me an unofficial second chance and I could not – dare not – fail. As it turned out, I passed out top of the class and was duly congratulated. This was incidentally the first praise I had ever received in all my life and I wallowed in it. The defining moment was being awarded the cap tally with 'HM Submarines' on it. Not quite the same as the Sword of Honour at Sandhurst, but to me it was everything!

Having passed out it seemed wise to volunteer, despite the service adage of never volunteering, for one of the overseas bases. The choices were Malta, Australia or Ceylon. The last two were ruled out because they were for a minimum of three years' duty, which I didn't have left to serve. So Malta it was to be, and home for two weeks' overseas leave. As we were still living in Yorkshire, I took the opportunity to contact a friend from Eton, James Wilson, who also lived in Yorkshire and who I knew often holidayed in Malta, and we agreed to maintain contact.

I had a wonderful leave and went out again regularly with Maureen, who had looked after me when I had had my hernia operation. Maureen was my first ever girlfriend and we had kept in touch all the time I was under training. I was really sorry to say goodbye. Our last night out together was to see the Western film *Shane*. It turned out to be one of the top Westerns ever made, and although I have seen it many times since, that first time was special.

I had received my draft instructions through the post, together with the necessary travel documents, and was to get myself to the transit camp in the deep shelter at Goodge Street adjacent to the tube station. Goodge Street was horrendous, but fortunately my stay was only for one night before we caught the flight from Northolt to Luqa Airport in Malta. I have had many memorable breakfasts in my life but this one was truly outstanding. We had two options; porridge or scrambled egg, the former made with water, the latter with dried egg. Whichever you chose, the mix came from a forty-gallon drum stirred with a dinghy paddle. The cooking area was verminous, but this was something we were soon to get used to, with cockroaches everywhere one looked.

This was also my first ever flight and I was quite looking forward to the experience. We boarded a Vickers Viking twin-engined plane and were on our way. As we crossed into the Mediterranean I was surprised to see how blue and clear the water was and how much you could see from the air, both on the water and below it. I quickly realised why all submarines in the Med are painted two shades of blue, one to make the boat difficult to see on the surface and the other difficult to see from the air. We eventually arrived at Luqa, where naval transport was waiting to take me and John Gardiner to HMS *Forth*, the depot ship for the 1st Submarine Squadron. As it was quite late we bedded down (hammocked down would be more appropriate) for the night. I don't recall how, where, when or even if, we got fed. I slept well, despite the twin emotions of excitement and apprehension. As John and I were both well-spoken public schoolboys we had to put up with the usual crap, about what use upper-class twits – and part-timers at that – were likely to be to operational submarines. The 1st flotilla was at the time fully operational with highly experienced crews, and no one had any experience of people like John and myself.

I was drafted onto *Trenchant* and John to *Sanguine*, both as spare hands – or 'spare pricks', as we were more colourfully described. It was to transpire that most of the senior hands on *Trenchant* had seen war service with one of the more colourful commanders AC (Crap) Miers. I clearly had a lot to live up to, especially as I was not only the youngest but also the only man who had no trade qualifications. I was assigned to blue watch as spare hand, this watch being one seaman short.

CHAPTER X
HMS/M Trenchant

I was put under the control of the Torpedo Instructor (TI) Petty Officer Oxley and his leading hand, Sid Hicks, and given a quick guided tour of my new 'home'. *Trenchant* was essentially a steel tube sixteen feet in diameter and two hundred and seventy-five feet long. She weighed approximately 1,400 tons on the surface and another 160 tons dived. *Trenchant* was ten years old with a distinguished record in the Pacific against the Japanese. Her most famous trophy was the Japanese cruiser *Ashigara,* the largest enemy warship sunk by a British submarine in the Second World War. The T-class carried the heaviest torpedo load of all the Royal Navy submarine fleet. *Trenchant* was designed to carry a total of seventeen torpedoes, six internal forward with six reloads, two external forward, two external amidships firing at an angle off the beam, and one stern tube aft. The external tubes had no reload facilities for obvious reasons. At this time of peace, though, only the internal forward tubes were used, giving a capacity of twelve 'fish'. The most forward compartment was the tube space, and then heading aft came the torpedo stowage compartment or fore-ends, seamen's mess, chiefs' and petty officers' mess, wardroom, Captain's cabin, control room, telegraph office on the port side, galley on the starboard side, engine room, motor room, stokers' mess, and right aft the steerage compartment. The total ship's company at that time was sixty-three, an increase of twenty-five per cent over the original design figure.

Having completed my quick guided tour I was then put to work, or more accurately, given my initiation test, viz. greasing the runners inside each torpedo tube. The removal of chaff and cavings from a threshing drum was the filthiest job I had done yet or could imagine ever doing. Greasing torpedo tube runners was in an altogether different category. I think it must have been the ultimate test for claustrophobia. Whether that was the intention I deliberately never asked. The tubes were twenty-one inches in diameter, and as I could just get down to twenty-one inches diameter myself I was equipped with a bucket of grease and a torch. A rope was tied round my ankles so that I could get back, some ramrod device was placed against my feet and I was then pushed twenty-five feet up to the end. I began applying the grease as instructed and called out when I needed another pull back. I did all six tubes without complaining; at least I had been pulled out each time. My only real fear was being left up a tube! I must have passed the test alright as there were no more horrors in store for me. We were not due to put to sea for a couple of days, so I was given a more detailed tour of the boat and had my watch-keeping duties explained to me. I was to be control room messenger when dived, and bridge lookout whilst on the surface. My diving or action station was to be in the fore-ends as one of the torpedo team.

In general terms the seamen lived and mostly worked forward, the stokers lived and mostly worked aft, and the commissioned and non-commissioned officers did their stuff amidships. There were various bunks in the vicinity of the messes, and in the T-class there were usually enough to go round, although sometimes when we were carrying extra mouths either for training or special forces landing parties we had to 'hot bunk'. In the smaller boats, hot bunking was the norm.

Between the fore-ends and the seamen's mess was one loo known as the 'heads' for all twenty-six of us, no doors, screens or anything. The first thing any newcomer had to learn was how and when to use it. Unlike the more modern A-boats, there was no tank system; our waste could only be discharged directly to sea. The act of discharge was one to learn thoroughly, as too little air pressure meeting a greater amount of water pressure resulted in 'getting your own back'. As each use of the heads whilst dived resulted in telltale air-bubbles on the surface, they could only be used with the express permission of the OOW (Officer of the Watch). This was only grudgingly granted, and consequently we all developed well-trained bodily functions, which only performed at night when we were usually on the surface charging batteries.

Whilst on the subject of body functions it should be noted that there were no effective or reliable water makers in those days, and we only carried a very limited amount of fresh water. This water was only for drinking and cooking. There was very little water for washing, so consequently we didn't wash. This was not as bad as it sounds as we all grew smelly together and no one noticed except the depot ship's company, and then only when we returned from a patrol of several weeks' duration. However, the pleasure from a long hot shower at the end of a trip was almost orgasmic. Although we all grew beards, only two or three kept them on, the rest of us rejoicing in feeling clean-shaven at last. The fresh water discipline was relaxed if we were visiting a foreign port, as we were able take on extra fresh water there.

The seamen's mess was where we ate our meals and it could also sleep eight hands in great discomfort. The fore-ends or torpedo stowage compartment took the remainder and also doubled up as a food storage and preparation area. The chiefs' and petty officers' mess, together with the wardroom, was where the commissioned and non-commissioned officers slept and ate. Only the Captain had his own cabin.

The control room was the nerve centre containing the helm (steering position) on the forward bulkhead, with the control room messenger seated alongside. Situated down the port side was the fore and after hydroplane position, with accompanying depth gauges, and aft of that the diving panel with all the hydraulic levers used for opening and closing vents, raising and lowering the periscopes and so on.

Down the starboard side of the control room was the chart

table, the 'fruit machine' for calculating targets' range, speed, direction, angle and the timing at which to fire torpedoes. The Asdic (Sonar) operator had a little cubicle, as did the radar operator. The two periscopes, main and attack, filled a large section of the middle part of the control room. Moving aft, on the port side was the wireless and telegraph office and on the starboard side the galley. We had one chef only, and no matter what the weather conditions he always produced at least one good hot meal each day.

Proceeding aft was the engine room. Two large six-cylinder diesels were set on either side of the main passageway; these were started with compressed air and equipped with the schnorkel (snort) system, allowing them to be run whilst the boat was below the surface at periscope depth (thrity-two feet). The 'snort mast', as it was called, was a twin tube device allowing air to be drawn down one half and exhaust gases expelled through the other. It was fitted with a flap valve which automatically closed if it dipped below the water. Snorting in choppy seas was an extremely uncomfortable business; if the sea covered the flap valve it would close so as not to suck in water, and the air required for combustion would be sucked out of the boat instead, giving rise to a sharp drop in pressure until the flap valve opened again.

The constant tugging at the eardrums was very painful in itself and under certain conditions exhaust fumes frequently made breathing difficult. Snorting was not a popular pastime and put great pressure on the planesmen to keep very accurate depth control to avoid the snort mast dipping below the water.

Further aft again were the main motors which provided the underwater propulsion via nearly three hundred tons of storage batteries. The main motor switch gear was also aft of the main engines.

Next came the stokers' mess, and finally the steerage compartment from where, in theory at least, the boat could be steered manually, and which contained the main propeller shaft bearings.

Below the main deck were various smaller compartments, like the bo'sun's store, the rum store (very important), ammunition store, pumping positions, and so on.

Above the waterline the main deck over the pressure hull was called the casing. Here was mounted the three-inch gun, the conning tower and bridge superstructure. Between the casing and the pressure hull was space for stowage of mooring wires, ropes and fenders, both fore and aft of the conning tower.

It all sounds pretty simple when you say it quickly, but in fact there was an immense amount of detail to absorb, especially from the point of view of mechanical and electrical operational efficiency.

Having been willingly accepted into the ship's company (much to my surprise), I was determined to justify their confidence in me. It was also an interesting psychological situation. I made no attempt to disguise where I came from, but equally I didn't volunteer information as to what on earth I was doing as an ordinary seaman. However, I always answered questions honestly. The entire ship's company knew that my father was a general in the British Army, they knew I had been educated at Eton, and far from pouring ridicule and scorn, were curious to know what it was really like at an English public school. The officers were equally puzzled, especially when a signal came through requesting me to go to Sunday lunch with the Governor of the island, who was the stepfather of James Wilson. Having given my explanation of the connection, I was told to invite James on board for one of our day trips.

With all this extraneous stuff out of the way I simply got on with my job, which was increasing in responsibility every day. I was befriended by virtually every member of the crew, especially two brothers, Ron and George Etherington from Liverpool. We became firm drinking partners and used to go ashore together whenever we were in harbour and our various watch-keeping duties allowed. They introduced me to the notorious 'Gut', Valletta's answer to Soho, both in terms of dens of iniquity and fabulous eating houses. Very early on in our friendship Ron and George introduced me to their friend Lena, a local prostitute who they apparently knew intimately. She told me she had a special treat for me and ducked under the bar-room table. Before I knew what was happening I had received my first 'blowjob'. Rather public but great fun, it caused much amusement!

A few weeks later I had my first Christmas away from home and I have to admit to feeling slightly homesick. However, we had an excellent Christmas lunch and the rest of the crew who were required for duty and still on board shared their 'tot' with me. The daily issue of rum was a major event, the ritual and security equalling that of issuing ammunition.

In the Navy, surface ships issued ordinary ranks with rum diluted with water at a ratio of two parts water to one part rum. Submarine crews were allowed a one-to-one ratio, and chiefs and petty officers drew neat rum. It had to be drunk there and then, approximately a third of a pint. Saving it – known as 'bottling one's tot' – was highly illegal, as indeed was sharing it with anyone else. I was too young at nineteen to draw my own tot, and was the only one on board not 'drawing'. Although it was not strictly allowed, my fellow crew members all felt sorry for me and I was often allowed some of theirs, either 'gulpers' or 'sippers', to define the amount you were being offered. Fortunately I had a good head for alcohol and never disgraced myself. Navy rum was a mighty powerful brew, not at all like the insipid apology served in pubs and hotels today.

One advantage of being the youngest came on New Year's Eve. It was my 'perk' to ring in the New Year on the ship's bell. Forty-eight years later on a trip to the submarine museum at Gosport I saw, amongst the various displays, the very same bell on which I had rung in the New Year all that time ago…

Other perks were cigarettes, pipe and even chewing tobacco, and whilst these had to be bought they were so cheap as to be virtually a non-cost item. At sea, smoking was not allowed whilst dived, except occasionally when the announcement of 'one all round' would come over the tannoy. Food at sea was excellent compared to that in surface ships, but the diet was fairly limited. Submariners lived basically on 'babies' heads' – the name given to the tinned steak and kidney puddings still sold today. Some liked 'brains', as the meat section was called; and some liked 'skull', as the suet crust was described. The all-time favourite though was 'pot mess', which was stew, dumplings and vegetables all mixed in together. Another staple was pilchards or herrings either 'in' or 'not in', to describe the absence or otherwise of tomato sauce.

The way we lived depended entirely on the duration of each trip we were to make. As much as possible we relied on fresh food, certainly for the first few days of any patrol, and thereafter on tinned. Bread and potatoes we could make last a bit longer, although after a couple of days the outside of the bread was mouldy. Removing the outer layer of mould revealed reasonable bread underneath. The reason for such a short shelf life was the very damp conditions in which we all lived, hence also the compulsory chest X-rays every three months to guard against TB. Potatoes would last for all but the longest patrol. *Trenchant* was kept fully stocked most of the time, but when on an exercise supposed to simulate active service we had to 'store for war'. In simple terms this meant loading stores and supplies for a minimum of six weeks' duration. The dummy warhead torpedoes were offloaded and replaced with live ones, and a false deck of canned provisions was laid throughout, except in the control room and engine room. This made getting around inconvenient to say the least; the normally stooped movement became virtually a hands and knees job. This encouraged us to eat rather more during the early stages of a patrol to get the deck level down as soon as possible.

I have often been asked what life in a submarine was really like. It is a difficult question to answer as my experience was limited entirely to peacetime operations. A significant number of *Trenchant*'s crew had, however, seen war service so I was able to form a fair picture from them. In essence it was exactly the same as I experienced but with a greatly raised fear factor. I understood that being depth-charged was not much fun, but then I imagine the same could apply to all the armed services, where the motto had to be 'kill or be killed'.

As far as our daily life went, it was as realistic a repeat of the real thing as could be achieved. The greatest personal memory is one of comradeship and trust; an awareness of being responsible both to and for your colleagues.

Living conditions were fairly spartan but no worse than at boarding school, whilst the food was a great deal better. Possibly the hardest thing to contend with were the cockroaches. They were absolutely everywhere and would collect in virtual swarms round the deckhead and bulkhead lights. We were fumigated every six months to get rid of them. Other than cockroaches, the only downsides were the lack of fresh air, high humidity, and in the motor and engine rooms, very high temperatures; and always the stench of oil fumes and stale bodies. Always living in artificial light, yellow by day and red by night, was certainly no worse than a modern-day office environment. *Trenchant* was of course a large submarine, and conditions were nowhere near as good on the S-class or U-class. The conditions on the German U-boats were even worse and I was quite shocked when I went aboard one.

Initially my duties varied between bridge lookout, helmsman, foreplane operator and torpedo man. I used to spend quite a lot of my spare time sitting with the watch-keeping electrician in the motor room studying the operation of the switch gear, and was allowed to operate the controls under supervision. There were two sets of control gear, one for the port motor and one for the starboard motor; all changes of speed were rung up on the motor-room telegraphs, and changes were made first one side and then the other. One day during a particularly active period I found myself operating the starboard side and the duty electrician the port side. This became an almost daily occurrence and eventually when one of the electricians reported sick and there was no electrician available in the spare crew, the Leading Electrician was asked whether he thought I could do the job just for a day trip, only a few hours of which we would be dived. He concurred, and so with constant technical training I eventually became an official watch-keeping electrician.

From then on I relinquished my other duties, except to occasionally act as relief lookout during meal times. This gave me a regular opportunity for fresh air, and on our flag-waving trips, which were largely spent on the surface, I could also get some sunshine.

As the two remaining electricians were both married men with their wives in Malta, I eventually started doing their weekend duties and would also relieve for them during the nights we were in harbour. These nights in harbour were when the main standing charge was put on the batteries. The state of the charge had to be monitored every hour by taking the specific gravity of acid in the batteries and the rate of charge adjusted accordingly. This could take up to sixteen hours a night – quite a long spell of duty. I well remember one night sitting on the motor room stool wondering whether this was really happening; here was I, barely nineteen, with total control of the boat, complete responsibility for its safety although considerable quantities of hydrogen gas were given off during a heavy charging period. I was also in charge of the engine-room staff, who had to obey my orders for speed settings to drive the generators. I felt king of all I surveyed. I was a totally happy man, and with all the extra pay made up as submarine pay, 'hard liers' extra for sea time, and extra for weekend and evening duties, I was very well-off financially.

Malta, known to the world at large as the George Cross Island for its stubborn survival in the face of the German onslaught and less deferentially to 'Jolly Jack' as the island of smells, bells and pregnant women, was no more than a lump of barren rock inhabited, apart from its human population, almost entirely by 'shoats' – the Mediterranean beast between a sheep and a goat. It was primarily a naval base, complete with dockyard repair facilities; but with every other building being either a bar or a brothel, we were never short of entertainment. Three of us shared a flat near the dockyard which was a form of escape from always living on board a warship. It was especially valuable when we went into the dry dock ourselves for repair work. The Maltese climate was typically Mediterranean but never uncomfortably hot; there was always a sea breeze.

At the time I was there, the island was virtually controlled by Mabel Strickland, who fortuitously also owned the *Malta Times* newspaper. This degree of right-wing political control was not to everyone's liking, and a certain left-wing firebrand was appearing on the horizon in the form of Dom Mintoff. Long after I had returned to England he eventually gained power and effectively kicked the Brits out and invited Gaddafi in.

The Maltese were a friendly and likeable people and I made friends with one particular family who used to have me to Sunday lunch occasionally, which was a great treat to look forward to. As it was a Roman Catholic island there were magnificent churches in every town, and there seemed to be a saint's day to celebrate at least once a week, with truly spectacular fireworks displays. These displays were especially vivid when viewed from seawards. Somehow lights reflected in water seem to have a special beauty, and I would spend hours leaning over the bridge just gazing at harbour lights or at night when at sea doing the same, watching the fluorescence created by the dolphins swimming and leaping alongside us.

Most of our work was to act as 'clockwork mouse' for the anti-submarine forces to practice on. This basically consisted of our trying to avoid detection, carry out a simulated attack, and then getting away as fast as possible. The frigates and destroyers obviously were doing the opposite, hunting us down with small explosive charges, mercifully not real depth charges. Aircraft were also ranged against us as part of the anti-submarine forces. I managed one day to mistake a seagull for a Shackleton reconnaissance aircraft. As bridge lookout, I had called out, 'Aircraft bearing green two-five.' The OOW had quickly sighted it through his binoculars and pressed the diving klaxon. Once at periscope depth the aircraft was identified as a seagull! I apologised profusely and was told 'better the mistake is that way than the other'.

One of my first patrols was exercising with the American Sixth Fleet, especially a carrier group, where our 'target' was the USS *Lake Champlain*. Incredibly, we passed through the destroyer escort screen undetected, surfaced alongside our 'target', where the glow of sailors' cigarettes could be clearly seen, fired a Very pistol saying '*bang-bang, you're dead*', dived and disappeared whence we had come, still undetected. The realisation of how vulnerable these large ships are has never left me.

Sleep deprivation was the most serious problem. During periods of high activity one learned to make do on as little as two hours in twenty-four, taken in perhaps ten lots of ten minutes. At least it taught me to catnap, something I've been doing ever since.

We were also required to land raiding parties. One of these which is still stuck in my mind today was having a party of what later became known as the SBS (Special Boat Squadron) on board, whom we were to land somewhere along the Adriatic coast. They were not comfortable companions in a confined space. Mostly they never spoke at all, and if they did it was to utter some irrelevant expletive. One spent all seven days taking his machine pistol to bits; then he oiled and polished it and put it together again. Another just sharpened his killing knife and after seven days it was a pleasure for me to be part of the casing party responsible for launching them over the side and see them paddle off into the dark. We all thought you had to be nuts to do this sort of work, but they scared us to death and we were glad to see the back of them. Goodness knows what they did to the enemy!

We had wonderful flag-waving trips to Sicily, Beirut, Tobruk, Gibraltar and several to Italy. One Italian trip saw me organising a coach trip to the Italian Grand Prix at Monza. Seeing the Mercedes team streaming across the line in the first three positions was to me, an avid follower of Grand Prix racing, a rare treat. On a different day of the same trip, I went to Florence and Pisa, where I climbed the famous Leaning Tower, but I had to stay on board for the trip to Pompeii, which was a great disappointment to me as I never had another chance to visit.

We paid many other visits to Italy but my memories are confined to beggars and pasta. I cannot, however, deny the beauty of its coastline, none more spectacular than sailing past the island of Capri at four a.m. in the middle of June on a virtual millpond.

Sicily was a pleasant port of call, made memorable by my purchase of a donkey for two Maltese pounds after a drunken run ashore. I was proposing to take it on board and succeeded in getting two front legs on the gangway, but mercifully it would go no further and eventually escaped back whence it came.

Beirut was a favourite, and has a particular memory for me as the place I really lost my virginity. This event had been well planned, and during the bucket-wash under the casing I had informed that certain part of my anatomy that I had a treat in store for it. Pete Redman, who had set me up for this, knew exactly where to go: yes, sailors really do have one in every port! He was met by the Lebanese procuress and we were escorted up the stairs. At the top Pete went left and I went right. After about two minutes this rather delightful little Lebanese blonde in a red dress came in to the room. She asked me in perfect English for two Lebanese pounds, took off her dress, lay back on the bed – and the rest, as they say, is history…

A wonderful experience. Pete was first out of his room but I was no more than fifteen seconds behind him; we compared notes and headed for the nearest bar. Fortunately the pleasure was worth the ensuing weeks of anxiety, but I am not sure whether I would have I felt the same way had the morning 'short arm' inspections turned positive!

However, it was not all fun, and we had at least three dodgy experiences.

We were to exercise in the Gulf of Genoa, a notoriously fickle sea; the weather forecast was for force eight or nine gales for the whole week. We sailed from Malta in a very rough sea; I was violently seasick and so ill I couldn't possibly keep a watch. After twenty-four hours of this indisposition my fellow crew members had had enough, and Sid Hicks, with whom I was eventually to lodge as a student at the Royal Agricultural College, announced that I was to be cured of seasickness. I was to have a tot of rum poured down my throat! I protested there was no way, I should bring it straight up again.

'Oh no you won't,' he said, 'because we are going to keep your jaws clamped together for five minutes!'

'Kill or cure?' I said rather weakly.

'Something like that,' came the reply.

I really thought I was going to choke to death, but after literally five minutes I felt better. In another five minutes I was up and walking, and I've never, from that day to this, felt seasick again!

Then followed the roughest trip I was ever to endure at sea. Mountainous seas, lookouts lashed to the bridge, and the elephant's foot, a canvas structure to catch the water pouring down the conning tower, rigged and constantly pumped out. This was a high-risk period, as sea water in the battery compartment would give off choking fumes of chlorine gas.

On arrival at the exercise area we had no choice but to dive. Diving was not too risky, but surfacing in these seas was highly problematic as a heavy wave at the wrong time from the wrong direction could roll the boat over. We were still rolling quite heavily at nearly two hundred feet down, but after twenty-four hours of battery conservation we had to surface to recharge the batteries. Mercifully the weather was calming down, so all was well. The sea was still very rough and after a night of battery charging we dived again just before dawn. By now the weather was definitely improving and there were no further crises.

Two other occasions were also memorable as being slightly 'hairy'.

We had been snorting, and in order to go deeper the valves to the snort mast had to be closed. The main induction valve for the starboard engine had jammed open and sea water poured into the engine room. In no time we acquired a very acute stern-down angle. I was in the motor room keeping watch and could see the depth gauges heading rapidly towards our safe diving depth. Both motors were by now full ahead group up, i.e. maximum power; all the after ballast tanks had been blown but still the water poured in and it really looked like curtains for us all. Suddenly the engine room staff got the offending valve shut, we gradually started climbing and before long we had assumed equilibrium. Panic over, but we all needed clean underwear!

Returning to harbour after another exercise, we surfaced around six p.m. and I took my turn as bridge lookout. I volunteered for this as I used to love the sight of the fireworks on the island as we were approaching. There was a saint's day and accompanying fiesta every night somewhere, and I knew this night was a very special one. I saw a big orange flash and thought, That was a big one. Then suddenly there was a splash in the water about thirty yards out from my side of the bridge. At the same instant there was another bright flash and it suddenly dawned on the three of us on the bridge that we were under fire. The diving klaxon was activated and we literally all jumped down the conning tower hatch. As we were moving we saw the splash about thirty yards the other side. Safely down, we immediately sent in a report. The upshot was that the cruiser *Glasgow* was having a night practice shoot and had mistaken our conning tower on the radar for the battle practice target towed by a tug. An interesting five minutes!

Although we worked reasonably hard and spent a large proportion of our time underwater, it was not always so. We enjoyed considerable freedom and time to enjoy life.

Whenever we were off duty in the evenings, Ron, George and I would head off for a 'run ashore'. This invariably consisted of a slap-up meal of rump steak in one of the many restaurants in the 'Gut' after which we would adjourn to a bar, where Ron would buy a bottle of gin, George and I would have a bottle of whisky each, and we'd drink it whilst putting the world – and the Royal Navy especially – to rights, and then solemnly walk back to *Forth*, having drunk a pint of milk each at a milk bar halfway between Valletta and Msida.

The arrival of the US Navy would be a great occasion for a punch-up. Nobody cared much either for them or their attitude to the rest of the world (once again, what's changed in half a century?), and a bar-room brawl between the RN and the USN was looked forward to as much as any boxing match. Apart from once having a pint beer bottle broken over my head I escaped unscathed, and as far as I recall the RN always won!

My tour of duty was not without its sadder moments. The most anxious was receipt of the dreaded signal 'Subsmash one'. One of our sister ships, *Tudor*, was overdue. We all knew everybody on board and every one of us could visualise the worst. All we could do was wait and pray that 'Subsmash two' didn't come. To everyone's relief it didn't. *Tudor*'s radio had broken down so on that particular day they couldn't report their position at the appointed hour. Ships were already heading for her last known position when they finally repaired it. The other moment of personal sadness was when the *Sidon* blew up in Portland Harbour. My cousin was the torpedo officer and he was killed in the explosion. The cause of this was alleged to be a new torpedo propellant under the name HTP. We had some on *Forth*, but after this incident they were never used.

Just before I was due to come home for demob, the coxswain told me that Captain SM1 wanted to see me. He had no idea why, so with some trepidation I presented myself to the 'Boss'. He told me he had had good reports on me from my Captain and First Lieutenant and he wanted me to go back to England, take a commission and switch from National Service to the regular Navy. This was a considerable shock, as I had already got my place booked at the RAC at Cirencester.

Here I was just twenty years old, five thousand miles from home, with nobody to consult, so I asked, 'How much time do I have for a decision?'

'Twenty-four hours,' came the reply.

I went ashore that night with Ron and George as usual and they advised against changing my plans, as whatever happened the Submarine Service would never be a career, as you had to leave at thirty-five – and then what? In any case, they said, submariners – being oddballs – never get on in General Service. I took their advice, which in my heart I knew was sensible, although I had many regrets in subsequent years.

I came home on the *Thermopylae,* a so-called Super T, with a high fin instead of the more usual squat conning tower. In the control room the hydroplane and steering controls were T-bars instead of the usual spoked wheels. She also had a much higher underwater speed and was driven more like an aeroplane than a conventional submarine. I thought, If this is the future, why on earth am I giving it up?

We had a very rough passage through the Bay of Biscay and the sea conditions rapidly worsened as we turned into the English Channel, so much so that we had to 'heave to' outside the entrance to Portland Harbour to allow conditions to ease up. As I walked over the gangway for the last time, I shed more than one tear and I think I realised even then that I had made the wrong decision.

CHAPTER XI

The Royal Agricultural College

After I left the Royal Navy, the RAC agreed that as I had had practical experience of agriculture over the full farming year for a number of years, they would not insist on the formal requirement of a full twelve months' continuous posting, and I was allowed to enter the college in the following September. Sid Hicks, our leading torpedo man on *Trenchant*, who lived in Cirencester, was leaving the RN after twelve years' service that summer, and he had kindly agreed to take me as a student lodger for my first year. Older students were expected to live out, the college accommodation being for those joining straight from school. It did not take me too long to work out that I had already acquired a considerable amount of practical knowledge, probably more than most of the lecturers, but I buckled down to learning the theory which would be required in order to pass my exams, especially the NDA at the end of my two years. In those days there were three basic courses to take: the so-called Agricultural Science course, for those who were intending to farm; the Estate Management course, for those who were primarily landlords or budding land agents; and a special short course intended as a quick guide to theory for those going to work with family who were already farming. The first two courses were of two years' duration and the short course was for one year. The principal was Professor Robert Boutflour, who was and will be, forever associated with the RAC.

I am ashamed to say I was not really any better a student than I was at school. I found it all a complete waste of time, as I hadn't really got the Royal Navy out of my system yet and the call of the sea was still stronger than the call of the land. Perhaps lodging with Sid Hicks was not such a good idea because we spent too much time reminiscing.

I was able to restart my rifle shooting activities and became captain of the RAC club, and also shot with the Cirencester Town Rifle Club. My brother by then was at Cambridge, not having had to do any National Service, and had been smitten with the Match Rifle bug.

This was a rather eccentric sport, shot at ranges between 1,000 and 1,200 yards, mostly lying on your back shooting between your knees. I never took to this position and remained one of the minority 'belly gunners' as we were called. Apart from the universities, the only range in the country which could accommodate these extreme distances was at Bisley. To shoot this sport at Bisley it was a requirement to be a member of the English VIII Club; quite fortuitously the secretary, Wing Commander Whitelock, was also secretary of the Cirencester Town club. As happens in life one thing led to another, and I was soon an active participant in the Match Rifle competitions at Bisley.

I passed the first year's exams, and for my second term changed digs to be with friends I had made during my first year. During the long holidays I worked for Bruce Seton for the first two holiday periods, either winter ploughing or harvesting cabbages. I had been well off financially in the Navy, but was now getting chronically short of money, so as well as a daytime job with Bruce Seton I also worked at the GPO sorting office from ten p.m. to six a.m. sorting Christmas mail. As it got dark so early in midwinter I was able to get some sleep in the evening and also an hour in the morning. I have always been a 'catnapper' so I did not suffer unduly. During the Easter holiday I helped Bruce with the spring drilling programme, but this was to be my last time with him, he having taken on another student.

From then on I worked for Bells of West Bergholt, who had been threshing contractors and indeed still had one outfit.

They, like many others, had taken on contract combining and I worked on the Claas combine, bagging off the corn and also worked as relief driver.

I was already having doubts as to the wisdom of trying to farm, for clearly I was not going to ever have one of my own. Moreover, I wasn't too sure that I wanted to be a farm manager, even if I could get a job as one. I had also done contract work for Bruce Seton during the summer before going to the RAC and was beginning to cast my eyes in this direction. I was also aware of developments with chemical sprays, and the weird-looking machines in Fisons Pest Control yard at Feering nearby appeared interesting. However, we had another year to get through at the RAC before any decisions had to be taken, and there was enough contract work in the holidays to keep me busy and the money coming in. By this time my father had retired from the Army and had moved to West Yorkshire to a job with David Brown of gearbox, Aston Martin and David Brown tractors fame. As I wanted to see more of my parents, realising I should soon be kicked out of the nest, I spent more time with them and gave farm work a miss for a couple of holidays. My father was by now convinced that my ambitions did not extend beyond driving a tractor, which I found irritating as well as untrue, and I felt a change of emphasis might please him a little.

College exams were due at the end of June, and provided these were passed I was then to go on to Leeds to sit the NDA (National Diploma in Agriculture) in August. At the beginning of June I learned that my grandfather, who was by then approaching his eightieth birthday, had bought another four hundred and fifty acres to add to the two hundred at Crabbes Farm. This would make a very viable holding; being the only member of the family other than him who knew anything about arable farming, I assumed that I would be asked to run it. I thought it would be a wonderful thing to do. Imagine the shock of receiving a letter from my father enquiring whether I had got a job, as in case I thought I was going to walk into

Grandfather's farm I should think again! I don't know whether I was more incensed or mortified, but pride prevented me from saying anything.

I immediately wrote to Fisons Pest Control, enquiring whether they had any vacancies for trainee managers, explaining that I had had experience of general contracting, although not any crop spraying. To my utter amazement I had a positive reply by return of post summoning me for interview in two days' time. I presented myself as requested at the company headquarters at Felixstowe, where the interview was to be conducted; when asked if I had any formal qualifications, I replied quite truthfully that I was taking the NDA in six weeks' time and could see no reason not to expect to pass. They paid my petrol expenses and promised to let me know. To my even greater amazement a letter arrived the very next morning confirming my appointment as trainee manager from August 1st at the princely salary of £560 per annum! The terms and conditions would be amazing in this day and age: they were virtually the same as the RN, in that you were to be available at all times, seven days a week, except for three weeks' holiday which could not be taken during the operating season.

I signed on the dotted line and in the same post went a letter to my father saying, yes, I had got a job; with Fisons. As the Vice Chairman of the company was a personal friend of his, and I had done it entirely on my own, Father was moderately impressed. As far as the enlarged Crabbes Farm was concerned, Father was now leaving David Browns and was going to farm it himself! I left the RAC at the end of June, and went home to swot up on material for the NDA exam in six weeks' time.

CHAPTER XII

The Chemical Revolution

Whilst at home studying for the NDA exam, I was instructed to report to the Downham Market branch of Fisons Pest Control (FPCL) at the end of August when the exams were over. About two weeks later I received a telephone call from the branch asking if I could start earlier as they were very short-staffed and in the middle of a particularly severe outbreak of potato blight.

I jumped at the opportunity, as this would let me off the NDA exam, which I was increasingly less confident of passing. As the main purpose of this particular qualification was to help me get my first job, which I now already had, I had no real conscience about missing it. Surprisingly my father didn't veto the idea, so I duly reported to Bexwell Airfield the following Monday. The manager, Peter Perrow, was out on site and was called up on the RT. I was told to get booked into my accommodation and wait for him. He duly arrived at high speed, greeted me with special delight when he saw my Land-Rover, and immediately asked if I could make it available to the firm, as they were not only short of men but vehicles too. I readily agreed – as long as I drove it. I then jumped into his car. His dog, a dreadful little mongrel called 'Ichabod', jumped into my lap and we shot off for a lightning tour of the Fens, visiting operational sites, with the constant babble of the RT combining with his equally constant chatter. The whole afternoon and evening were totally manic and I was still loading vehicles for the next day at midnight. Peter's enthusiasm was, however, highly infectious, and this whirlwind of activity on my first day at work I thought bode well for the future. A hot meal was waiting for me at the Crown Hotel and I flopped into bed, exhausted but excited for the next day, which started at six a.m.

A summer of almost continuous rain had produced a major outbreak of potato blight, which was similar to that which had caused the Irish potato famine over a century before. The Fens, being the major potato growing area in the UK, were in serious trouble, as the ground was too wet to take the ground sprayers onto. Another major crop in the fens was celery, which was also susceptible to potato blight. Instead of being what had previously been regarded as a bit of a luxury, aerial spraying became the only way to apply fungicide. The Downham Market branch were running three aircraft, an old de Havilland Tiger Moth, a modern Piper Pawnee and a Hiller 12C helicopter. There was enormous pressure on everyone, as running one aerial spraying team was a big enough logistical task; three had never been done before. A typical 'team' consisted of at least four ground markers, one aircraft and pilot, and one tanker to supply water and aviation fuel, the latter in forty-gallon barrels. There was a tractor-drawn sprayer, in which the chemical mix was made and pumped into the aircraft, and a van on the landing site to ferry ground markers, provide a back-up man to refuel the aircraft, clean the pilot's wind shield and generally act as motorised 'gopher'.

On the second day I was designated as the 'man with a van' – my own Land-Rover, to boot, to back up the helicopter operation. Talk about being thrown in at the deep end! I had never even seen a helicopter before! In the morning I helped load up the lorry with fungicide and barrels of AVGAS for the helicopter. Then I climbed into my pristine Land-Rover, destined never to be pristine again, with two ground markers and followed the lorry to the landing site. At this stage I didn't have a clue about the geography of the Fens. This was not to be too much of a problem in the end as the whole process worked on the Ordnance Survey system of six-figure grid references. The operation was a bit like pit discipline in Grand

Prix racing; time on the ground was time wasted. The helicopter was hired at an hourly charge, and we were paid by the acre; the cost clock was continually ticking, so we had to keep the earnings clock ticking even faster. The best way of doing this was to keep moving the landing site in order to keep the flying time to the spraying site as low as possible and to cut the time on the ground refilling and refuelling to the minimum. This was much easier to do with the helicopter, as all it needed was the corner of a field.

Payloads and consequently spray-run durations varied with each aircraft, but generally averaged thirty gallons, allowing ten acres per load to be treated. Target acreage was five hundred acres per day per plane. To achieve this everything had to go smoothly right from the start, and indeed on one day we achieved over seven hundred acres with the helicopter. The most difficult part of the operation was positioning the ground markers. These were invariably casual workers, and often they weren't too bright, otherwise they would never have done such an awful job. Two were positioned at either end of the field, the pilot lined himself up with them, dropped to crop height and switched on his spray bars. As soon as he was lined up, the markers had to move fifteen paces and position themselves for the next run. Frequently there was no time to get out of the way, as a heavy crop of potato tops is nearly impossible to move through quickly; in this situation, if the marker couldn't make it in time he had to make a choice between getting his head chopped off or laying down between two rows of the crop and getting sprayed. It was not unusual for the younger and more daredevil pilots to come back with potato tops hanging from the undercarriage, so most usually chose the latter!

The landing site was a fairly hazardous place. Not only were the rotor blades to be avoided, although they were at least fairly obvious, but the main hazard was walking into the more or less invisible tail rotor. By far the greatest risk was to the pilots. The Fens especially have few trees, and what trees there are can be easily seen, so they tend to cause few accidents; but there are a great many electricity cables. These are very deceptive and are the main cause of accidents.

I had a month of flat-out work with the helicopter, which was to prove absolutely invaluable when the time came for me to set up my own aerial operation. By this time some of the crops were beyond redemption and the only solution was to burn off with sulphuric acid. Acid had the advantage over other chemicals of actually destroying the blight spores on the soil as well as killing any on the remains of the tops.

The greatest fright I ever had with Pest Control was during that September whilst acting as acid tanker driver. The Matadors were very crude vehicles to drive. They had a crash gearbox, and the steering was so heavy that in an adverse camber situation it was necessary to stand up in the very high cab just to turn the wheel. Very sharp and effective air brakes completed the fun. I had driven the Matadors with water on board and was conversant with the special skills required to drive liquid loads rather than solid, so I set out from the depot with my first load of acid, proceeding confidently on my way.

I arrived at the turning where I had to go right, and even with no oncoming traffic I naturally slowed down for the turn… but evidently not enough! I had not allowed for the extra weight of acid compared to water, and she wouldn't turn. I stood up, putting my full weight behind the wheel. She was turning, but not enough, and I realised I had two choices: either end up in the river at Denver, or try to stop before I got there. I applied the brakes as gently as I could and she stopped dead. Why the vehicle didn't roll over I shall never know. But it had four-wheel drive, so I extricated it from the wide soft verge and no one ever knew.

I seemed to have passed my initiation satisfactorily as I now had the rest of my year's 'training programme' confirmed.

I was to spend approximately six weeks at a time at various establishments to get a thorough grounding in all the company's workings. The value of these experiences depended entirely on how much effort the branch staff, especially the managers, made.

I was expecting to be allowed to be useful as I had been in the RN, but with certain exceptions this was not the case. Interestingly, on the day I am writing this, *The Times* is running an article on the utter uselessness of 'work experience' schemes where the employer just uses trainees as cheap labour and/or cannot be bothered with them.

By and large I thoroughly enjoyed my time at Downham Market and was quite sorry to have to move on. Peter did his best to get my move to Holbeach cancelled so I could stay with him. I think this was partly that he appreciated me and partly because he knew those at Holbeach would not.

I did not enjoy the Holbeach experience at all. I lived at the Black Bull, which was an horrendous pub. With short days and long nights it was not an enjoyable experience at all. In the end I attached myself to a muck-spreading gang and drove a muck-spreader for them for six weeks. I don't think any of the staff either knew or cared whether I was there or not and I was pleased to move on.

The next port of call was to Fakenham branch, ostensibly to learn about the company's spreading operations. This was the company's largest fertiliser spreading branch, operating about a dozen two-ton Atkinson twin-disc spreaders and three muck-spreaders. I had seen enough of muck-spreading at Holbeach so I concentrated on the other activities. Norfolk was one of the largest sugar beet growing areas in the country, with three British Sugar Corporation factories at King's Lynn, Wissington and Cantley. As well as being a very important cash crop it also provide the 'root break' in a predominantly cereal cropping programme.

The Norfolk soil is mostly slightly too acidic for sugar beet and requires regular applications of lime to keep the soil pH at the correct level. The liming operation at that time was fairly simple in that the material was collected from the quarry nearest to the site of operations in ten-ton loads, and hand shovelled into the spreader. Once again, good transport management was vital to keep the spreaders moving. The branch used to spread about ten thousand tons a year.

A large quantity of sugar beet sludge, a by-product from the factory, was also spread, not only to neutralise acidity but also to add body to Norfolk's predominantly light soil. However, the principle spreading operation at Fakenham branch was the application of Kainit to land to be cropped with sugar beet in the forthcoming season. Kainit was a mixture of potassium, sodium and magnesium, all especially beneficial to Norfolk's mineral soils. Kainit was a mined product imported from Germany, both East and West. It arrived in small cargo ships in anything from two hundred and fifty to five hundred tons. We used four ports: King's Lynn, Wells, Yarmouth and Norwich. The company had no control over these imports, as they were all organised by the merchants. Especially in the middle of the season it was possible that we had to have to offload from four ports on the same day. Suddenly we had to find up to a hundred tipping lorries at a day's notice. Not easy, but somehow Jack Wykes always managed it!

I used to accompany Jack on his regular visits to the markets to meet his customers, and also used to spend quite a lot of time with the lorry drivers collecting materials. I had absolutely no idea that I was to take over as manager less than a year later, but when I did I found this field experience of huge benefit.

After Christmas I was posted to Metheringham in North Lincolnshire, one of our principal drainage branches. Although I knew the theory of land drainage, herringbone systems and so on, I had had no practical experience beyond watching the Essex and Suffolk River Board's draglines maintaining our watercourses. I worked with a drainage crew but seemed to spend most of the time offloading clay drainpipes. What a job compared to today's perforated plastic coils! At the end of my time there I had had a crash course on all aspects of drainage, including how to build a reservoir.

After Metheringham came time at Harston, near Cambridge, where the chemical factory as well as the contract operation's head office was located. Officially I was to learn general administration and get an insight into the manufacturing process. This induction lasted about one day; long enough to convince me for the umpteenth time that whatever I went on to do with my life it would not include working in an office – not any kind of office! Time spent round the factory on the production process was interesting but, like trying to understand a computer manual before you have learnt to use the computer, it was not especially instructive. Once I had practical experience and had repeated the experience at my own request, I was able to absorb a lot more detail.

We then moved onto Chesterford Park, our R & D department. The centre was run by Gordon Thompson, who made me very welcome, as did his charming secretary, Sylvia. For me it was definitely love at first sight and Sylvia and I went out together for quite a long time. This continued after I was posted to Feering; but eventually, having nothing in common except a mutual affection for each other, we drifted apart. We frequented the Red Lion at Whittlesford for a good dinner at least once a week. I sometimes go in now, accompanied by my very understanding wife, and the dining room still looks the same. I am sure that the table we sat at is still the same one too. I still frequently travel the A505 and always think of those candlelit evenings to be followed by Pat Boone, especially his rendering of 'Love Letters in the Sand'.

Not only was the setting at Chesterford Park beautiful but the work was totally absorbing. As a gross oversimplification, the processes all started with the research graduates' quest to make new compounds. These were then tested to see if they had any potential as either weed killers, insecticides or fungicides. Obviously the wastage was huge but once a product had a potential use identified, it would then be sent to the botany, entomology, mycology and toxicology departments for further evaluation. Assuming a consistent result, the next step was to see if the product was likely to be able to be made in commercial quantities and for this purpose there was a 'pilot plant' at Harston. If this was successful the product was sent out for small plot trials around Cambridge. The plots were harvested by hand and yields compared with untreated plots.

If the results looked encouraging the pilot plant had to produce enough product for larger scale trials to be carried out by the company's contract branches. Only after all these stages had been successfully completed would the product be put on general release. As in today's pharmaceutical industry, the pressure was always on to launch, and there were no prizes for coming second.

I was sad to leave Chesterford Park, not only for personal reasons but also because I found it so stimulating. We were at the front end of pioneering research and really felt we were not only improving the farmer's lot but the consumer's as well, helping to provide ever cheaper and more abundant food of much higher quality. All my generation can remember going to work in the morning and leaving the evening's vegetables to soak in salt water to remove the slugs and caterpillars. This was now, thanks to the agrochemical industry, a thing of the past. I, and no doubt all my old colleagues, bridle when we listen to the arrant nonsense talked about organic farming as we, unlike those who talk this nonsense, can actually remember the days of real as opposed to pseudo organic farming. I expect those working in the GM industry must have similar thoughts today.

I went from Chesterford to the Feering branch for my final training period on crop protection of cereal and other summer crops. At the end of this period I would have completed a full twelve-month cycle and would be told where I was to be posted.

Feering was of course where I first sighted the specialist machinery with which I was now associated. It also had the added advantage of being only fifteen minutes from Horkesley, so I had no accommodation worries.

I arrived at the beginning of the spring corn-spraying campaign and came under the wing of Doug Everitt, one of the older generation of Contract Spraying Representatives (CSRs, as they were collectively known). I walked many fields with him learning my weed identification, what to spray on what crop, when was the best timing for each operation and what level of infestation justified spraying at all. The majority of farmers knew little about chemicals and were content to trust our judgement. Fisons were of course an East Anglian firm with a good reputation, and Pest Control had been operating successfully for several years already as Pest Control UK before Fisons took them over. As at other branches I was required to fill any gaps caused by illness, pressure of work or other exceptional circumstance. Otherwise I would join up with one or other of the three CSRs for crop inspections, weed and pest identification. I had the best all-round training of all here. I was given more responsibility than anywhere else, and being in home territory, living at home, life was pretty good. Although I still missed Sylvia desperately, my head still ruled my heart sufficiently to realise that there was no long-term future for us together, so I gradually let the memories fade. Faded they may have become, but forgotten – never!

Unbelievably, the first job I was entrusted to on my own was to spray spring onions with sulphuric acid for weed control on a farm near Manningtree. When given the address of the farming company I innocently enquired who the owner was; the reply came back – Sir Clavering Fison. He was no less than the Group Chairman! I was assured that this wasn't a wind-up. I said, 'Why me, for goodness' sake?'

'No one else available for a small one-off job,' came the reply.

I was to meet the acid tanker there, so I set off on my own down the A12. Under the circumstances it seemed a journey without end. Who was to meet me on arrival but Sir Clavering himself. What an utterly delightful and charming man he was. I didn't really know what I was doing, but fortunately neither did he on this occasion. I cheekily suggested he leave the field when I was ready, as acid spray was not that pleasant to be caught in, a bit like being flagellated with stinging nettles. He laughed and left. Mercifully, everything went fine; the main problem we were trying to eradicate was the standard market garden annual (chicken) nettle. Highly susceptible to acid, they had all shrivelled up, leaving the onions standing up like guardsmen by the time I had finished.

I thoroughly enjoyed my time at Feering, not least I expect because I was in home territory and knew a lot of our customers socially anyway.

I was notified that I had passed my training course and was to take up a post as Assistant Branch Manager at Downham Market.

I wasn't aware of any reason why Peter should need an assistant but I quickly learned that I was being groomed to take over as manager at Fakenham.

The then incumbent was one of the original Dr Ripper appointees. Dr Ripper, who founded Pest Control, had decided not to continue with Fisons and had been offered the responsibility for setting up a new operation for Dow Chemicals from the US in King's Lynn. He wanted Ted Barrett from Fakenham to go with him. After eight weeks at Downham Market, spent almost entirely on the responsibilities of management, I was offered the post of Acting Branch Manager at Fakenham, which needless to say I took. Although Peter and I had had a number of spats over my love of rifle shooting and his hatred of it, because of his war experiences, we nonetheless worked well together, and I appreciated his advice.

I realised that yet again, as in *Trenchant,* I was to be the youngest and least experienced member of a team. But this time I was the CO – a rather daunting prospect.

CHAPTER XIII

Norfolk

I had many mixed feelings about the prospect of taking over the Fakenham Branch. I had not particularly enjoyed my time there as a trainee. It was marginally better than at Holbeach, but that was all I could say in its favour.

It was certainly not the largest branch in the company but believed itself the most important. Even at that early period of traineeship I was conscious of the Norfolk air of disdain towards everyone and everything not Norfolk. It's an attitude with which I now can identify, having completed more than the obligatory forty years' residence!

In Pest Control terms it probably was of great significance, as this was the county of residence of the founder, Dr W E Ripper. Norfolk was also a county of equal significance to the Fisons parent company. My predecessor was a Norfolk man, well known and respected in the area. I was young, inexperienced and worst of all a 'furriner'.

I left Downham Market after the day's work, having been wished every success by all the men, the supervisors, Peter the manager, and Molly and Daphne, who ran the office.

I had decided not to book into the Crown Hotel where I had stayed before, until I had seen how the land lay with me wearing my 'new hat'.

I had let the staff at Fakenham know that I would come in at nine a.m. rather than the usual time of seven thirty, to give them time to get the men and machines out. I had booked in for three nights at the Hoste Arms at Hillington until I had got my new bearings. All the staff and operators were the same as had trained me nine months earlier. The first problem we had to get round was their method of addressing me, I was not prepared to continue with Christian-name usage so we had to find a mutually acceptable term of address. As my surname was unpronounceable to most – we had a significant number of non-English staff, recruited initially from the POW camp at Hempton – the term 'Mr D' was arrived at.

In contrast to the previous summer, which had been very wet, leading to the previous year's blight outbreak in the Fens, 1959 was hot and dry. There had been nothing like the panic of the year before, but I walked into a different type of panic at Fakenham.

Corn spraying was the company's bread and butter but the cream came from anti-blight spraying on potatoes and celery, and insecticide spraying on sugar beet and brassica crops. As far as Fakenham was concerned there were relatively few potatoes grown but there was a vast acreage of beet, cabbages, sprouts and carrots; these crops were Fakenham's cream. This year the sprout and cabbage crops were heavily infested with insects of every kind. Those first few weeks were to prove a very steep learning curve, and to give credit where it was due, my staff were good teachers. I was acutely aware that our fledgling industry was on trial: could it deliver pest-free crops in adversity? We had to prove that the days of soaking cabbages and cauliflowers in salt water over night to get the livestock out were gone. We certainly didn't deliver one hundred per cent clean crops, but we did a lot better than would have been remotely possible without chemicals.

Eventually the Indian summer came to an end and we then had the difficult task of assessing just how successful or otherwise we had been in protecting the brassica crops. Customers were well aware that whilst all our treatments carried a guarantee of success, in recent weeks some had been less than totally effective. The majority were understanding about the exceptional circumstances, but a hard core decided to turn the screws by not paying. They also took advantage of my personal inexperience to turn the screws even tighter. One

I remember well had a beautiful daughter living at home, who was always around when I called to have another set of negotiations with her father. I was always given lunch, and managed to drag the negotiations out. I wasn't too sure of the wisdom of this as here was clearly another relationship going nowhere, even if it were to ever start.

One day Jane wasn't there and her father got me in a metaphorical armlock, and I am not sure to this day whether I gave away more than I should have.

Immense hours of overtime had been worked and a lot of money was earned all round. It was only when the work died down and the earnings dropped to basic wages that we had any strife. The Fakenham branch was the only unionised one in the company, and the shop steward and I had many differences of opinion; but we never allowed it to develop into open warfare.

The company was becoming seriously worried by the competition coming from farmer-operated sprayers using safer chemicals. It was unrealistic to expect to live for ever on the use of harsh and dangerous poisons, however effective they were. My staff, with the exception of Jack Wykes, who was in charge of the spreading operations, were not salesmen. They were extremely able and competent technical supervisors, but to get them 'out on the road' was very difficult and it appeared to be somewhat beneath their dignity. This was a problem all through the Fisons Group. A high percentage of staff had been reared in a climate where demand always outstripped supply and manufacturers and wholesalers had developed an almost civil service-like attitude, whereby if there was but one reason not to do something and a hundred reasons in its favour then it still wouldn't get done. One of my briefs was, as one unspoilt by the old days of 'rationing', to think up new campaigns, which would at least dovetail into our existing operations and put us into a better position to withstand the competition that was surely coming.

This was the first time in my life that I had experienced

commercial pressures and I was far from certain that I could handle it. I was not at all happy within myself and was really missing Royal Navy life, so much so that I enquired into the possibility of 'signing on' again. The Submarine Service was not an option as I had lost too much seniority over the previous three and a half years' absence for any meaningful career to be possible. However, a short service commission in the Fleet Air Arm, with an option to sign on for twelve years, was possible. I chose this option and discovered that I had to lose a stone in weight and also attend a pre-medical in Norwich before making a formal application. All this was done and I was eventually summoned to RAF Hornchurch for the flying aptitude tests, which took two days, and then on to Lee-on-Solent for the rest. All this went really well, but having been warned at Norwich that I had a slightly suspect blood pressure, I was becoming increasingly apprehensive of the looming medical on the last day. However, this passed off alright, with no blood pressure readings being taken. However, I had not escaped – after the final lunch came the blood pressure exam – I failed and my world fell apart.

Despite a formal appeal against rejection, it was not to be, and I decided to get my head down and make the best of what was after all a pretty fantastic opportunity for me. Crunch time came after my return from my so-called week's holiday, when it was time to renegotiate the contract with EARP (East Anglian Real Property Co.). This was the second largest farming operation in Norfolk at the time, comprising some 12,000 acres of arable crops. The largest concentration was at Cantley, with other farms at Swaffham, Paston, Southrepps and Guestwick. Currently the contract was held jointly by ourselves, with the Cantley Group and the farms at Swaffham, while our competitors, Westwick Distributors, held the remainder. I was extremely nervous about the proposed meeting. Not only did EARP represent nearly a quarter of our total business, which was a frighteningly high proportion, but it was my first ever contract negotiation. I was impressed that my masters allowed me to handle this on my own without any head-office involvement. Having pored for days over the figures I decided to make no changes to the previous year's prices, hoping thereby to at least maintain the status quo. The meeting lasted three hours, after which I and Chris Hammond, who looked after the day-to-day operations at Cantley, were told that they would let us know in due course. 'Due course' turned out to be the longest three weeks of my life, but the positive result made it all worthwhile.

EARP were a Dutch-owned company who were primarily responsible for the introduction of the sugar beet crop and the establishment of the first UK beet factory at Cantley. The General Manager was Adriaan den Engelse, with John Cock his deputy. Quite apart from the money, it was a total pleasure doing business with these two gentlemen. They were always firm but fair and never, ever tried to put one over you. They taught me the meaning of 'my word is my bond', and I am extraordinarily appreciative of all they taught me about business ethics. What was so special to me was being allowed the run of their entire farming operation. The steady fraternisation with all their staff which ensued was like having one's own farm only far, far better. Indeed, I maintained regular contact for more than ten years after I left, right up to the time that the farms changed ownership. Landmarks of their presence were huge barns, which in the 1930s during the run-up to the war were suspected of housing German planes! Such was, or indeed still is, the Norfolk man's suspicion of 'furriners' that a Dutchman soon became a 'Hun', and a perfectly innocent farm building, the like of which admittedly had never been seen before, became a store for weapons of war. Adriaan den Engelse was in fact interned as an undesirable alien, but for all that never held it against the English. To me he was a wonderful man and I am still grateful for all he and his staff did for me over the years. I like to think that the relationship between us was reciprocated, as two years later the whole contract was awarded to us – much to the chagrin of Westwick Distributors. This of course hugely improved my personal standing within the company, but I was acutely aware that EARP now represented an even more unhealthy proportion of our business – a most dangerous situation. Happily, it all worked and the company still had the whole contract when I left some seven years later.

One of my less enjoyable tasks was having to compulsorily retire Charlie Hewitt, our yard man and van driver. The personnel department had found out that on his original employment application he had understated his age by five years and was in fact now way beyond the company's retirement age. He was utterly devastated by the decision, and to soften the blow I arranged for him to go on to part-time employment and also gave him an official retirement party, which we held at the Crown Hotel. This degenerated into the usual Pest Control drunken orgy, which had significant after effects. Halfway through the party, my secretary and right-hand mentor, Mary, and I decided to go back to the office on some pretext which I do not recall, and fell into a somewhat inebriated embrace. This was to be the start of a passionate love affair which lasted throughout the next six months, during which more and more eyebrows were raised, as she was a married woman – albeit unhappily (surprise, surprise).

The next morning I was confronted by Bert Eke, shamefacedly apologising for his behaviour the night before but stating he had lost his false teeth and could I ask if anyone at the Crown Hotel had found them, as he was too embarrassed to ask them himself. No luck from that direction, but as the heads cleared during the day one of the others remembered seeing Bert throwing up over the car park drain... A fishing expedition ensued and after about half an hour a set of false teeth came up! The ensuing hilarity allowed my own escapade with Mary to be forgotten.

The spraying season had been successful and I felt I was settling in quite well to the job and thoroughly enjoying it. I was still living at the Crown, and used to go home to

Horkesley on Saturday afternoons, returning by seven thirty on the Monday morning. At least two weekends a month I used to fly out to Holland and crew a converted MFV (motorised fishing vessel) for Ingram Capper, a wartime Royal Navy officer. All expenses including flights were paid for. We used to sail her across from Wivenhoe to Rotterdam Yacht Club every Easter, and back again at the end of the summer.

Throughout this time my love affair with Mary went from strength to strength, and despite her protestations that she was unable to have children I managed to resist the ultimate temptation. I realised I was getting into ever deeper water and couldn't reconcile my behaviour with my current responsibilities. For my summer holiday I was to spend two weeks on *Shemaun,* as the yacht was called, and Mary and I decided to make a decision on our future on my return.

CHAPTER XIV

Romance, Courtship and Marriage

There were normally three of us available as crew for *Shemaun*; Bob Stirling, related to the founder of the SAS; Ed Puxley, an ex-submariner like myself; and of course me. Normally we permed two out of three to get the crew and on this occasion I was to relieve Bob Stirling. A friend of the Cappers, Mandy, was also holidaying on board. With a maximum of eight people at any one time, it didn't take us long to get to know each other. Rosemary Capper took me to one side as soon as I joined and confided that Mandy was having a totally unsuitable relationship with Bob, who was old enough to be her father, and could I try to talk some sense into her. I thought, Oh no, this is all I need – given my own equally unsuitable relationship with Mary.

We cruised all day up the Dutch canals and ate ashore each evening, a wonderful water-borne pub crawl. As soon as we came back aboard, Mandy and I would take ourselves off to the upper deck, in a most unsociable fashion. Everybody tactfully left us alone, assuming we might be getting something together under the stars. In fact copious quantities of whisky and tobacco were consumed by us both whilst we wondered how two people could get in such a mess, and above all, should we get out of the mess or go with it? Neither of us wanted to end our respective relationships, but by the final night we had both resolved to let our heads rule our hearts and accept that the bullet had to be bitten...

After a lot of tears from both of us, Mary left Fakenham with her husband and I never saw or heard from her again. This was a truly terrible time for me, as not only had I lost the girl I was totally in love with but I'd lost an extremely competent secretary and above all, my only close friend in Norfolk. Mandy had done the same thing with similar results, and although we sought solace in each other's company for a while nothing was to come of it. I remember almost nothing of the next few months, except having to find a replacement secretary. Not only did no one suitable apply, each applicant was less suitable than the last; however, I finally managed to plug the gap in the office – and that's as charitable as I can be, even forty years later.

At the beginning of the hunting season my parents had engaged a new girl groom, Jacqueline; the first time we met she was pushing a wheelbarrow… wow, what a figure! So began another love affair, but this one survived all the way to the altar. After a year's courtship my father demanded to know my intentions, to which I replied, 'Marriage.'

He was furious, as apparently her way with horses was the best he had ever experienced in forty years. I don't think he ever even wished us luck! The courtship itself was far from smooth. Her parents did not approve of me and mine didn't approve of her. One of my earliest, if not my first meeting with her parents was Sunday lunch.

I earned a few brownie points by shelling some fresh peas but promptly lost them when I observed a roasted earwig on the Yorkshire pudding and was foolish enough to point it out to my future mother-in-law before she actually put it in her mouth. This invited the caustic comment that surely I knew the difference between a piece of black from the oven and an earwig. The rejoinder that I had never seen a piece of black with pincers on it before ensured that my score of brownie points reverted to zero.

Relations between the two families deteriorated further when my mother tried to insist that the wedding ceremony and reception should be at Horkesley. This made sense to me, as we had all the facilities and all previous family weddings had taken place there. However, Jacqueline's family flatly refused to let the de Havillands hijack the occasion and we settled for her local church at South Benfleet with the reception at a hotel at Westcliffe. Because my terms of employment insisted that time off was only allowed in mid winter, we decided on January 17th, a Wednesday. Further expressions of dismay followed, and my explanation that Wednesdays were not shooting days and January 17th was the day when one could finally see the days lengthening, marking the beginning of the end of winter, did nothing to calm the atmosphere. My half of the family insisted on wearing morning dress; her half refused. However, we ploughed on – and in any case the great day was still six months away and there were more urgent problems to address, such as where we were going to live. Jacqueline had made it quite clear by now that with her went her horses!

Her parents were having a new house built on a six-acre plot near Chelmsford, which included horse accommodation on site. My running off with their daughter had thrown a real spanner in the works and it was incumbent upon me to provide nothing less. Colin Beck, auctioneer and estate agent in Fakenham, found us an old farmhouse with thirteen acres of land and stabling for up to four horses. This was in the small village of Foxley on the main Norwich to Fakenham road, about fifteen minutes' drive from my office. Jacqueline approved totally, but there were two quite significant hurdles to get over. Colin Beck told us there was a main road improvement scheme coming through the property at some date in the future, but he had no idea when. As the scheme had been first mooted before the turn of the century and before the first motor car had been invented he didn't want me to worry too much as it would probably never happen! My employers had a helpful mortgage scheme but were not too sure about thirteen acres and a stable block with a potential road improvement scheme. However, they generously went ahead and we took possession on August 1st 1961. We were both so thrilled to have not only a home of our own but one with considerable potential.

The house was dated between 1560 and 1590, and was heavily beamed inside. The outbuildings consisted of three stables, a barn and three small stores around the perimeter of a 'crew' yard and separately a range of pigsties; separate again was a pack house. Turnpike Farm was surrounded by mature orchard of mainly dessert cherries, apples, pears and plums. The rest of the land was paddock and barley, plus half an acre of rhubarb. At this stage Richard Briers and Felicity Kendall had not embarked on 'The Good Life', and it was not until some years later when the TV programme was made that we were able to laugh at ourselves.

Jacqueline came up each weekend and we were able to make a start clearing up – and what a task it was! The vendor had only had the property a very short time, and apart from the current crop of barley, which he retained, everything else was the legacy of a smallholder referred to only as 'Pickles', so called (we believed) because he was always in one! Initially we concentrated on making the house habitable, and after a couple of weeks it was liveable in – just. It didn't take long for the locals to establish that we were not married and the fact that we lived together at weekends was a cause of much sucking of teeth in the rather puritanical community of Foxley. I very soon learned that like most men of my generation I didn't like coming home to an empty house during the week. Jacqueline was still employed by my parents, and with the hunting season rapidly approaching, her weekend visits got fewer and fewer. Friends of mine from Essex had acquired a farm near Fakenham, and out of sympathy for me kindly allowed me to live as a guest with them until we got married. Relationships between myself and Jacqueline gradually deteriorated to a level whereby the whole question of marriage was being called into question. I had thought that both sets of parents were trying to sabotage the event, but while there may have been some element of truth in this, the real problem was my friend's daughter. Apparently she had an undesirable reputation regarding men within the equine fraternity. I was totally ignorant of this but when Jacqueline learned that my bedroom adjoined hers she freaked out. I can't remember exactly how I got out of the predicament but eventually we got back on an even keel. The basic furniture and fittings for Turnpike Farm were acquired and all was set for the 'off' on January 17th.

The day before was spent 'hedgerowing' for cock pheasants at Horkesley as the weather gradually got colder. I remember plodding slowly up the lane at the end of the day with George Gant, our keeper, and brother John, and the pair of them banging on non-stop how my life would never be the same again, and was I sure I was doing the right thing?

To my horror I woke up on the great day to a completely white world. We'd had about five inches of snow in the night. Accompanied by much grumbling from my family, we had to bring the departure time forward by half an hour. I went out to my car before breakfast, for some reason I don't recall, found the door frozen up, gave it a good pull and broke one of the hinges! As we were driving to France for our all too brief honeymoon – just five days, Fisons having booked me on a sales course in Hampshire starting early the following week – I had no choice but to beg a friendly garage in Colchester to mend it whilst I waited. Driving into Colchester one handed, the other holding the door shut, in ice and snow, made me wonder whether this was an omen or merely the normal operation of sod's law.

Spurlings Garage were wonderful and turned me round in twenty minutes. I collected John, who was to be my best man, from King's Farm, and proceeded to South Benfleet. At the Rayleigh Road roundabout I had a severe attack of self-doubt and went round it four times before deciding I had already passed the point of no return and carried on. Uncle Hugh, the Bishop, married us; we froze nigh unto death for the inevitable photographs before reaching the sanctuary of the hotel for the reception. Jacqueline's parents had done us proud. Nobody fought or made a scene and we eventually departed for the Chaucer Arms in Canterbury, where we were to spend our first night before catching the ferry from Dover to Calais. I had asked the travel agent to book us into a hotel in Calais to the equivalent standard of the Castle Hotel in Norwich, but all we had was a dosshouse – a total disaster in every way. After a night at Rheims we eventually found a good quality hotel in Le Mans, which we made our base. The company's Hillman Minx was thrashed round the racetrack for ten laps, which was a great thrill, particularly down the Mulsanne straight. I did ease off the throttle after the second lap, as I didn't fancy having to explain a blown engine at this particular site.

The crossing home was horrendous, very rough with vomit bowls skidding back and forth with the ship's movement. Far worse, though, was the huge number of illegal Pakistani immigrants. No, they are not a new phenomenon! The immigration authorities sent them straight back and told us that the smallpox scare which was gripping the UK was still increasing, and as none of them had vaccination certificates any of us who were unvaccinated were at very high risk.

To my horror Jacqueline announced that she had never been vaccinated. I rang my doctor from the quayside and arranged to have her done as soon as we got back to Norfolk. He did say that we might be too late, but he thought it was unlikely and we were not to worry.

We did, of course, and spent an anxious period waiting for the worst but fortunately it never came. Life improved rapidly thereafter and by the spring we were kept busy homemaking. Jacqueline had sold her scooter, and her parents very kindly gave her not only her horse but their Land-Rover and its accompanying Rice trailer as well. The horse, Grey Castle, was an enormous beast standing at seventeen hands, which more than kept her busy. Much as I disliked horses, always likening them to reincarnated Trade Union leaders doing just enough to get fed and kept on the payroll for another day and not one iota more, it was needless to say an opinion I kept to myself.

Accordingly, I settled willingly into pleasing my bride by horse-proofing all the fences, securing feed supplies, finding a local blacksmith, a good vet, and above all somewhere to ride. She had been an extremely successful junior show jumper, but like most girls when they came out of juniors, found the transition into seniors a whole new ball game. Not only were there the pressures of working for a living to contend with, with the consequent shortage of time, but above all, as in all sports, the senior game is far, far tougher and more competitive. I built a mounting block in the stable yard, sourced poles and assorted timber to make practice jumps, and finally managed to find some decent hay. The latter was extraordinarily difficult in the springtime, but John Cock, Deputy Manager of EARP, came up trumps with some superb quality tripodded hay. Indeed, he was our source of hay for many years until the economics involved forced him to drop it as a farm crop.

With some trepidation we went to the first show of the season at Fakenham, where in front of many of my colleagues Jacqueline won the main event. I was as thrilled as she was, and everyone was amazed at how she managed such a huge animal. Elation was short-lived, however, when the next piece of publicity was a half-page photograph on the back of the *Eastern Daily Press,* of her out of control, jumping clean out of the ring and clearing a small car parked at the ring side in the process! Eventually Grey Castle had to go and we placed an advert to that effect in the *Horse and Hound*. Sir Charles Gooch, of Wivenhoe Park at Colchester, who coincidentally was in the process of selling a large part of his estate on which to build the new Essex University, was our first respondent. Appointments were made and on the appointed day he duly turned up after lunch with his vet, whilst we also had ours in attendance.

Both advisers were the worse for drink, which I was assured was quite normal, and there followed a scene of total unreality. Charles Gooch, a very big man who I believe rode at sixteen stone, got aboard and really put Grey Castle through his paces. He was thrilled, and immediately offered the asking price; his vet then carried out the usual post-exercise examination and pronounced that he had a weak heart – a diagnosis promptly denounced by ours. Then followed a fairly inebriated discourse between the two before both buyer and seller had had enough and the deal was done, with the proviso that if Grey Castle had a heart attack within twelve months we would agree, with arbitration if necessary, to an appropriate level of compensation. In fact he gave the Gooch family twelve years of devoted service hunting with the Essex and Suffolk for an average of three days a week. Some heart defect! A replacement was soon found, and over the next ten years I became a reasonably proficient attendant at shows all over Norfolk and the neighbouring counties. I cannot pretend that I enjoyed it as I was permanently worried about Jacqueline's safety, or how well or badly she had done. It is said it is always worse to watch than to do, but it was to be a full fifteen years before I had to leave her unconscious in an ambulance and bring the horse home on my own.

We worked steadily to make a nice home and garden until the Cuban Missile Crisis blew up. Peter Hancock, a farmer customer, had given me a hundredweight of daffodil bulbs and I remember as if it was yesterday how we planted them on a beautiful autumn day thinking how unreal it all was, as there appeared no way in which the world could avoid World War III. This appeared to be certain to go nuclear from the start, and with the almost saturation coverage of American airbases in Norfolk, we all realised we would be somewhere in the Russian target area. In all other ways life was idyllic and we were very upset to think it was all going to end before it had barely begun. As the world approached the seemingly inevitable Armageddon, some of the men asked if they could spend the last few days with their wives and families. Somehow I managed to have enough 'faith' and assured them that when confronted, all bullies turn and run, and they too must have that belief. I didn't say no to the request, but within hours the bully, Khrushchev, had indeed turned and run. If

CND had had their way, does anyone really think the Russians would have walked away?

That crisis gave way to a somewhat lesser one in the form of a bitterly cold winter.

As still happens today to most families, we all seem to have to spend Christmas where we don't want to. On this occasion Jacqueline spent Christmas Day with her parents and I spent it with mine. I did see hers over the period and she saw mine, but in neither case was the visit longer than either of us could get away with. On the day after Boxing Day, the weather was starting to deteriorate badly and we were at last able to come home to Norfolk. How we made it I shall never know. The snow was several inches deep in Suffolk, although in the days before privatisation the snowploughs all worked, and additionally of course each lengthman with his handcart of sand was also diligently at work. As we crossed the River Waveney the snow completely vanished in the space of a few hundred yards, and indeed that set the pattern for the rest of the winter. Norfolk had little snow but several degrees of 'permafrost' instead, which had the potential to do serious damage to crops with no protective snow blanket.

Economic survival that winter was far from easy, and work which we could actually do was in very short supply, but somehow we managed without laying off any staff. At home it was no easier, as I had had a wood-burning hearth installed, which of course was useless for burning coal, and poor Jacqueline had to start trying to get a fire going with green apple wood (all we had) at about midday every day so that there was some warmth by evening when I came home. It was impossible to ride, but the horse always had some exercise, if only being led round and round the field.

As always the seasons come round, and soon we were back in the normal routine. Again, as is normal, the frost damage was not as severe as the ever-gloomy countrymen expected.

CHAPTER XV

All in a Day's Work

One of the earliest jobs I had to do was arrange the aircraft hire contracts for the aerial spraying during the coming season. The branch had previously done very little, and although an expansion of this activity was a priority for me I found it very difficult to forecast what would happen. Certainly there would be very little activity on potatoes, as in this part of Norfolk – unlike the Fens – very few were grown; although there could be some demand in an aphis year for use on sugar beet and peas.

In the end I decided against committing to a helicopter as they were far more expensive than a fixed-wing plane. I decided to rely on the spare capacity of an Italian Aero Macchi, which was going to be the company's reserve aircraft. Any jobs which were not suitable for a fixed-wing would have to be done either by hoping a helicopter could be spared from a neighbouring branch or putting a ground machine in instead.

It was whilst we had a borrowed helicopter that I had the most unpleasant job I have ever had to do. I had a call from the police at four o'clock in the afternoon telling me that the eight-year-old son of one of our drivers had been killed coming out of school, did I know how to contact him? I knew he was out on the King's Lynn marshes, and as only the cars had radios and not the tractors, the answer was no. Quite fortuitously the helicopter had just returned and I got the pilot to fly me out to the marshes, where our green and yellow machinery was easily identifiable. I had rehearsed what I was going to say all the way in the helicopter, but it didn't make it any easier when the time came. Both the driver and his mate on the tanker knew instinctively that there was a crisis. In fact it was a double blow, as the tanker driver was also the boy's uncle. The boy's father went back in the helicopter and I rode back in the lorry, leaving the tractor out on the marshes for someone else to take over. A devastatingly awful time.

Not long after this tragic accident I called for the fixed-wing plane to come and do a few days' spraying. It was much larger than I expected but the skill of the pilot, Paul, overcame any apparent lack of manoeuvrability, as he demonstrated to me one Sunday morning when we flew over Turnpike Farm... at zero feet. Jacqueline was shocked to see me leaning out of the cockpit and downright cross when she learned of the effect on the neighbour's chickens!

Paul had the strange habit of never getting out of his cockpit during his hours of duty. He said it was the only way he could maintain concentration. He sat there chain-smoking surrounded by 'No Smoking' notices while he was refilled with chemical. He did refrain whilst Av Gas was pumped in, however.

Some ten years after I left Fisons I called in at the air operators' HQ at Bourn to see how everybody was and was quite shocked to be told that many of those I knew had killed themselves – but not Paul, who by then had graduated to 747s. Crop spraying certainly had a high rate of attrition amongst the pilots. Fakenham branch was only involved with one fatality. I had personally briefed the pilot at an early breakfast in the Red Lion, handed him the map with the power lines clearly marked, and explained that on that day we would only be using one landing site and that for a large part of the day he would be crossing these power lines to and from the landing site. 'Please go *over* them, not under' earned a reassurance that he would do just that. Indeed he did, until the last acre had been sprayed, whereupon he switched off his spray bars and was returning to the landing site to refuel for the final journey back to base. The landing site crew watched him fly straight into the cables he had been flying over all day. At the inquest it seemed to be accepted that loss of concentration was to blame, as presumably he had just relaxed having finished the day's work. He was an older man than most, very calm, and didn't deserve that end.

The younger ones were all a daredevil breed, none more so than Mike Napier, a young helicopter pilot who I often flew with. I remember one day, whilst still a trainee, racing a train between Chelmsford and Colchester with him. We hedge-hopped on a level with and as close to the carriage window as he dared, but I had to spot the telephone or low-voltage electricity wires, so missed most of the passengers' reaction, which Mike told me was 'mixed'! We never heard any more about it, but I think we were very fortunate. Mike was the maddest of them all but I did get really cross when he flattened me in a sugar beet field and I actually felt the skids on my back. To my stream of invective that he could have killed me he merely laughed and said, 'Well, I didn't!' Only when I threatened to deck him did he apologise and the incident was over. We remained good friends until I left.

The chemical revolution was now getting into full stride. New chemical companies were springing up and with the switch to the newer, safer chemicals which could be applied at low volume, the spraying operation itself was becoming simpler, encouraging not only farmers themselves but other contractors to climb on the bandwagon. This put the company under severe competitive pressure, nowhere more so than at Fakenham where there was still a huge pool of labour on the farms with no industry to draw them off the land. I made a couple of staff changes to reflect the growing emphasis on selling, as opposed to relying entirely on technical expertise to bring in the orders. On the whole this was successful, but we had to work very hard indeed to even maintain our position, let alone improve it. At the same time Rachel Carson published her book *Silent Spring,* which was a blatantly undisguised attack on the fledgling agrochemical industry.

Much uninformed criticism was laid at our door, including

accusations of 'poisoning the face of the nation'. Today those in the biochemical and GM industry can take heart: it's all happened before. We did *not* poison the face of the nation but we *did* play an enormous part in increasing food production and putting cheap food on the nation's plate. That, after all, was the agricultural industry's brief. Not only the big names – Fisons and ICI – but others too, had highly sophisticated R&D departments, and I am unaware of anything finding its way on to farms that should not have. As a result of the drive towards newer and safer chemicals the company signed a marketing agreement with Dupont for the distribution of the new pre-emergent weedkiller 'Telvar' and later with Geigy for their new 'triazine' group of chemicals. They were all soil-applied herbicides and within this group there were opportunities to use products selectively on certain crops or alternatively to give total control of all plant life for twelve months. The selective usage fitted comfortably into our normal operations and as a result we could now, to give one example, achieve control of weeds in carrots cleanly and safely, whereas before we used to spray with paraffin.

It was in the non-selective field, however, that we were able to open up a totally new area of operations which was christened 'Industrial Weed Control'. One of our earliest customers was Shell, who used them to create vegetation-free firebreaks round their refinery sites, as well as British Rail and the Air Ministry. The company had developed a special 'spray train' which kept all the railway lines in the country free of weeds. Neither I nor Fakenham branch were directly involved, except on occasions when we provided staff when it was operating locally. It didn't spend long in Norfolk, as after Dr Beeching had wielded his famous axe there was very little rail service left.

The Air Ministry contract, however, was all mine and although the contract was for every RAF and USAF base south of the Humber it was all carried out by Fakenham branch and kept staff occupied for at least six months every year. In the main it consisted of eliminating weed growth in the cracks of main runways, perimeter tracks and overshoot areas; plus fuel and armament stores, ballistic missile silos and around buildings. One of the things that struck me very forcibly was the different levels of security. With the exception of the ballistic missile sites, RAF security appeared relatively lax. To work inside the missile bases, however, the operators all required the highest level of security clearance; only myself and two others at Fakenham had this level of clearance. We employed a high percentage of foreign nationals and they were not allowed on the operational sites as a matter of principle. In general, though, the Americans had far higher levels of security, which they enforced ruthlessly, if necessary at gunpoint – as I was to find out at first hand one Saturday morning at Lakenheath.

Of necessity our operations on main runways could only be carried out when there was no flying, and frequently this meant working weekends. On this particular occasion I went to Lakenheath on the Friday morning and checked with the control tower that the runway was not going to be used that weekend. I arranged for the crew to be on site at eight a.m., collected all the necessary passes and arrived myself at seven thirty, checked in at the Guard Room and drove down the main runway to have a detailed inspection of the overshoot area next to the main road, as I felt we might have to use a stronger mix in view of the amount of weed growth after a relatively wet spell. I had got about halfway down when I heard a siren wailing. I looked in my mirror and saw a Jeep with a flashing red light. I stopped and out jumped an enormous black American sergeant waving a pistol at me and screaming at me to get off the f—ing runway! I didn't hesitate to do as I was told. As I turned the engine off and prepared to get out, a squadron of Sabre jets screamed in to land.

Once I had produced my security pass he calmed down and explained that the planes had come from Germany and were supposed to have landed in France, but the French – as they frequently do – had other ideas. They had been diverted to

Lakenheath without warning, catching everyone by surprise – including me! We both reckoned I had been within less than thirty seconds of disaster!

I was thoroughly enjoying life by now, but after two or three years of working very long hours, which of themselves were no problem at all but in the context of married life were highly questionable, we began to wonder where we were going. As we had acquired an old nursery we thought we might do worse than see if it could be resuscitated. Sweet peas were one of my favourite flowers, and a friendship with Alec Stark, the local florist, whose father had a variety named after him, encouraged me to try growing them. I bought two hundred plants from him, grew them as cordons (a single stem per cane), and was sufficiently pleased with results to enter some at the local show. To our astonishment we won the class; convinced this could only be beginners' luck we nonetheless entered again in a couple of weeks' time with the same result. We now began to think that rather than beginners' luck perhaps we were rather good at the job. Meanwhile the plants were so productive that when we couldn't get any more flowers in the house, we thought that rather than throw them away perhaps we should try to sell them. It was no good trying to sell them to Alec Stark's florist shop, as he grew his own; so I thought I might try Woolworth's, who had just opened a new store in Fakenham. Woolworth's were highly enthusiastic and took a consignment every day, but it was still not enough. I then approached the other florist in Fakenham, Mrs Fuller, who was also very pleased with what we had grown, and agreed to buy what we cared to bring in. I took the day's consignment, bunched and wrapped in newspaper, in my car each day on the way to work. After a few days Mrs Fuller offered me a second-hand flower box to put them in.

The horse show calendar was to take us to Tendring Show in Essex and there in the horticultural tent was the finest display of sweet peas that I had ever seen, either before or since, by L J Everitt of Little Clacton. I cannot recall how the jumping went, but I do remember announcing on the way home that that was what I was going to do.

'What, exactly?' said Jacqueline.

'Grow sweet peas like that,' I replied.

'Good,' she said, 'I'd like to too.'

'Commercially?' said I.

'Yes,' came the reply.

No matter how many times I look back on my life, that conversation was unquestionably one of its defining moments. I had picked up a seed list from the firm, and over the next couple of weeks we pored over it and finally sent in an order for five thousand seeds in ten varieties, including the star of the show, 'Orange Wonder'. This variety was the giveaway, as it apparently had to be shaded and could only be grown under glass. Joe Everitt himself rang up to query the order. Did we really mean five thousand, or had we got a nought wrong? I assured him we were serious and to his question of what were we going to do with them I nonchalantly replied, 'Sell them.'

He was not satisfied with my answer and enquired whether I had actually ever done this sort of thing before. I couldn't lie, so he very kindly said that as I clearly had no idea what I was taking on he would help me all he could to grow them, but selling them would be up to me. I would be on my own, and had to undertake not to go anywhere near his wholesaler, Collingridge, in Covent Garden. I never seriously expected them to grow, so marketing was not really on my mind. I recalled the label on the end of Mrs Fuller's box – *F J Forster, Wellington Street, Covent Garden* – and thought, If we do get a crop, they will handle them. However, let's grow them first...

We built the requisite cold frames, ordered two thousand three-inch clay pots from Sankeys and the necessary John Innes seed compost from Coltishall granaries, and on the first weekend of October set about sowing the five thousand seeds at three to a three-inch pot.

By the end of the month we seemed to have had a good germination, but we were soon to learn that this was the easy bit. First the sparrows had a go, so black cotton was spread everywhere. Then came the short-tailed voles. Initially I suspected mice but traps with cheese were never touched. I now had to seek the first of many pieces of advice from Joe Everitt. He diagnosed voles, and told me to bait the traps with apple. Magic! Several voles in traps, no more damage. I knew one mustn't coddle, but how severe did the frost have to be before taking precautions? The answer that first winter was obvious once the plants were frozen in the pots. The danger apparently was sun through the glass thawing the plants out in the daytime, only to be frozen again at night. The answer was straw over the covers to keep the sun out and keep them frozen. Despite their being frozen solid for nearly a month we never lost a plant. How valuable a lesson that was to be in later life – it's the thawing out and re-freezing which does the damage. During the late autumn the ground where they were to grow had been deep ploughed and copious quantities of stable manure buried.

The plants looked really well in their frames and I was thrilled. Then came planting out time in mid-March. It was done over two weekends; Jacqueline knocked them out of the pots, threw out any substandard ones and brought the rest to me to plant. We completed the task and then waited for them to grow.

While waiting, we erected the framework of supporting posts and training wires and carried on waiting. I didn't realise that it took a month to get their roots down before they really started to grow, during which time they were attacked by partridges – not pigeons, surprisingly – and of course sparrows. We ended up with every type of bird-scaring device known to man, which did in the end prove to be fairly effective. By far the worst predator was myself. Every morning before I went to work I used to dig up a few plants looking for cutworms or leatherjackets feeding on the roots. Eventually growth spurted ahead and I stopped worrying about that and concentrated on worrying about what we were going to do with them all, as in truth Joe had always said we would.

Throughout April and May they grew happily. We got all

the canes stuck in and secured to the straining wires, the windbreaks erected and plants ringed to the canes. After her morning ride, Jacqueline spent all her time every day among the sweet peas and by the beginning of May it was obvious that whilst she could just cope now, if they were to flower and there was to be a crop to pick she would need help. Once the flower buds were obvious I thought I could stop being an Eeyore and accept the fact that we were going to get a crop after all, and had better find a home for it pronto. I wrote to F J Forster to ask if they would sell our crop or part of it. To my surprise I got a letter straight back explaining that as their sweet pea grower in Guernsey had recently died they would be only too pleased to take me on. I couldn't believe my luck and rang straight back to talk to Ronnie White, who had signed the letter on behalf of Forsters. He told us exactly how to pack them, the colour coordination in the box, the condition of the flowers and so on. On June 6th I rang Ronnie to say that our first consignment was within twenty-four hours of being ready. I was greeted with the statement that the market had 'fallen out of bed' and he didn't think he could make anywhere near the price he had quoted, of three shillings and sixpence (about eighteen pence). Eeyore came back and said gloomily 'Shall I not send any, then?'

'Oh no, let them come, but not too many to give me time to build up a connection for you in the market.'

They actually hit the market on June 8th, Jacqueline's twenty-sixth birthday. I had to go to a Branch Manager's conference at Cambridge that day, so I rang up from a call box during the lunch break to learn our fate.

'Wonderful sample, well done, three shillings and nine pence (nineteen pence) made.' It made the birthday complete and we celebrated both events that evening.

Within two weeks the unbelievable happened. Ronnie rang up to ask if we could do a special order for Moyses Stevens. 'Who are they?' I asked in all innocence.

'The Queen's florist,' came back the reply.

I enquired whether he was winding me up but he assured

me he wasn't. They wanted three hundred stems of our mauve variety, Leamington, plus foliage, for the banqueting room at Buckingham Palace for the state visit of King Hussein of Jordan. Naturally we experienced the twin emotions of fear and elation; but we did it, and their buyer, Miss Adams, was delighted.

We received a letter a few days later from the Chairman of Moyses (Monica Simonds) saying how pleased the Queen and Prince Philip were, and thanking us for our efforts. This letter remains one of my most treasured possessions.

This particular display featured in the film named *The Royal Palaces of Britain,* and when I finally met Monica Simonds personally some twenty-five years later, long after she had sold the Berkeley Square business, there over the mantelpiece in her drawing room was an enlarged photograph of the display.

She confided that in forty years of working for the Palace this was one of the best jobs she had ever done. The tragedy for me, though, was that by this time the chief architects of this success, Jacqueline and Ronnie White, had both died, so they were never able to know what they had achieved.

We decided on a similar cropping plan for the following year and quite unbelievably got another royal order, but overall the season was not so successful. The summer was very wet with a lot of storm damage and high wastage. After some serious soul-searching and long discussions with Ronnie, we were persuaded to start cropping under glass. We thought the best idea was for mobile greenhouses on runners, with extra high gable ends to clear the seven-foot canes. This would give us two crops of sweet peas a year; the first grown entirely under glass, cropping through April and May, and the second being grown in the normal way with the glass moved over them to crop during June and July. Everyone thought we were mad but we ordered two aluminium houses from the Cambridge Glasshouse Company, each of them three thousand square feet (one hundred by thirty). We doubled the area of cold frames and sowed the first batch the second week of September and the next, three weeks later. We also bought

Bill, aged ten days

Bill's introduction to John. That night he tried to kill him with a poker

Bill picking daisies

Bill watering the sweet peas, aged three. He's still doing it sixty-five years on

Horkesley Hall

Part of the kitchen garden at Horkseley Hall

Bunde, margarine magnate's house

Lindhoft, Gauleiter's house

Front door of Lindhoft

Sybil milking Frau Ziege

Bill and John with German helmets

Bill and John's play zone

Hitler's bunker, Berlin

Call-up – off to Prtsmouth, 15 March 1954

Control room of HMS Trenchant. Periscope on the left; hydroplanes on the right; diving panel furthest

Turnpike Farm House

Turnpike Farm, the garden

Poinsettias for Christmas

Family group: Sam, Jaqueline, Bill, Susan, Eskimo

Grand Prix of Lopik, 1983

Marion – Savoy Ballroom

Arndale Centre, Luton

Circus and crew

John Carter, Judith Charmers and Anneka Rice on Circus

Cheryl

Marion in the Sheik's swimming pool

deHavilland Maritime Company ownership, July 1988

'Flying' Bridge. Bill, Michael and Nick

Elephant disapproving of our company and spraying our van

Bill and Harry

Leopard, Kruger Park

Lion called up by the ranger, Kruger Park

Lions full of giraffe

Fossilised trees at Lake Kariba

Pavarotti at Tiger Bay, taken from our chalet

Bill in Chalet Three at Tiger Bay, from where Pavarotti was photographed

Among the crocodiles, Zambezi River

Elephants at Chickwenga

Car park at Linkwasha

Impala jumping the road

Black rhino

Our room at Linkwasha

African Wild Dog

Dagga Boys

Marion's friend

Fifteen-year-old elephant killed by lions

Kariba Dam, Zimbabwe

Paul

three thousand second-hand, three-year-old rose bushes from Peter Warmerdam to crop during the Autumn, on the third site for the mobile greenhouses. They also served as an introduction to rose growing for us. I could sense that with the UK's main rose production area in the Lea Valley being developed for housing, there might be an opportunity to fill this gap.

I felt confident that we were heading in the right direction, as things were beginning to fall apart at Fisons and I felt my career with them was coming to an end. The straw which broke this camel's back was the imposition of a layer of middle management. The branch managers were no longer to be directly responsible to the Managing Director but there were to be three Area Managers imposed between us. When I discovered that my new Area Manager was to be none other than my previous mentor and tutor at Downham Market, I had to readjust, as there was clearly a serious clash of personalities coming. Up to now I had devoted all my efforts to Fisons' business and only the occasional weekend to the flower growing, all the rest of which had been done by Jacqueline. She did the growing, employed the staff, supervised the packing and took the boxes to the station.

Breaking point came when Peter, wearing his new Area Manager's hat, decided that Fakenham branch should tender for a massive tile drainage scheme for Weasenham Farms. I did enquire whether he'd gone mad, as we didn't even run a drainage operation from Fakenham, as unlike many other parts of the country, the Norfolk soil was predominantly free draining. This contract was so huge, something like one hundred and fifty miles of pipe in virtually undrainable terrain, that nobody wanted it. I said to Peter, 'Doesn't that suggest this may not be too good an idea?'

'Rubbish, you are being defeatist!'

'None of my staff even know what a drainage machine is, let alone being trained in its use.'

'That may be so, but you do, so get on with it,' came the reply...

CHAPTER XVI

Changing Course

Having received a direct order to tender for, and if successful to carry out, this drainage operation for Weasenham Farms, I went to see Eric Thorsen, the manager, whom I knew well, especially from his previous tenure at Raynham Estates. Indeed I knew him far better than I did my Area Manager. We spent a whole day walking around the fields to be drained, which though very wet, as one would expect, appeared to present no special problems. However, I had by now learned that it isn't what you *can* see but what you *can't* see that matters. In another context I had come across an example in my first few weeks at Fakenham. We used to spread farmyard manure by the cubic yard. It was not that difficult to cube up a heap, or so I thought, until I had a summons from the loader driver on a job in West Norfolk, which I had measured up myself. This particular heap had been built in an old silage pit, the farmer conveniently forgetting to tell me this, and that what I could see and what I measured was but the tip of the iceberg, with over half the heap below ground! Presumably he felt he had got one over this upstart youngster.

Eric Thorsen was a gentleman, though, and made no attempt to mislead me. He had no objection to my arranging for some test borings, and it wasn't long before I found what I was looking for. The two greatest hazards to trenching machines in those days were always below normal ploughing depth. They appeared as prehistoric bog oaks, especially in the Fens, and very large flints in certain areas of Norfolk. The flints we found were not just large, they were mega. I reported back to Peter yet again that I really thought we were being very foolish to venture into such uncharted territory. Again I was accused of being negative, so this time my attitude changed to one of, 'Sod you, I *will* do it and on your head be the financial consequences!'

We were into late summer, and now came some light relief in the form of George Cushing. George was a road building contractor with a fleet of genuine steamrollers who also farmed some three hundred and fifty acres which we were responsible for spraying.

I was in his yard one afternoon when a rusting steam traction engine appeared on a low-loader. This was at the time when there were many of these once proud and beautiful machines just left to rot in farmyards and scrapheaps. When I enquired what he was going to do with it he told me he was going to restore it to its former glory and it was to be the first of a collection for a new steam museum which he was going to create so that these examples of a bygone age could be seen by future generations in full working order. The collection was to include the engines which drove the threshing drums, ploughing engines, fairground engines, road rollers and steam lorries, and so on. I thought it an exciting idea, as even I had a strong sentimental attachment to the age of steam. A few weeks later I had a call in the office asking if I would like to come down to the farm to see his latest acquisition.

There was his first fairground organ.

Over the years I was privileged to watch at first hand what has now become the famous Thursford Museum being assembled. I was a frequent visitor to this wonderful place and never ceased to be amazed at what he had achieved. George used to be there every day and he must have seen many thousands of visitors over the years, so much so that as he got into his nineties he was not always sure who was who. More than thirty years after he started it I met up with him again and we spent a wonderful half-hour looking back to those early days when he reminded me of our first meeting. He told me that he never, ever in his wildest dreams imagined that it would become world famous, and said how pleased he was that the collection had given so many people so much pleasure. George was not of course the only one to do this, although I believe Thursford has a special place in all steam enthusiasts' hearts.

Being included in what he was doing was a pleasant diversion from the hassle at work. In the meantime I pressed on with the drainage project, working on the assumption that we could hire in the equipment, and I knew there were two volunteers from the existing staff who were willing to go to other branches for training. I now had to set about pricing the operation. Costs were fairly standard for everything except the trenching machine. There was only one machine in Europe considered suitable for digging in the conditions these very large flints created. It was a twin-engined rig on thirty-six-inch tracks. The digging wheel had some two hundred specially hardened steel teeth which we had to be prepared to renew every day whilst working in the worst areas. These were expensive, very, and had to be air-freighted in from Holland when we were unable to keep up with rebuilding them in our own workshop. I consulted my colleagues at the other drainage branches, and they reckoned I should price it at between five and six pounds a chain (twenty-two yards). However, the Ministry of Agriculture would only pay grant on a figure of one pound ten a chain. To my surprise I was told to quote the Ministry figure. I argued with my superiors that this was madness and would bankrupt the branch, and surely no prestige project was worth that. I lost the argument, so I gave them an undertaking that I would see this very challenging project through but also gave them nine months' notice (this was the anticipated duration of the contract) that I would quit on completion or on May 31st at the latest.

Unsurprisingly, we won the contract, and as I had nothing to lose I threw myself into it one hundred per cent. I selected key personnel and sent them for training to other drainage branches and interviewed casual workers from the labour exchange for the less skilled work. Everything was in position to start at the beginning of November. It had not been too bad an autumn weather-wise, but on November 1st it started to rain and as far as I can recall it never stopped until well into the spring. Even on thirty-six-inch tracks the machine would get stuck, so I hired a Field Marshall tractor (the successor to the steam traction engines) to winch the trencher back and forth across the field. If I had been able to get an old steam ploughing engine I would have done so just for devilment. The pipe trailers, as well as those delivering clinker and shingle, all had two tractors to keep them moving. Despite the enormous difficulties we were able to maintain a clean, firm trench bottom for the pipes, so I was not unduly worried about whether the drains would flow. Indeed, once we had completed the first field we were able to see the drains really working, and myself, Eric Thorsen and his foremen were all quietly satisfied.

The wettest winter in memory eventually gave way to more normal conditions and we were able to dispense with the extra towing tractors. The drains all worked and the customer was more than satisfied – as well he should have been.

Unfortunately the money was flowing out of branch funds nearly as fast as the water out of the drains. Interestingly, in the *Eastern Daily Press* thirty years after the completion of this scheme, it was reported as the largest tile drain scheme ever done in Norfolk under their 'Thirtieth Anniversary' column. I took the opportunity to drive round the estate after I had read this and was proud to see the drains still flowing as they should.

I was still committed to leaving the company at the end of May, despite attempts to dissuade me otherwise. The early sweet pea crop was performing well, and my first job as a self-employed nurseryman was to be to move the greenhouses over the second crop. I was to have my farewell leaving dinner on May 31st, and to my utter disbelief I woke up that morning with chicken pox! This was the only day I had ever had off, and within twenty-four hours I thought I was going to die. Jacqueline didn't know whether to look after me or the sweet peas; bravely she managed to do both and even kept the horse exercised as well.

Eventually I crept back to work and the season finished up successfully. My dealings with Moyses Stevens as their preferred supplier had given us a massive 'edge' in the market, and we soon added all the top West End florists and hotels to our customer list.

During the five years we had lived in the village, I had perforce lived an almost absentee existence, and it was Jacqueline who had made friends there and got to know some of its history and its characters. Foxley was a lovely little village with a population of about a hundred and fifty. It had an ancient Norman church, heated with an underground coke boiler, which did more to asphyxiate the congregation than it did to heat them. The irascible vicar had flaming red hair and reminded me of Basil Brush; he spoke like him, laughed like him and held not dissimilar views. We had an old-fashioned village shop, owned and run by 'Arkwright'. The fish man called once a week; the only fish he ever carried were herring and cod and when we had the temerity to ask if he could bring a bit more choice one day he replied, 'Oh no, my customers would think I was being pretentious, they wouldn't know what to do with anything else.'

The baker had the unnerving habit of arriving long after we had gone to bed and earned the nickname of 'The Midnight Baker' as a consequence. On the rare occasions when we saw him he was a caricature of Steptoe, complete with knitted mittens and a drip on the end of his nose, the bread being carried in a wicker basket with a waterproof cover over it. We all thought he was an old man of seventy, but as he is still around forty years later looking exactly the same, we were clearly mistaken. For all that, the bread was excellent, and he was a real Norfolk character, with whom we had many a laugh – alternating with some sharp arguments, usually about nothing.

The community was almost entirely agricultural, and whilst I was fully conversant with the Norfolk dialect, Jacqueline found it very difficult to understand, and every night I had to explain the meaning and context of some new word she had come across. The local farm delivered the milk and they were especially helpful if we needed to borrow a tractor or spare manpower. Foxley used to have two pubs, but by the time we arrived it was down to one. All village people are nosy and like to gossip, and Foxley was no exception.

I think the classic was shortly after we were married when Jacqueline's parents came up for Sunday lunch. As neither of us drank alcohol we didn't keep a well-stocked bar – unlike her parents who were always most hospitable. So Jacqueline's father took himself down to the pub to get some beer.

About four o'clock, when they had gone, there was a knock on the door, I opened it and their was mine host from the Chequers.

'I hope you don't mind me asking, but was he your father or hers?'

'Hers,' I replied.

'Thank you,' said he. End of conversation!

The 'Big House' in the village, once the Rectory, housed our nearest neighbour, General Sir Ian Freeland, later to become GOC Northern Ireland at the height of the Troubles. His family and ours became good, if not particularly close, friends. Jacqueline and I were appalled at the effect NI duty was to have on them, especially his wife Mary, but more of this later…

Foxley itself was often rudely referred to as a suburb of our larger neighbour, Bawdeswell, referred to in Chaucer's *Canterbury Tales*. There was always considerable rivalry between the two villages, which the Silver Jubilee celebrations brought to a head a few years later. Bawdeswell challenged Foxley to a soccer match for the men and a netball match for the women. Being a village of at least four times the population, they clearly fancied their chances. They already had a village football team, which we did not. We scratched one together, and when Bawdeswell offered us the loan of a man who had just moved into the village and wasn't needed in their team, we readily accepted. What we didn't know, and neither did they, was that he had been a professional goalkeeper for one of the lesser football league clubs. He kept a clean sheet for the whole match, which Foxley won by the only goal. When his past came out, Bawdeswell cried 'Foul!' They made a similar miscalculation for the women's game, as Jacqueline had been a very skilful player in her youth, and being at least six inches taller than the opponents, frequently put the ball through the hoop, resulting in another victory. At Foxley we were unbearably cock-a-hoop and enjoyed rubbing our rivals' noses in it. It never got out of hand, though, as a number of us were aware that the last challenge match between the two villages in the Middle Ages had resulted in thirteen fatalities.

Bawdeswell had two village shops and a pub, garage, butcher and blacksmith. The population was about four times that of Foxley and we shared the parson. Their church had been demolished by a shot-up de Havilland Mosquito coming in to land at Swanton Morley during the war. Interestingly to me, Swanton Morley accommodated the RAF's first Mosquito squadron. Sir Geoffrey de Havilland's son, young Geoffrey, is alleged to have personally delivered the first one and given a demonstration of its capabilities. By the time we arrived in Norfolk it was no longer an operational base, having only a grass runway, and the buildings and facilities were given over to administrative purposes, with a small contingent of RAF technicians.

It was, however, the home of the Norfolk and Norwich Aero-Club with a large number of gliders and small private aircraft. The chief instructor was a delightful character typified in the cartoon figure of Flying Officer Kite, complete with handlebar moustache, who drove a vintage three-litre Bentley, sometimes seen parked at the Crown Hotel. In addition to the

Bentley he also owned his own Spitfire and a Messerschmitt 109. With these machines he did some of the flying sequences in such films as *Reach for the Sky* and *The Battle of Britain*.

Old age beat him in the end and I believe his planes went to the Confederate Air Force in America for preservation.

The 'Big House' in Bawdeswell was home to Quentin and Mrs Gurney, at that time the head of the Gurney family banking dynasty, which had been acquired by Barclay's Bank. Both were extremely kind to us, and Mr Gurney, although well into his eighties, would ride regularly with Jacqueline and show her where the local rides were and keep her up with all the local history. His wife's family were friends of my maternal grandparents in Essex. One of her eccentricities had been to travel in a trap pulled by white donkeys. Another colourful local character was Sir Dymoke White, who frequently took his coach and four out for a spin around the local roads.

At the other end of the social scale was Dick Fox, weaving down the road on his bicycle, blind as a bat and clothed in plastic fertiliser bags on a rainy day. He was a 'higgler', and amongst his pastimes was gathering up unwanted puppies and kittens for the Chinese restaurants in Norwich. It did not pay to get downwind of Dick on a warm day.

We had a good social life and a genuinely warm greeting from everyone. Many of my customers would ask us to dinner and we in turn would reciprocate. At that time home entertaining was the norm and eating out was but a rarity.

CHAPTER XVII

The Good Life

Although the television series of this name had not been made when we set out on our new venture it was not too long before it was, and then we were truly able to laugh at ourselves. Whilst 'self-sufficiency' per se was not the object of the exercise, our respective families were every bit as disapproving as Margot and Jerry, albeit for different reasons. It was an act of total irresponsibility on my part, in all their eyes. My father by now had decided to become a farmer – running the family unit – and had made it quite clear that I would never walk into a ready-made business. Consequently I decided I would have to do it the hard way and set out once again to prove them wrong and start my own business from scratch.

Our two existing mobile greenhouses would certainly not be able to provide us with an adequate full-time living, so it was our intention to build a new half-acre static greenhouse in which to grow roses as cut flowers. We had had a little experience of roses in the autumn crop in the mobiles, sufficient, in fact, to feel confident about having a go on a larger scale. We were by now getting advice from Peter Warmerdam, who described himself as an English Dutchman. Peter had a large nursery in the Lea Valley growing nothing but roses, and a visit there had had the same effect on both of us as the visit to Tendring Show two years earlier. As Joe Everitt had done, Peter took us under his wing and set out to make a rose grower of me.

In the meantime there was the question of planning permission, made doubly contentious on account of the proposed bypass. Although it appeared to be no further forward, nonetheless it was there as a proposal which couldn't be ignored. As yet no route had been formally agreed, but unofficially one had been indicated to me earlier so that I could site the mobiles parallel to what was likely to be the new road to avoid land wastage. As our nursery was not deemed to be a traffic-generating operation, the highways authorities raised no objection, and neither did the planners to this new expansion. We went ahead and ordered the glass and materials for August delivery, erection to be completed by the end of September 1967.

The greenhouse was to be twin span, each of forty-five by two hundred and thirty feet long; steel and aluminium structure, as the mobiles were, and again supplied by the Cambridge Glasshouse Company using their own erection contractors. Now the problems began; somewhere in the corridors of power it had been decreed that in order to reduce the chances of steel beams buckling under the heat of a fire they were all to be encased in concrete in new buildings! A greenhouse was a building, the structure was metal, therefore it all had to be encased in concrete. Even by bureaucratic standards it wasn't very practical. The Cambridge Glasshouse Company told me not to panic, it would all get sorted out. I was sure it would, but to us time was of the essence. We knew that in the first year roses produced very light crops and the priority would be to build up wood on the bushes for the subsequent years.

It would be nearly eighteen months before we started to see any positive cash flow, so to lose the planting window because of some idiot bureaucrat would have been a catastrophe. The Cambridge Glasshouse Co. were sufficiently confident that all would be sorted, and we carried on with the infrastructure. Indeed, long before we needed to get materials on site the necessary exemptions for greenhouses had come through. George Cushing was called in to build the roadways as not only did we need to be able to receive large articulated lorries with the greenhouse materials but we needed larger oil storage with access for bigger tankers. I had a three-phase electricity supply put in, and we'd recently had mains water arrive in the village, without which we would never have had enough water for the expansion. Once these infrastructure works had been done we were ready for the materials to be delivered. There seemed to be an awful lot of steel and aluminium, but it was the nine tons of glass which brought home to me the enormity of what we were taking on. The erection gang came a few days later, headed up by an Irishman rejoicing in the name of Mick Murphy. I don't believe it was ever his real name. He was a devil for the girls; no one was safe. I remember one morning having to jeopardise the completion of the contract by telling him in no uncertain terms that I didn't care who else he f—d but could he please leave *my* girls alone!

During the three weeks he was with us we must have had calls from half a dozen different Mrs Murphys wanting to speak to him. Whatever his moral shortcomings, he and his crew did a wonderful job, and completed on time with no defects requiring a return visit. They were like spidermen, walking along the ridge or even up the glazing bars with sheets of glass under their arms. During October and November we worked flat out fitting the automatic ventilation and installing three large hot-air blowers, each of half a million BTU capacity. All the watering system also had to be fitted, and in those days headers and mains were all made from galvanised steel. Cutting and threading two-inch pipe was extremely hard work, plastic piping being then only available in small bore sizes. Peter Warmerdam kept an eye on us, imploring us not to fit air heaters and offering us a pipe system from a contact in Holland. I had no choice; I couldn't afford a pipe system.

Once the contractors had left, the ground was ploughed over and tons of muck and peat were added. It was whilst I was doing this one morning that George Cushing rang to see if I would like to come and shoot with him. I was slightly nonplussed as I didn't know he had a shoot; I enquired when

186

and he said, 'Now.' I must have gone quiet so he said that Tom and Anthony, two large landowners, were coming, so I accepted and said, 'Give me half an hour and I'll be right there.' I rang Tom to enquire what this was all about, and he was as much in the dark as I was. I asked his idea of how many cartridges we needed – twenty-five or two hundred and fifty? He was going to take two hundred and fifty, so I did the same. Suffice it to say we needed them and we had a wonderful day. I still don't know what was behind it and he never did it again. Such was the eccentricity of the man!

I elected to take a chance and did not sterilise the soil the roses were to grow in; this was an extremely expensive job which did not seem to be justified on virgin soil.

We encouraged a germination of weeds before planting and then sprayed them off, hoping that the subsequent growth would be manageable by hand. It wasn't! To keep them under control we recruited Phyllis, who was to be our very first full-time employee. Phyllis had worked in the gangs, mainly pulling carrots in the Fens.

This gang work was always piecework, with no allowance for travelling, and if it was too wet she would have to go home again: a whole day without pay. Instead of eighty miles a day in the back of a van she had a ten-minute bike ride to us, working in the warm. She was almost pathetically grateful for such an improvement in her lot. I say it was only a ten-minute bike ride, but she didn't have a bike. The whole family worked, paid six shillings (thirty pence) a week rent and never had a penny to their name. She played bingo every night, and so as to be ready to go out in good time, fed her family entirely on instant meals – in those days a very expensive option.

Phyllis also smoked for England and had the unusual habit of carrying the packet between her extremely large boobs. Whilst she was bent over weeding, it was a toss-up which would fall out first! Both frequently did, but Phyllis was quite unabashed. Our twenty thousand rose grafts duly arrived, split into three consignments to give us time to plant them. They had to be damped over frequently until they were established. We lost very few, but by the time they were established so were the weeds. Phyllis was a very quick weeder, but glasshouse roses planted about seven inches apart were very vulnerable to her rough and ready ways. I had to explain that this half-acre of roses was worth about the same as a hundred acres of sugar beet, and would she please slow down and take more care, as she wasn't on piecework now.

The crop survived and grew away well, but there was always too much to do. The bed supports and retaining wires all had to be erected and we still had two crops of sweet peas to look after as well. At the peak that year we were employing thirty-five women, all part-time, and two full-time. This was the moment the tax authorities decided that all part-timers had to have a tax deduction card, even though no tax was payable. This was an administrative nightmare but it got done, with much grumbling. This was also the first year that the dreaded pollen beetle appeared. These got into the keel of the sweet pea flower and although they did no damage, when the buyer took the lid off the box it looked as though it was full of caterpillar droppings. There was no cure for this, and as it got steadily worse in following years we eventually had to stop growing them. Norfolk has always had a large acreage of 'host' crops – mustard, kale and nowadays oil-seed rape – and consequently a high population of pollen beetle. In Pest Control days we mounted a big spraying campaign against them, but only the most toxic chemicals achieved control. Gradually these chemicals were phased out and there has never been a satisfactory replacement. I don't think they do that much damage to the host crop, but sweet peas are difficult to clean up enough even to bring indoors.

It was very sad to have to give them up but it was a great relief to be able to do without the large number of part-timers, not to mention the tax deduction cards which went with them. We sold the canes to a runner bean grower in West Norfolk, and for many years afterwards I would see them next to the

A17 just beyond King's Lynn. Consolation came many years later (unfortunately after Jacqueline had died) when I saw Joe Everitt for the last time, just before he too passed away. 'You were better than me,' was all he said. Under the circumstances, even I became quite emotional.

We were now in a position to concentrate full-time on the roses and on raising a family. By this time my brother had had two children, with a third on the way, although he had married some two years after me. Mother came to see us at a horse show at Ipswich, and whilst Jacqueline was doing her stuff with her horse, Mother confronted me with my failure to provide her with yet more grandchildren. She even went so far as to volunteer to pay for any medical services we might need.

I was able to assure her that we had been too busy to worry about children, and no, we didn't need to see anyone.

She was concerned that as Jacqueline was now over thirty we might be leaving it too late. I told her to stop worrying and reported the conversation to Jacqueline, who was inclined to agree that perhaps now was the time. So that night we did the deed and our daughter, Susan, appeared nine months later. Had we known what dramas 1969 was to produce, I am sure we would have postponed the event. Thankfully we didn't, and Susan now lives nearby. In order to help the cash flow whilst the roses were establishing, we started a wholesale flower round in the Norwich/Fakenham area, recruiting Wendy as van salesgirl. This developed into a highly successful operation, with F J Forster supplying us with market flowers, some local growers supplied us with bulb flowers and chrysanthemums, and of course our own roses were freely available. We kept the van sales for about four years until the roses were generating sufficient funds and we were then able to sell it as a going concern.

By the autumn of 1968 Jacqueline's pregnancy had been confirmed and the roses had been pruned so as to give a first flush for Valentine's Day and a second flush for the first week of May, the baby being due about the third week of April. If everything went according to plan, the birth would be at home. We would be in a relatively quiet period and a domestic routine would have been established before the next crop of roses hit us.

That was the plan – clinical, possibly, but essential. Everything went well until after Christmas when we were visited by very heavy snowfalls. So bad were they that the valley gutters in our big new house were beginning to buckle under the weight of snow. I panicked and rang the Cambridge Glasshouse Company to enquire if there was anything to worry about. There was. Get them supported with pit props or similar, at once, or the whole thing could collapse! All this time the crop was growing satisfactorily, but we were suffering from lack of humidity. The hot-air blowers were keeping the temperature up alright but the downside was this terrible dryness, which is of course why they are utterly useless for serious growing. Constant damping down was the only solution, and all the time Peter was reminding us, 'I told you air heaters are not suitable!' – which didn't help. January 29th 1969 is imprinted on my brain for ever. The previous night had been very cold and when I went down at eleven o'clock to check everything, I couldn't help but admire all the rows of new rosebuds, just beginning to show colour, perfect for Valentine's Day.

I just hoped the heaters would keep going, but having three of them, even I reckoned that they wouldn't all break down together. I was covered against power failure with a standby generator, which I had run up only that morning. Going into the greenhouse at seven o'clock the next morning I couldn't believe my eyes. All I could see were rows of brown sticks and a greenhouse full of exhaust fumes. The heat exchanger on one of the heaters had a large hole in it, and a mixture, lethal to plants, of ethylene and sulphur dioxide had been pumped round the houses all night. I literally cried for about five minutes and dragged my way through the snow back to the house.

'What's up?' said Jacqueline.

'They are all dead – we are bust, finished,' I replied.

'They can't be!' she said.

'Go and look,' I replied.

On her return she asked, 'What are you going to do?'

'I really don't know,' said I.

She suggested I ring Peter Warmerdam, as he had answers to most things. When I told him, he said – very kindly – 'I did tell you hot air heaters are worse than useless.' To his enquiry of what was I going to do, I told him I would probably shoot myself.

He thought this was a rather dramatic solution and told me not to do it yet, as after all, money was only money, and you could always get some more. In any case it was not like losing a leg or an arm; they really were irreplaceable. He said, 'Give me half an hour and I'll get back to you.'

As promised, he rang back some twenty minutes later and reassured me that the ripened wood would be undamaged and the bushes were not dead, we'd just lost the current flush. I was to cut everything back to the previous year's growth and he would send over all the necessary pipes and a proper oil-fired hot water boiler, with a gang from Holland to install the system we should have had in the first place. I told him that if I had no money eighteen months ago I certainly hadn't any now.

'Don't worry about that, pay me back when you can – even if it takes a couple of years or more.' To my remonstrations he merely told me not to argue; the equipment was all in stock in Holland and was being loaded as we spoke.

I had one week to cut everything back, and his men would be on site at the end of that week. They would take two weeks to do the job and we would have a new crop growing at exactly the same date as would have been the case if we had cut for Valentine's Day. What could I say? We both wept at such generosity. We all buckled to, including my heavily pregnant wife, and sure enough the heat was turned back on February 20th. The new boiler ran on black oil rather than gas oil, so we had to get rid of a tank full of gas oil, fit pre-heaters into it and find a source of heavy oil, as this grade was not available locally. Otherwise there were no hiccups – and the new crop looked as though it would probably be a week at the most behind schedule. Our wholesale business turned up trumps and did really well in what is admittedly the best time of the trading year, covering as it does Valentine's Day, Mother's Day and Easter. We now seemed to be finally back on course.

The next item on the agenda was to be the birth of our new baby. The intention all along had been for Jacqueline to have the baby at home. However, when the due date had come and gone, with no sign of anything happening, the midwife thought somewhere else would be more appropriate. Accordingly she arranged a place in a nursing home at West Runton, near Cromer.

We started cutting roses during the first week of May and still there was no sign of a birth. It was a heavy crop, and indeed the benefits of a proper heating system were readily apparent; with the new crop looking so good I think Jacqueline was able to relax a little and after a few days I had to drive her to West Runton. It was her time now to say, 'Worry about the crop, not me,' as I had said to her two years earlier when I had chicken pox.

I saw her on the Saturday afternoon, but Sunday was a double packing day so I didn't visit that day. The next thing I knew was a call at three o'clock on Monday morning telling me all was well and that I had a daughter. We were both delighted it wasn't a boy and that she was 'sound in wind and limb'. I saw her on the Wednesday and brought mother and daughter home on Saturday. I drove very slowly home in case she woke up, as neither of us were sure what to do if she did! Jacqueline had elected to bottle-feed, and I soon ended up with the job of head bottle-maker – a duty I performed well, except that I always managed to get the wrong size teat. I remember saying very early on, 'Why can't she drink out of a cup instead of all this nonsense?'

'Try it and you'll find out,' came the reply.

I did, Susan drank and she never had a bottle again.

I am ashamed to say that was my total contribution. I certainly never changed a nappy or indulged in any 'new man' activity. It was a gloriously happy time on all fronts. Everything was going really well in the nursery, and eventually October came round and it was time for the christening. She had been registered Susan Frances, the latter name after my uncle, which she still refuses to use. We decorated the church with the help of the local flower club using mainly pink roses – a whole day's cut, in fact – and had a marquee on the lawn which accommodated all our friends and family. Uncle Hugh did the actual baptism, but sadly it was the last time I saw my grandfather's generation together.

We had one scare about an hour before the service when a neighbour dashed in to tell me the local motorbike boys had bailed out of the coffee bar in the village and were in the church en masse. I went steaming down for a confrontation to be met by the ringleader saying, 'Hope you don't mind, guvnor, we had heard there was something special to see and we have all been admiring the flowers.' Yet another lesson on not judging by appearances!

By the following year Peter Warmerdam had been paid back, we had an excellent reputation in Covent Garden and we decided to build another half-acre of glass and expand our rose production. There was enough spare capacity on the new boiler to allow this and it seemed the right time to do it.

The memories of the horrendous weed growth two years earlier determined me that this time we would not plant into unsterilised ground. There were two choices; methyl bromide or steam. I chose the latter but had no practical experience of the technique. After further investigation and because we were merely trying to kill weed seeds, I settled on the simpler sheet-steaming rather than grid-steaming method. At its simplest, this involved digging in a large polythene sheet over a given area of soil, pumping steam under it and keeping it ballooned for about an hour. I gleaned all this information from Hector Eastell, the manager of Pordage's nursery at Reedham; he also offered me the services of his mobile steam boiler and Brian, the steam engine driver.

The technique apparently was to create a good head of steam, just below the mark at which the safety valve blew off, and then open up the steam valve under the sheet. In theory this would take all the excess pressure in the boiler to blow up the sheet, and normal firing would maintain enough pressure to keep it inflated thereafter. Hector impressed upon me the need for good quality steam coal; household coal was no good. I consulted the local coal merchant who advised me that the best steam coal you could buy was 'Thoresby Hards' – so that was what we got.

The first two sheets were in position, Brian was stoking away and commented that this was the best coal he had ever used, the pressure rose quickly and at the psychological point I opened up the first steam hose. Far from taking twenty minutes to inflate, the sheet was up in about three, with the boiler pressure still rising. I opened up the second hose. In another three minutes sheet two was up and the boiler pressure was still rising. Clearly we had a problem! Brian just had time to say, 'What the hell have you got for coal?' when the safety valve blew and he yelled, 'Run for it!'

I wasn't so much worried about his steam engine, but I knew that if it did blow up our brand new greenhouse would go with it. We got to a safe distance and decided the only thing we could do was to laugh at the situation. Eventually the safety valve shut down. We crept up to it to see what was happening, but all was now under control. From then on we treated 'Thoresby Hards' with a great deal of respect. I eventually discovered that that was the coal used on high-speed railway engines, such as *Mallard* and the *Flying Scotsman*!

By now the sell-off of nurseries in the Lea Valley for housing was gathering pace. This was where most of the nation's rose growers were located, and many of them were pocketing the cash and leaving the industry altogether. Indeed, the market for cut roses was quite firm and we had some very good clients. All in all, the future looked quite rosy!

I felt now that I couldn't really manage this whole area on my own and took on an assistant, who was quickly nicknamed 'Diprod' on account of his extreme height. We fitted him up with a residential caravan and this did enable us to go away periodically without prejudicing the security of the site. Live-in staff – however you define 'live-in' – have their downside. Diprod was not good in the morning; in fact I sometimes wondered whether he was 'on' something. Coming as he did from the Isle College in Wisbech, it was quite likely that he was indeed 'on' something. One evening we came home much earlier than he expected. He had visitors, and a strange smell was emanating from the caravan. The visitor was a relative, I discovered, from Wisbech! This happened two or three times more until I was absolutely certain that my suspicions were correct.

A quick call to the police established that there were no drug squad officers on duty that night... so what's changed? However, if the suspects were still there in the morning could I let them know? I was fairly certain they would be and said I would ring and confirm. This I duly did the next morning; I told them specifically to come to my house and not to the greenhouse. Surprise, surprise, they did exactly what I asked them not to and the birds flew while they were walking up to the house. They did in fact later make some arrests and Diprod left soon afterwards.

England in general, and Norfolk in particular, were still very insular in those pre European Union days. We weren't used to looking over our shoulders any further than Holland for foreign competition. We entirely failed to recognise the threat from Israel and the aggressive marketing arm of their growers, Carmel. The English growers carried on with their expansion, but so did the Israelis, with their more favourable climate; we were all soon to reap the whirlwind, aided and abetted by the effects of the Arab/Israeli quarrels in the Middle East and the consequent effect on the price of oil. A sudden five-fold increase in the price of oil, combined with the sheer weight of Israeli imports in the winter when the UK growers traditionally made their money, had a devastating effect on the market price for roses. Rose growers were all caught between a rock and a very hard place. We, like most of the others, decided not to panic, as the flower market was traditionally so volatile that it could, at least in theory, recover. So for another year we decided to sit tight.

CHAPTER XVIII

Sugaring the Pill

F lower growing, especially roses, was a fairly speculative pastime. The lead time from planting to harvest was long, expenses were high and there was absolutely no guarantee of any return at the end of it. I confess to having a gambler's mentality. Indeed, Havilland Hall, overlooking St Peter Port in Guernsey and once a family home, was lost to some form of speculation after the war, only to be sold recently for over seven million pounds! There must be a rogue gene somewhere, part of which has infected me.

Ever since a speculative investment made at brother John's instigation in a tea and rubber company – London and Asiatic Rubber, I believe – immediately after the Conservative election victory in 1959, I easily made the progression from gambling at cards and horses to something more serious. John was my mentor, or leader astray, this first time, as when I protested that I couldn't afford it, he replied, 'Don't worry, you won't have to pay for it until it's gone up, and then all you have to do is pocket the profit.'

'Supposing it doesn't?' I replied.

'It will, trust me,' was all he said; so I did and – hey presto! – he was right. It seemed quite easy, as a certain well-known banker opined in a certain Singapore saga some thirty years later.

Eventually I made the transition to commodity futures, where trading on 'margin' enabled one to hold positions way beyond one's means with relative impunity so long, and only so long, as you guessed the market right. I stuck initially to copper and sugar, the largest and most liquid of the commodity markets. The large volumes traded in these markets meant that any adverse moves could be liquidated quickly without too catastrophic results, unlike the narrower and less liquid markets in precious metals like cadmium or bismuth, for example. These speculative but unspectacular trades were steady profit-earners on which I paid capital gains tax like a good boy should. However, one evening in '74, on the day of my daughter's birthday, whilst walking down to my nursery I was hit by a swarm of greenfly. I quickly identified them as Myzus persicae, the carrier of virus yellows in the sugar beet crop. Because sugar beet had been a very important crop in my previous time with Fisons, I was well aware of the potential impact of such a very early infestation on the UK crop, made all the more interesting because with the light breeze from the east these had clearly come from mainland Europe, also a large beet-producing area. I rang John up straight away and he questioned me at length on the potential impact on yield. As this infestation was at least three weeks earlier than ever seen before, I told him that it could be as damaging as to reduce sugar yields by as much as fifty per cent. I should explain that the UK crop on its own accounted for a very small part of the world sugar crop, the great majority of which came from sugar cane. Even in that section accounted for by the beet crop, the UK was a small player compared to the Russians and the rest of Europe. However, a dramatic shortage at the margin would so seriously affect the balance of supply and demand in an already very tight world supply situation that a significant price rise was likely, and I felt we should gear up for some fun.

He undertook to research the market in the morning and said I 'should stick a toe in' at the price of just under two hundred pounds per ton. John bought me two 'lots' (i.e. two times fifty tons) representing a total outlay of £1,000, equal to the five per cent margin required. The essential arithmetic was that if the price went to zero we'd lose £20,000; if it doubled we'd make £20,000. If the price did double then a profit of

£20,000 for an outlay of £1,000 would be a good earner. I was so sure of my identification that I could easily see the price doubling, so with a strategy of adding to the position as soon as the news got into the market, I waited.

How I wished that I was back in my old job, with official access to the farmers and sugar beet fieldsmen working for the British Sugar Corporation so that I could monitor things! I drove round and round the county looking for evidence of an early insecticide spraying programme. I found none, but did find greenfly on the crop. The market had not moved but, hoping I was not confusing wishful thinking with fact, I was sure that infestation levels were building and staked another £1,000. Suddenly the market started to creep up and before long I was showing a good profit. The secret of successful speculation was to run the profits and cut the losses: obvious, and very easy to say but much harder to do. Human nature says you're never wrong to take a profit but it also tells you a losing situation will be better tomorrow. I was also aware of the adage that the only difference between a sheep and the average investor is the number of legs. When one runs they all run; look at the recent behaviour of the stock markets. Equally, trying to buck the market can be a very expensive amusement, so caution was for ever the watchword. I had already become a student of charts and tried to balance their behaviour against fundamentals to avoid any catastrophes. Gradually more options and margin positions were acquired until I had a total commitment of a thousand tons (and a liability of £200,000). The market steadily rose until by the middle of July there were clear signs of virus in the crop and I was feeling ready to really go for it.

Now a new (to me) phenomenon appeared in the form of official communiqués of disinformation that the yellowing of the crop was due to magnesium and manganese deficiency. This unsettled the market and it started to fall back. Fortunately I was highly skilled in the ability to identify mineral deficiencies and was able to reassure John, who was trading on behalf of a much larger third party, that the official communiqués were lies. I cannot think how many times he sought reassurance, to the extent that at one time I began to doubt the evidence of my own eyes and sold a few lots so as to lessen the exposure. John suggested he and I should go to France, Holland and Belgium and get a continental flavour.

We flew to Amsterdam, hired a car and went looking. We started in the Dutch polders of Flevoland, the reclamation of which I had studied as part of my drainage course at Fisons. This was exceptionally fertile soil producing much higher yields than the UK, but the evidence of virus yellows was very plain to see. On we went through other areas in Holland and down into Belgium. Again the same result. Whilst driving in Brussels, John nearly had us cut in half by a tram and I suggested he let me drive from then on! We drove down to Mons and the area where the battle of Waterloo took place, and he took the opportunity to give me a history lesson, having got a degree in the subject at Cambridge. I was fascinated to find how agriculturally productive the old battlefields were, especially those of the First World War. Whether this was due to the enforced 'deep cultivation' by exploding shells or other more distasteful causes, I don't know. We lunched in the restaurant in the museum to the Battle of Waterloo, where I ordered a steak. Quite the best I had had so far. On my congratulating the waiter, he told me it was horse! Definitely the best thing to do with a horse!

On down to the Somme, where some of the best crops I have ever seen, including wheat, are grown. Certainly the sites of the heaviest fighting and greatest loss of life produced outstanding crops; coincidence, or…?

I succeeded in convincing John that we were looking at a near total infestation of virus yellows, whatever officialdom was saying to the contrary. Now the fun was about to begin, during the peak of which I was to hold sugar positions to the value of some £5 million for an initial outlay of £1,000. So intense was the adrenalin flow that I was losing all touch with reality. Jacqueline was marvellously supportive, although she had no real idea of what I was doing, and was sufficiently content with Susan and the horses (now increasing in number) to let me get on with it. It was anything but a straightforward situation as numerous cross-currents of political origin were now confusing the issue.

We had arrived at the stock exchange crash; the oil crisis was upon us; businesses were going bust; and general mayhem was about to overtake the country. In those days very few people understood what futures trading was all about and it came under intense attack from the politicians and industrialists who only saw the adverse side of the 'game'. Essentially, futures markets were set up to enable producers and consumers to buy and sell forward (up to two years or more), thus locking themselves into a known financial position so that their operations would not be blown off course by sudden changes in the price of a given commodity. Sellers always want the price up and buyers always want it down, so to maintain a lively and liquid market a certain speculative element was required. The speculators, or specs as they were known, were mostly private individuals and other small operators who fancied a punt. There were a great many of them and their numbers injected a sufficient divergence and fluctuation of viewpoint to oil the wheels of the markets. During this particular time virtually all commodity markets were bullish, partly because the stock markets were a sea of misery and green faces, and partly because inflation was roaring away at twenty per cent p.a. Cash shaken out of a bearish stock market always has to go somewhere, and in the early Seventies it went into commodities. This current decade sees it going into property. The great majority of commodities are produced in the Third World, to be consumed in the Developed World. The bull run in commodities during the Seventies undoubtedly was an enormous benefit to the much poorer producing countries, but the consequent rise in the price of our imports was causing a great strain on the Western economies which, when added to the recent five-fold increase in OPEC oil prices, were really beginning to suffer. So much so that there was even talk of shutting down the commodity markets. The battery manufacturers, for example, were seeing the price of their basic raw material (lead) escalating out of control, and were at the forefront of cries to curb the speculators; indeed, deposits were raised to discourage new entrants to the fray. In reality it had the opposite effect of merely drawing the attention of new, very big name players into the picture, who helped to drive the price even higher. Very few of the original small-time speculators had the power to move markets on their own, but the new generation could. One of the names which come to mind is the billionaire Hunt family in the United States, who effectively cornered the world's silver market at the time when the newspapers were full of pictures of old ladies taking their Georgian teapots to be melted down at twenty pounds per ounce. Little good it did them in the end, as at the day of reckoning even they couldn't prevent a catastrophic collapse of the world price and they were driven into near bankruptcy.

At the time it was a very scary situation and one lived with the prospect of the then Labour government under Harold Wilson, who had no love for capitalism – especially in its raw, unbridled form as exercised in these commodity markets – actually closing them down.

We consoled ourselves with the thought that were they to do this there was always America, to whom everyone would turn; although quite how wasn't too clear.

Both John and I decided that despite the bluster, action was unlikely, and so it turned out to be. As my sugar position increased and the world became aware of the likelihood of a very poor crop in Europe, I was sitting on what was to me a large fortune, and I could not foresee a price collapse, especially as the Russians were now reporting poor crops as well. We never knew whether they were genuine or not, but as they would have a vested interest in talking the market up we both took the view that so much the better if they were. With a comfortable cushion under me I had a go, with John's guidance, at cocoa, coffee and silver. The first two were profitable but silver was a disaster. Just for fun and to say I'd done it I bought a small quantity of 'greasy wool' and 'pork bellies'. To my subsequent regret, John dissuaded me from 'live Omaha steers on the hoof'.

Having got this little bit of fun out of the way we set about considering the sugar position. We had reached the stage where instead of risking what I had never before even dreamed about we should seriously review not only the financial prospects but the political risks of the game. The price was now sitting at well over £400 per ton, and returns of more than three thousand per cent were there for the taking on some of the positions. All gamblers are greedy and I was no exception, and neither were John's principals. We chartered a light aircraft with long-range fuel tanks to do a circuit of Europe's beet-growing areas to compare with our own in England. The pilot was a crop sprayer who I knew from the past, and was confident that he would not confuse sugar beet with any other crop. He had the Norfolk crop as a yardstick, and I asked him to bring back his best overall comparisons of each area on a scale of nought to ten, with the Norfolk crop on the five mark. I specifically asked him to take in the areas we had visited a month earlier, so that we were comparing like with like. We would be going back to these areas for field samples of root weight as soon as the BSC started weighing in the UK.

At about this time John asked me if I would take the Vice-President of The Great Western Sugar Company (part of the Hunt empire referred to previously) on a tour around East Anglia's main beet-growing areas. I duly met him and one of his colleagues at Norwich and spent all day with them. The most memorable part of the trip was his propensity to spit out of my car window; for such a supposedly high-powered individual he was fairly basic, to put it mildly. He did however give me great comfort when he described his method of crop evaluation, which was, 'Open your eyes and drive through as much beet territory as you can; if you know your crop you will soon know what you are looking at.'

As this was my preferred method, which John told me was too broad-brush, I was reassured that I wasn't just being idle. Having spent the whole day with them I formed the opinion that they liked what they saw and could see good speculative opportunities.

Despite my preference – and the American's – for the 'broad-brush', John thought otherwise and we made another trip through France and the Low Countries. In England the BSC had started crop weighings which were starting to confirm the outcome I had predicted in May.

We armed ourselves with a set of scales, hired a car at Schiphol to be returned at Charles de Gaulle in Paris, and set off. I was scared of being arrested if we were caught digging up a farmer's crop, but John said if you look as though you have every right to be doing it the farmers will not ask any questions. He was right until the very last site near Paris, where we were caught with the car boot open full of wet and muddy sugar beet. We drove off with the Frenchman still gesticulating, and before we knew it were in the outskirts of Paris, still with a boot full of mud and sugar beet! We couldn't empty it in the street, so returned it to Avis with its load intact and scarpered quickly. Thankfully no more was heard of the incident.

Once again the results confirmed our suspicions, and although the crop weight was substantially higher than in England it was still well below normal, by as much as thirty per cent, and on poorer land even more. We were in such uncharted territory that it was impossible to guess where the peak might be.

All this time the political opprobrium was growing in intensity and John and I decided to stay with it until the price reached £500 per ton and then get out. I duly did, but whether he did on behalf of his principals I never knew. I was able to bank a cheque for £250,000, which gave the manager heart failure. I said, 'Don't ask questions, but it's legitimate.' But after he'd threatened to report me to 'the authorities' I came clean and told him! It was quite a lot of money in the Seventies. Neither John or myself could believe it when the price ballooned to over £600 per ton! I couldn't bear to think of what might have been. We were never tempted back in, as the market was in 'blow off' mode, when the next move is likely to be vertically downwards. Next came the decision of what to do with the proceeds. A significant amount went to pay off the nursery overdraft which had ballooned out of control as a direct result of the Arab-Israeli War, the subsequent five-fold increase in the price of oil and above all, the infamous three-day week.

Some of the profits had funded a new block of glass for the nursery, and as there was still a reasonable amount left in the kitty, even after new cars and household goods I went to see a top firm of accountants for advice. Their suggestion was to put the tax on one side and become a Lloyd's 'name'. The idea of unlimited liability in an area over which one had no control and the inability to get out if you didn't like the look of things did not appeal at all. Thankfully I never joined. I used the rest to stay in the market, with reasonable success but nothing like what I had been used to.

Then, on July 20th in that glorious summer of 1976 came the bombshell after which life was never to be the same again: a tax demand for £196,000, payable in fourteen days. The Revenue had changed the rules and instead of CGT at thirty per cent I had been assessed under Schedule D Case VI at ninety-eight per cent. Jacqueline saw me turn from my normal ruddy hue to a deathly white. Was something wrong? I could only show her the contents of the envelope. I hadn't got anywhere near that sum left.

I have no recall of the next few days beyond the extreme heat, and my beloved mother's slow death from cancer nearing its final outcome. What jerked me back to reality was a further turn of the screw by the tax collector reminding me of the penalties for late payment.

I decided to go to see the collector personally and try to talk my way out of it. He suggested I pay a significant deposit and as I was so clearly aggrieved I should lodge an appeal. After nearly two years of negotiation I had the rate reduced to eighty-three per cent, Schedule D Case 1. My activities had been reclassified as 'an adventure in the nature of trade' and I was able to offset nursery losses against the profits. This helped, but the net sum was still very considerably larger than CGT would have been. It took me another five years, and relatively successful commodity trades before we were finally clear. I had to keep trading to have any hope of paying off the taxman and after a while I gave up worrying about losing it, as if I stopped speculating we would have to go bankrupt anyway.

Strangely enough the trading was quite profitable and I was beginning to build another cushion. Sugar was still the mainstay, as after its 'blow off' it fell sharply to earth and then bounced, aided this time by efforts to manufacture fuel from sugar cane. Perceived wisdom was that if this process was successful it would sharply decrease the availability of sugar for conventional purposes, so the price was rising once again!

There were other opportunities which kept popping up as, for example, during the time it took me to drive from Norfolk to Nottingham the coffee market had obliged sufficiently that I could get a brand new Perazzi shotgun out of the morning's trading. This little win was to be more than cancelled out by the behaviour of the aluminium market. I relied heavily on Ceefax for price information but was finally caught out when I had been away all day and on return there was a perfectly normal call to ring my broker 'when it was convenient'. I didn't even panic when I saw that aluminium had 'fallen out of bed'. So bizarre was the quoted price that it had to be a misprint. I was to be out of contact all the next day, being due to take my wife and daughter to a gymkhana starting early in the morning before the broker's office was open, but I intended to ring in from a call box (no mobile phones in those days) later. The showground was very near to Sculthorpe, the American airbase, which although no longer fully commissioned was on that occasion hosting a visiting squadron.

As Susan's class was entering the ring a plane took off, and when exactly over the showground switched on his 'afterburners'. The place exploded, there were ponies running amok, small children howling on the ground, mothers screaming; total bedlam. By the time the tumult had died down it was some three hours after the market had opened before I could get to a phone. Ceefax was right, I was indeed looking at a massive loss just short of £100,000. As my broker couldn't get hold of me he hadn't sold, as in any case I had no stop loss order on at that time. Mercifully the market had firmed up quite a bit overnight, so I left it to him to decide what to do and we finished up having recovered more than half our losses. It was painful but not a disaster.

In the early days commodity futures markets existed only in England and America, with a potato market in Amsterdam and a wool market in Australia, so that in reality a man could go to bed solvent and know he would still be solvent when he got up. This was all changing; twenty-four-hour trading and globalisation started to appear, and this comfort factor was disappearing fast. Additionally, the day of the small speculator was also going; it was all the big boys now who dealt in millions, not thousands. So ended my days as a serious commodity speculator. In spite of all the dramas it was one of the few profitable periods of my life. A crazy roller-coaster ride, but in a masochistic way rather fun!

I still wish I had traded 'live Omaha steers on the hoof'.

CHAPTER XIX

The Not So Good Life

As can be learned from the previous chapter, the early 1970s could best be described as 'interesting'. Our version of *The Good Life* took us through the whole gamut of emotions from hope to despair, disaster and death, riches and poverty and just about every other emotion one can think of. I had always believed that I might have made a mistake in leaving the Royal Navy, and certainly there were times when I looked back with nostalgia and thought what might have been. On the credit side I had a wonderfully happy marriage, a lovely daughter, and we were, I thought, 'getting there'.

The economic situation after Harold Wilson's Labour government was awful. 'Grocer' Heath made it worse. Wilson's second bite, followed by 'Stoker' Jim Callaghan, did nothing to stop the rot, and neither in truth did Margaret Thatcher give much for us to jump for joy about. By the time Mrs T was to deliver the 'goods' I had given up the unequal struggle.

The period had actually dawned with the issue of a compulsory purchase order for the long-planned 'bypass' to come straight through our holding, leaving the house and buildings on one side of the road and the nursery on the other. We were of course prepared for it, but not for the alteration of the route. This meant that not only had our greenhouses been built at the wrong angle, but even worse, the road was coming within a few feet of our front door. With patient negotiation I persuaded the Highways Authority to move it nearer to my neighbours, who – poor souls – had no say, as it wasn't on their land anyway. Looking back over that period I am amazed

208

that I didn't end up in jail. It was the high-handedness of the 'little' men passing as civil servants that sharpened up my total contempt for government officials, which has not diminished in any way even in my more mellow old age.

The bitterness between us started when I went out one morning and found officials sticking stakes in the ground on our land. I enquired politely what they were doing, and when they said it wasn't necessary to either ask permission or to undergo the normal courtesy of even informing me, I was a long way from being happy. I reminded them that it was still my property until they had paid for it, after which they left in high dudgeon. They were back the next morning in double strength. This time I met them with my gun under my arm, dressed in all innocence as if to go shooting. Once again they left. Jacqueline was not pleased and reminded me that this was Foxley in the 1970s not Dodge City in the 1870s! Once the adrenalin had stopped flowing I began to think my next visit might be from the Old Bill and was quite relieved to get a call instead from the County Surveyor, who very diplomatically suggested I come in to see him for a chat to find a better way out of both our dilemmas. He apologised for the behaviour of his officials and we had a surprisingly amicable discussion. We came up with a compromise, whereby I would let them stake out the route, but no more, until our claim had been agreed.

Both parties kept their side of the bargain and lived in a state of reasonable harmony throughout the construction process, until I discovered that their plans took no account of reinstating the main watercourse through the divided village. I had become a Parish Councillor in 1971 and now had to don my Parish Council hat to prevent what I saw as an environmental disaster, for by this time the storm water drains had been laid two feet higher than the natural drainage system.

Mr Forrester, the local Highways Engineer, informed me that they would connect the village watercourse into these drains. I tried to explain that water wouldn't flow uphill, but he would have none of this and said of course it would! I didn't want another falling out as the Highways Department had built me a beautiful roadway and security fence, so I kept quiet. Two years later, after the village had been flooded several times, they accepted that perhaps I did know what I was talking about. With much grovelling by the highways authorities, and at huge expense to the taxpayer, the situation was rectified. All this, however, was merely an irritation as by now my beloved roses had been pulled up and burnt and we were painfully making the transition from cut flower production, trading with the best florists' shops in London, to something far more vulgar in the form of 'potted plants'.

With hindsight, regardless of the role played by Carmel and their Israeli growers in the destruction of ninety per cent of the UK rose market, we would all have had to change our ways anyway. Flowers were no longer the preserve of the rather 'snooty' high street florist, and were being stocked by garages and supermarkets, whose sole criteria was price. Perhaps for too long we had relied on quality. Anyway, there we were trying to carve out a niche in an already overcrowded market and having to trade with greengrocers, supermarkets and the like. Reluctant though I was to admit it at first, I soon came to enjoy it, as much as anything for the diversity of crops, but our greenhouses, being designed for roses, were not ideal for pot plant production with the need for different regimes of both temperature and humidity.

We were also putting a very large quantity of plants from an unknown 'pot' grower into the marketplace. Fortunately our reputation as cut flower growers stood us in good stead and most of our customers stayed loyal, although their individual uptake of pots was much lower than had been the case with cut flowers. We started with the basics – cyclamen, poinsettias, geraniums and fuchsias. At this stage we were growing on the floor, hand watering, and working on our hands and knees. This was neither pleasant or efficient. However, we gradually benched out the houses and increased our cyclamen production to seventy-five thousand plants a year, with the season stretching from late July to early April. Poinsettias remained at around ten thousand for the main Christmas crop, but we also experimented with 'blacked-out' crops for flowering earlier than December. All sorts of other crops filled in, whilst we searched for the right 'mix'. Our oil consumption had dropped as the cyclamen crop, which had a much lower heat requirement, had increased. Now came the next hammer blow: oil was to go on ration. Our December ration was to be ninety per cent of what we had had delivered the previous December. Panic, total panic! Our previous year's oil deliveries were five thousand gallons on November 29th and five thousand gallons on January 2nd, therefore our allocation was ninety per cent of nothing! What made it even worse was that in the meantime we had built a new block of glass so our actual requirement was thirty per cent up on the previous year! First of all I spoke to Shell, our suppliers, to remind them that the previous year's *scheduled* delivery was for December 31st, and it was at their request that I took it two days later. They didn't dispute this but said their hands were tied.

I grovelled to the Ministry of Agriculture, I asked our MP, I consulted the National Farmers' Union and anyone else I could think of. Everyone was terribly nice and very sympathetic – but no prospect of any oil. I calculated that on a frost protection basis I could just get through until Christmas Eve, so I turned all the thermostats down as low as I dared.

There was nothing left to do except try to find a second-hand coal-fired boiler to join into our system. Nothing ventured, nothing gained, so I rang the National Coal Board number in Norwich and explained the situation.

They in turn explained that they only sold domestic fireplaces and suggested I should ring the NCB's headquarters at Hobart House. I was put through to their senior fuel technologist, Steve Byrne. Bingo! He told me he had a second-hand, coal-fired, automatically stoked unit, which had just been taken out of a district heating scheme at Edmonton, of 6.5 million BTU capacity. We could have it for £500 plus transport. No guarantees, sold as is, where is. I immediately sent up a boiler specialist to make sure that it was insurable and not likely to blow up. This seemed to me unbelievably cheap and the cheque was on its way before he could change his mind. The help and cooperation I had from the Coal Board was incredible. They found me an installer, they found me a hundred tons of coal – how, in the middle of the miners' dispute, I don't know – and gave me the spec for the base, the full electrical spec and everything I could possibly need to know. Even all these years later I can say I have never experienced technical back-up and support from any commercial organisation to equal that from the NCB. Without them we should have 'died' that winter.

The boiler arrived on a low-loader, there was a sixty-ton crane in attendance and we finally got our new acquisition into position. The signature tune whistled in the nursery was, of course, 'Any old iron' – which did my confidence, looking at this heap of rusting scrap, no good at all. The NCB-recommended installers from King's Lynn arrived the following day and reassured me I'd bought well and they would have it all up and running within two weeks. We were in the middle of random power cuts to conserve electricity, and Surefire, the installers, were relieved that we had our own generator, as there was no time to phase work around power cuts. Now came another hammer blow. The government announced an official three-day week. In essence, no business using electricity as part of its production process could operate for more than three days in the week. I decided to ignore it, as we could generate our own electricity. A few days later it was announced that the use of private generators was also not allowed. Again we ignored it, and finally all was complete and ready for firing up. Amidst great excitement we got her alight and she worked – except for the automatic stoker, for which spares were not immediately available.

We let the fire out, as I still had nearly three weeks' worth of oil in the tank, although we needed to conserve this in case the 'new' coal-fired boiler broke down.

We had not had time to build a boiler house, so I was

mentally prepared to spend Christmas in the open air, hand stoking. In the event it was not necessary, as on December 23rd a Shell tanker appeared with five thousand gallons of heavy oil. I rang the depot at Royston and thanked them profusely. To my enquiry about how they had managed it, I was told not to ask questions… I was profoundly grateful to whoever had arranged this. I never discovered who my guardian angel was, although I had my suspicions.

In the meantime, however, we had to cope with the Christmas market. The three-day week and constant blackouts had decimated sales. This wasn't catastrophic, as cyclamen would sell well in the New Year, but apart from a Christmas tree nothing is less saleable on Boxing Day than a poinsettia. The poinsettias were indeed almost unsaleable and I totted up our losses due to the three-day week at just under £60,000. The only consolation was that a significant portion of that amount would have gone in tax.

These losses certainly helped provoke my anti-Heath moves described elsewhere. As the days started to lengthen the country became resigned to political and trade union idiocy. Plant life, however, started to show new spring growth and our spirits began to rise. We had got the new part for the underfeed stoker and I was learning the mechanics of operating this huge beast when at ten o'clock in the evening there was a knock on the door just as we were going to bed. My visitor greeted me with, ' Good evening, Mr de Havilland?'

'That's me, who are you?'

'I'm the doctor.'

'No one's ill, I don't want a doctor.'

'I'm the Coal Board doctor, Bill Hicks, I've come to set up your boiler and do all the combustion tests.'

'What, at this time of the night?'

'Of course, night-time is when greenhouse boilers do their work, not in the middle of the day.'

Well, I couldn't argue with that, so I gave him a cup of tea and we were down in the boiler house, which had now been built, until five o'clock in the morning. After that I felt I knew more what I was doing. Bill Hicks and Steve Byrne gave customer service which now seems like the relic of a bygone age.

I was to need their services in dire emergency one day in late March. I went in to de-clinker at eight o'clock. The fans were off, as was the stoker, which was the condition required. However, when I opened the furnace doors the fire was white hot, so I decided to leave it to cool down and went back to the house for breakfast. I had noticed a slight vibration in the boiler but thought no more about it until I got indoors and heard a huge explosion. My instant reaction was that the IRA had finally got to General Freeland, but rushing out of the door all I could see was clouds of smoke and steam where the boiler house was! I approached gingerly and could see the safety valves, two huge eight-inch diameter units, had blown. Steam was still roaring out of them and I had no idea what to do. I rang the Coal Board at Hobart House and mercifully Steve Byrne was in. He calmed me down and said, 'At least we know they work – they have never blown before!' He told me to rake the fire out and thereby reduce the heat in the boiler. I think that was the hairiest thing I have ever done in civilian life. My boots were on fire, my clothes were on fire, and I couldn't breathe for sulphurous fumes, but I did it. I dashed out into the fresh air, found a hosepipe to put the fires about my person out, got my breath back and went back to the telephone.

It was all blindingly obvious with hindsight, for dawn is always the coldest time of the night when the boilers work their hardest. Combine that with, as on this occasion, a sudden very bright March sun, giving a combination of red-hot pipes, mixing valves on the circulating pumps suddenly all shut together, leaving nowhere for the energy to go except build up pressure in the boiler. Although the boilers – both coal and oil – ran together from November to the end of March, the oil-fired one simply shut down when up to temperature and I had never thought about the residual heat in the coal-fired boiler. We never had the problem again, needless to say.

I personally looked after the old thing for about seven years and she became my steam engine substitute. There is still something very special about the smell of coal and steam, which, no doubt, is a significant cause of the popularity of steam rallies. The downside of all this nostalgia, though, is the reality of the filth and the soot which goes with it. How Jacqueline put up with my filthy clothes I really don't know; perhaps she just saw it as a trade-off for the horsehair and hayseeds which she and Susan generated!

CHAPTER XX

Over and Under

In the summer of 1975 my father, for some reason best known to himself, decided to split up his matching pair of Watson side-by-side twelve bore shotguns and give one to me. Initially I declined because I was perfectly happy with my – or more correctly, John's – Churchill, which I had used for the past fifteen seasons. However, he was obviously going to be touchy about it, so in the end I accepted graciously, but still pointed out that as he and I were a totally different shape it would have to undergo major reconstructive surgery and they would never be a matching pair again. He was quite happy with that until two years later when he had an invitation to a double gun day and suddenly wanted it back. By that time I had sickened myself of shooting hand-reared pheasants and taken up clay pigeon shooting instead. The decision to give up game shooting was taken a few days before my forty-first birthday, which I am told is the approximate age at which the bloodlust either renews itself until old age, or as in my case, disappears altogether. Anyway, after a year of clay pigeon shooting with a cheap Miroku over-and-under, I had exchanged Father's side-by-side and the Miroku for a much more expensive Browning over-and-under. When I confessed that I had sold his 'gift', Father had a quite serious sense of humour failure!

The volcanic eruption which followed was a repeat of some ten years earlier, when unbeknown to me, he had invited the Essex and Suffolk hunt to a 'Lawn meet' at the Hall, assuring them there was a resident fox in 'the Marsh'. He had omitted to tell me this until after I had accounted for it during a day's shooting two weeks before the meet. I promised to get him a 'bagman' in good time before the meet, but all the keepers in Essex and a very good contact in Norfolk failed in their attempts. The Essex and Suffolk had a blank day, and Father felt he and my mother had been totally humiliated by their eldest son. And now here was history repeating itself. Father's double gun day at Raynham was still two months away, so I made extensive efforts to trace it to try to buy the gun back in order to calm him down. We traced it as far as Northern Ireland and then the trail went cold. I was eventually advised that it had probably had its barrels sawn off by now and I was unlikely to see it again! Father had to shoot with an unmatching pair about which I never heard the end.

Clay pigeon shooting opened up a whole new world for me. There were several disciplines one could engage in. I gave them all a try before settling on 'Skeet', of which there were three separate versions shot in England. The basic skeet discipline was 'English', with twenty-five targets constituting a 'round'. In an area such as East Anglia, with the large number of USAAF bases, there was also the American version enjoying equally popular appeal. The principal appeal of this version was that most competitions were shot with four different gauged weapons, twelve, twenty, twenty-eight bore and .410. The third version was by far the most challenging – Olympic skeet. The targets were much faster, and as its name implies it was an Olympic discipline.

Needless to say I ultimately specialised in the latter, not with any aspirations of achieving Olympic glory, I was far too old, but for the greater challenge. I was fortunate to find two very good coaches, firstly Jack Pennington at Holbeach, who had represented his country abroad on several occasions, and subsequently Eric Swinkels, a Dutchman who had won the Silver Medal at Montreal in the 1976 Olympic games. The first few years were an uphill struggle, but as this was the first competitive sport I had engaged in for twenty-five years it was hardly surprising. Jack frequently regaled me with his tales of overseas shooting. If only half of what he told me was true, the shooting grounds, facilities and camaraderie were superior in mainland Europe.

Eventually, at Eric Swinkels' suggestion I was to have my first taste of European competition. This was at an international event in Holland in early April. Not wanting to go entirely alone to face this rather daunting prospect I took Peter Simpson, a fellow shooter, and his girlfriend with me, not only for the company but moral support as well. The weather was absolutely vile, bitterly cold with frequent snow showers; Eric in his capacity as my coach had already told me what was expected of me. At the end of the first round I was heading for about half the score he had set me, and the prospect of another two days of this filled me with dread. Eric told me that however tough the opposition, that only concerned the top performers like himself. The only opposition I had was from each individual target. After a lesson in relaxation – not easy when you are frozen stiff – things went better and better and by the end of the competition I had exceeded his expectations by two targets out of the two hundred. It was an exceedingly modest score of 167 ex 200; however, it was a start on which I was able to build and marked the beginning of a period of about six years when I shot somewhere in Europe at least once a fortnight during the season. I had a few triumphs along the way but more importantly had acquired a very wide circle of friends, mostly Dutch, but including several from Germany, Belgium, Norway and Sweden, to name but a few.

The preponderance of Dutch acquaintances was partly due to Eric's influence, but also to the fact that by now my horticultural activities were being conducted more and more in Holland. The system of firearms legislation was complicated by the fact that the English shotgun certificate had no validity in any other country, and getting guns in for specific competitions required an International (FITASC) certificate for that particular event. I was able to circumvent this by joining the Dutch shooting association – the KNSA – whose certificate was recognised in other European countries. This made regular travel to Europe with my gun, for whatever reason, straightforward, or at least relatively so. We had a few excitements even so, such as on one occasion when my gun had been put on the flight deck for safe keeping, but the Captain had forgotten to offload it at Schiphol. It was retrieved just as the plane was taxiing onto the runway for take-off to the next destination! Frequently I was accosted by customs officers – mostly female – who accused me of cruelty! By far the most serious incident was at Munich, where I was arrested and held for three hours. Someone travelling on an English passport with a Dutch firearms certificate gave the blond-haired, blue-eyed Aryan immigration officer adequate cause to declare 'my papers were not in order'.

These exact words sent a chill right through me, for on my previous visit to Munich's Olympic shooting stadium I had observed factory chimneys behind the boundary hedge, and upon enquiring of one of my Dutch friends what they were doing stuck in the middle of the country, they turned out to be from the ovens at Dachau concentration camp – in which, coincidentally, most of his family had been done to death during the war. Dachau seemed to be a tourist attraction, but I was not tempted to visit.

Whilst I was being held I couldn't help thinking what people rounded up by the Gestapo must have felt. Eventually, word got to the shooting ground that I was detained and I was identified and released. A few days later the Pope was shot at, so quite clearly the authorities were justified in looking for anything suspicious. Even so, it was not a pleasant experience. Having said all that, our German hosts, a few of whom I knew from their visits to Holland, were absolutely charming, and on the first night took me to a beer festival.

This was not at the famous Hofbrauhaus but a lower-key outdoor venue. I had left home at five o'clock that morning and was starving hungry, so imagine my feeling at being confronted by seventeen one litre 'steins' of beer and no food! There were seventeen of us in the party and the majority did not speak English. The inner man eventually got the better of me and I enquired in my school-boy German of the possibility of something to eat. Everyone thought that a great idea – and on came seventeen whole roast chickens! No vegetables, no plates, no eating irons, just seventeen whole chickens!

We had a wonderful evening, I being intrigued at how many steins of beer the large-breasted Bavarian serving girls could balance on their boobs. This seemed an even greater feat than African girls carrying as much as they do on their heads. The 'oompah' music was mesmeric, and it really wasn't difficult to see how Hitler's rise to power was centred on Munich and its culture. All it needed was a mob orator, a bellyful of beer and this utterly stirring martial music – plus of course a real or imaginary sense of grievance.

It was my shooting activities which brought me out of the rather narrow horticultural scene and into the wider Dutch community. I had never previously realised how great was the hatred of the Dutch for the Germans, and how bitter the memories. There was one particular shooting club where at their annual championship one year a small contingent of German shooters turned up. At the prize giving, the club president, after thanking everyone for coming, turned to the German contingent and told them that whilst he couldn't welcome them with open arms, they were more welcome than forty years ago – and could he please have his bicycle back. I learned afterwards that he had had it stolen at the time of the Arnhem landings!

None of us quite knew how to react. Although I could understand some of what was said, the nuances escaped me. The Dutch suffered enormously at the hands of the Germans, especially around Eindhoven, Arnhem and Nijmegen, and they had neither forgotten nor forgiven. I managed to remain neutral and made quite a few German friends, even receiving a personal invitation from an eminent aristocrat to a competition in Hamburg. Some kind of sixth sense made me wary of this, and I sat on it quite a long time before asking my father whether he knew anything about this family. His reply shocked me: 'Don't go, I remember that name.'

It transpired that their estate had been broken up under Father's tour of duty with the CCG as part of the land redistribution programme.

The somewhat negative tone of these little anecdotes were more than compensated for by the good times I had, and I look back on them all with great affection. Particularly memorable was one October evening when Eric asked me if I would like to see his family's wild boar forest. Shooting wild boar is supposed to be one of the most challenging of field sports, and this estate abutted Prince Bernhard's in northern Holland. We climbed into the keeper's estate wagon loaded with maize, and on reaching a small clearing in the forest we got out and spread this maize around. In no time the pigs emerged. I could never have imagined what we saw.

The keeper kept a loaded rifle with him, as out of the undergrowth came about eighty or ninety animals ranging in size from massive old boars with their fearsome tusks to little *frieslings*. The latter made the best eating, while the old boars provided the best trophies. During that evening we saw over three hundred wild boar. The forest was notable for the lack of any other form of wildlife, as the pigs destroy everything. I was not invited to go on a wild boar shoot myself as this is a privilege which has to be earned over a long period of time. I did, however, receive an invitation from one of the Swedish shooters to shoot elk from a 'High Seat'. I declined this, as I had never really enjoyed deer-stalking, and I felt that killing elk for fun would be even less appealing.

I continued to train regularly at Jack Pennington's shooting ground at Holbeach in South Lincolnshire. Holbeach was the home of the Bailey family, who were destined to have more influence on my life than I could ever have imagined when I first met them. David was already in the GB junior team, and his young brother, Martin, was also a fine shot. The two boys were always at the same shoots around the country, having been driven there by their mother, Marion, who always very kindly provided me with coffee and snacks from their caravan, the facilities on most English shooting grounds being basic in the extreme. This friendship with the family resulted in my inviting them all to the Belgian Championships, which took place in Brussels each August. I used to take their grandfather out with me, Marion took the two boys, and after the competition, grandfather came back with me and the rest would tour France for about ten days. I tell this story slightly out of chronological order as the influence we all had on each other's lives was only to become apparent in later years.

CHAPTER XXI

Troubles

I had by now been 'dragooned' into the Chairmanship of Foxley Parish Council and endured seven years of 'responsibility without authority'. I don't know which left the deepest impression upon me – the pettiness or futility. However, I felt I was doing my public duty, and all the meetings were well attended. I have, however, no recollection of 'achievement'. A parallel attempt at public duty was to resuscitate the moribund Bawdeswell and District Conservative Association. With the help of many friends we created a really thriving branch, and I became one of the blue-eyed heroes of the Constituency Association. This area of public duty did yield unexpected rewards, in that a winning ticket for the Constituency 200 Draw provided me with a brand new car. I received the message on my answering machine and naturally assumed it was just a wind-up. Not so, it was for real!

Some three or four years later, when Edward Heath was at the height of his unpopularity, the branch membership, admittedly at my and David Sayer's instigation, instructed us to approach Paul Hawkins, our MP, to see what could be done about a leadership challenge. Paul was not anxious to take sides, as I think he was not as opposed to Ted Heath as was the right wing of the party, and suggested we talk to Ralph Howel, the member for North Norfolk, who was firmly aligned with the Right. It was my lot to make contact with Ralph, whom I did not know personally. He suggested we were far from alone, and promised to meet David and me at the home of one 'Happy' Tyrell in Dereham. 'Happy' was a flamboyant farmer who had been one of my Pest Control customers in the early years. He had a very nice house in Dereham and it never occurred to me that one day twenty years later we would be living in the same house. Be that as it may, we had our meeting and were surprised to learn the extent of parliamentary disaffection for Ted Heath and what many felt were his botched attempts to 'tame' the trade unions. Many of us, I more than most, had suffered terribly in the notorious three-day week. David and I were put in touch with some more malcontents and were promised that if we could come up with a name which was credible, and demonstrate that there was a real feeling at the grass roots of 'time for a change', Ralph and Paul would take the temperature at Westminster and see what happened next. By this time my own politics had changed from left of centre to right of centre, but I very quickly learned that my version of right of centre seemed almost left wing compared to those we were to meet up with.

After a couple of meetings we came up with Margaret Thatcher as, in our opinion, the most likely person to deal with Arthur Scargill and his merry band of brothers. Even then we had visions of her as a modern Queen Boadicea, and this view apparently was not confined to the East Anglian domain of this famous queen.

Ralph and Paul took this information back to Westminster and the rest, as they say, is history. I cannot claim that Bawdeswell and District Conservative Association were literally the first to start the ball rolling, but certainly we were in the forefront, sufficiently so that we, or more accurately I personally, were contacted by some real loonies. The National Front were the first on the scene, quickly followed by two more who were raising private armies with some grotesque idea of a coup. Jacqueline, who had been totally supportive so far, began to urge caution and questioned whether I was not getting out of my depth. I knew I was, and decided to resign from the little cabal we had formed. Without being over dramatic, some of the things I had heard and messages I received were, frankly, treasonable. Our private lives and those of the wider village community were now also coming under strain from outside influences.

Ian Freeland was the first GOC Northern Ireland at the start of the new round of the Troubles. Although the province had been simmering for some time, the posting there of one of the Army's most senior generals could only signal an anticipated escalation of the dispute. Although he continued with the ownership of his house in Foxley, there was only a modest police presence in the village whilst he was away. This presence was dramatically increased when the General himself returned home, either for a short break and especially at the end of his tour of duty. The Old Rectory, where he lived, with its large garden, field and outbuildings, resembled an armed camp, and even our occasional visits for lunch involved the most rigorous security checks. Even inside the house, armed police never left his side. We used to go shooting together occasionally, and even when he was my guest at Horkesley an armed detective travelled with us.

It is not an exaggeration to say that his family were mentally destroyed by the experience, especially his wife, Mary, who was of course a powerless bystander. I was woken about four o'clock one midsummer morning to the sound of shots ringing out. I looked out of our bedroom window to see a Bren gun carrier at the crossroads! Presumably some kind of 'D' notice had been issued to the press, as the incident was never reported. I believe one or more suspects were picked up, but again it was best not to ask.

Some time before all this my brother had arrived with my old stalking rifle plus five hundred rounds of 9 mm ammunition, explaining that it was no longer on his firearm certificate and as it was mine he thought I'd like it back. I had surrendered my own certificate when I came to Norfolk and had formally transferred all my rifles to him except, apparently, this one. I hadn't paid too much attention to it until the IRA business started to hot up. The government had had several amnesties for unlicensed firearms and I had simply waited for the next one. Unfortunately it never came, and I had become increasingly concerned about being in 'illegal possession' as the police presence in the village grew. By the time of the Bren gun carrier incident I had stripped it down and kept it in bits around the house, but now I began to think, If anything happens across the road and the police do a house-to-house search, I am going to be in a tricky position. I decided to own up and confess and after I had plucked up enough courage I went to see the Old Bill. They were totally unconcerned and said they'd send someone round. Three days later a constable turned up and put it, and the ammunition, in his car. I said, 'Is that it, then? Don't I get a receipt or anything?'

'Not unless you want to be charged with illegal possession,' came the reply.

In spite of all these distractions, normal life still went on. Susan was spending quite a bit of time with us in the greenhouses and at weekends there was always some equine activity to indulge in.

A chance encounter with my mother at a point-to-point meeting had resulted in us becoming the owner of one of her redundant cows, which was to provide us with Jersey milk, cream and butter for a few years until the waistline persuaded me this was not such a good idea after all.

On a subsequent occasion we learned that the little Welsh pony she had bought for John's children had proved unsatisfactory and was being sold the next week at Cambridge. The fact that John's children couldn't get on with it came as no great surprise. Even so, he was far too good a pony to go to Cambridge, which was simply a meat market.

After a long discussion with Jacqueline I rang my mother to see what she would sell him to us for. She said she wouldn't dream of selling him, we could have him for free, but only on condition that we didn't send him back to her. We asked Susan whether she would like him and she was absolutely delighted. So two months before her third birthday she became the proud possessor of, to use her own expression, 'My own, my very own pony.' His real name was Smokey, but all Susan could get out was 'Ssfmo', which gradually became 'Eskimo'. Many ponies came and went over the years but Eskimo was definitely 'not for sale' and he survived with us for seventeen years before old age got the better of him. By the time Susan was six years old she was riding on her own, getting the same pleasure and heartbreak from her horses as her mother before her, and my mother before that. At the time of writing Susan is nearly thirty-five and still horses are her life. I feel I have much to answer for.

In 1975 our lives became blighted by the dreaded Big C. First to succumb was one of the farmer's daughters in her early thirties; next was my mother, followed by another friend of ours, the wife of a neighbour in the village. After the third one we relaxed a little, only to find that the rule of three meant nothing, as Jacqueline was also diagnosed in 1982. After my mother's diagnosis, my parents took a final holiday together on a cruise to South Africa. They found Field Marshal Montgomery, with whom my father had served first in North Africa with the Eighth Army and subsequently in Europe with 21 Army Group, was in the next cabin. They had a splendid time of reminiscence, and overall the holiday was a great success; but sadly it was to be the last they ever had together. When my mother died. Father was absolutely devastated, as were we two boys. A friend of John's kindly asked my father to stay in Scotland. He made his private plane available to my father, and whilst flying up Father made the chance remark to the pilot that one of his great regrets was that he had never learned to fly. The pilot managed to convince him that it was never too late to learn and to our utter amazement father passed his PPL at the age of seventy-three!

We thought he must be the oldest man to have ever learnt, although there were plenty older who had been flying all their lives. An attempt to get him in the *Guinness Book of Records* established that a New Zealander had been six months older when he passed. I was seriously impressed with this achievement, especially father's ability to master all the instrument and navigational tests. The first winter after he qualified he quickly became frustrated with the weather and took himself off to the US where he flew with some members of the Confederate Air Force. His mentor on this occasion had flown P51 Mustangs off the airfield adjoining the farm at Horkesley during the war. For the next twelve years, flying was to become his life. Quite fortuitously he was the only de Havilland still flying. He was much in demand to open museums and the like, especially those devoted to preserving the old pre-war private aeroplanes, which specialist market de Havillands had made their own.

By now of course the 'private' market had been taken over by the American manufacturers, and Father acquired his own Piper Cherokee. To be more precise he had a half 'Timeshare Ownership', an arrangement which worked extremely well, and in truth had some bearing on my attempt to do the same thing with boats – of which more later.

In the meantime Father had married the lady he had engaged as companion/housekeeper. She was somewhat younger than him, in fact my age! I never knew how happy he really was in this arrangement. It certainly enabled him to maintain his independence, and for that I shall always be grateful. He certainly loved his flying, and it remains a moot point whether his aeroplane or his second wife emptied the coffers fastest. His flying companion was not his new wife but Bea Duthy, a widow whose husband had died a little earlier. The Duthys, de Havillands and Otter-Barrys (my mother's family) had been at war ever since I can remember, although Bea and my mother had somehow managed to remain aloof from the worst of the arguments. After my mother's death, Bea and my father became quite close; they should have married, life for all of us would have been much simpler. As far as I know my new stepmother never flew with him at all, and neither, to my eternal shame, did I. Father was not easy to be a car passenger with, as he was always farming over the hedge, but his concentration in a plane seemed to be one hundred per cent. He and Bea frequently flew up to see us, landing at Swanton Morley, which during the war was the first RAF station to have the de Havilland Mosquito. He handled his plane perfectly, was rigorous with his take-off procedures and flight planning, and there was nothing, even in his eighties, to give his age away, except his voice on the RT. He had regular CAA medicals every six months and had no difficulty renewing his licence, although the insurers did sniff occasionally.

Throughout his flying career there were only two potential dramas. The first was in poor visibility, when he missed the airfield he was supposed to land on and made his approach onto the A12, but realised in plenty of time the real situation. The other was when the aircraft was overdue to meet us at Swanton Morley. He had filed his flight plan with Swanton Morley and given us his ETA so that we could meet him. The control tower said he had diverted to Norwich Airport – they thought! I rang the control tower at Norwich but couldn't remember the registration number. I was told, 'We have a Cherokee with us and there appears to be an elderly gentleman accompanied by an elderly lady sitting under the wing and eating what looks like a bowl of strawberries.'

'That sounds like them,' I said, and stopped worrying.

It was in the days before mobile phones, but he rang later to apologise saying there was such a heavy haze, and Swanton having only grass runways was particularly difficult to see in these conditions and he didn't want to risk it in case it turned out to be an open field. Eventually at the age of eighty-three the insurers refused to cover him to fly solo any more, but it would be alright to fly with a qualified passenger. Father sulked and said if he couldn't fly solo he wouldn't fly at all. This lasted about two months, but he missed it so much that he took up accompanied flight again after all. His last trip was to fly a twin-engined plane from Mombasa to Nairobi in 1989 at the age of eighty-five. Shortly after this African adventure he drove up to bring our Christmas presents a few days before the festivities, and unusually for him he ate a very hearty meal, during which he was nagged incessantly by his wife about nothing in particular.

As he was ready to go, I leaned through the window and said to him, 'Don't let the women grind you down, Father.'

He looked at me and replied, 'I'm ground.'

Those were the last words he ever said to me.

Two hours later on arrival home he suffered a massive stroke and dropped down dead. It's the way he would have wanted to go. We gave him the kind of funeral he would surely have wanted, and then learned of our effective disinheritance. All rather sad. How did all this come about, the reader may wonder…

When our mother died her estate had been left to us boys 'in trust', with Father having a life interest. This 'life interest' was to be a problem, as Father told anyone who would listen that he had been disinherited by his wife and now had to ask his bloody children for permission to do anything! Almost immediately after my mother's death the only independent trustee also died. Father, John and myself, who were co-trustees, decided not to replace him and to make our own decisions. The first thing we did was effectively to tear up the life interest so the estate became his outright, but with the very clear understanding that it reverted to us upon his death just as Mother intended. This was to prove a terrible mistake, as Father remarried again quite soon. It is of course a dilemma which people come up against every day. We had a certain sympathy for Father, as he had in turn been disinherited by his mother and family via a 'deathbed' codicil drawn up by a priest in the Anglican Church. The thinking was that as he had married a relatively wealthy wife the needs of others, including this particular Church, were greater than his. Now history was to repeat itself, and John and myself were the victims. I certainly had sympathy for the position that a second wife should not be treated as a second-class citizen, but by the time my father died it was us who were the third-class citizens.

The blame for this debacle was not all his, however; we were thoroughly bad and incompetent trustees. Our mother knew her husband better than we did, and what we did was almost criminal. I am deeply ashamed at having flouted her wishes, but we paid a very heavy price!

CHAPTER XXII

KSM Flowers

The summer of 1976 was a torrid time for us on both the business and family front. My mother was declining fast and her demise was only a few months away at the most. We visited as often as we could, returning one afternoon to find a distressed and garbled message on the answering machine. It was a cry for help from Jacqueline's grandmother, mother-in-law having collapsed at Frinton while tending her aged parents, both of whom were well into their nineties. We eventually located her in Colchester Hospital where the prognosis was that she was unlikely to recover. She was a most distressing sight, with tubes coming from everywhere, especially as she had no idea who we were. Mother-in-law's sister and her husband came up trumps and took care of the Frinton end while we to and fro'd between our respective mothers. We were fortunate that both patients were at Colchester. Jacqueline's mother, against all the odds, recovered sufficiently to be moved to Aylsham to be nearer to us, but by no stretch of the imagination was she 'compos mentis'. Amazingly, on the night of my mother's death she apparently 'met' her and was told to tell John and myself, 'Keep an eye on your father, or you will regret it.'

We dismissed this as a trick of the imagination at the time, but as events unfolded as described in the previous chapter, we both wished we had taken the 'wanderings' of a seriously ill mother-in-law more seriously. A very strange occurrence indeed!

Miraculously, Mother-in-law recovered enough to be discharged from hospital and came to live with us for a few weeks to assist her convalescence. She eventually went back to her own home near Chelmsford where she led a normal life for another twenty-five years.

The very high temperatures of that summer had caused havoc in the markets and did huge damage, especially to the young cyclamen crop. I had become increasingly weary of this constant pattern of triumph followed by even greater disaster and was feeling the Good Life was an illusion. By October, when my mother finally succumbed, a deep sense of foreboding had settled over me, and by Christmas I was ready to give up the unequal struggle.

The nursery went up for sale, but so concerned were KSM, our main wholesalers in Covent Garden (now moved to Nine Elms), at the loss of one of their larger suppliers that they expressed an interest in purchasing. This period had seen the arrival of the 'roll-on roll-off' ferries, and KSM had rented a small nursery in Kent on which to store direct imports from Belgium via these ferries to feed into the market in smaller consignments. They were not 'growers' and had quickly discovered there was a bit more to it than they thought. If they could amalgamate the Kent operation with ours, they should logically have the best of both worlds. There was only one snag; they wanted me as part of the deal. I found I had no choice, and agreed a three-year management deal with them.

Jacqueline and myself were bitterly disappointed that we had had to throw in the towel but in fact the new era which was to dawn with the acquisition of our nursery by Colin and Vic, the proprietors of KSM Flowers, turned out to be far more interesting, challenging and enjoyable than we had ever expected. As is usual with hindsight, it is so easy to see how the UK horticultural industry had mortally wounded itself decades before I came on the scene, and the next six or seven years was to see it entering an almost terminal phase. The major blame must lie with our system of commission-selling through wholesale markets. The Dutch, especially, had established well-organised and efficient growers' cooperatives long before our own horticultural industry had even thought about it. Their auction markets were owned by the growers themselves, and whilst at first they were regional operations they gradually progressed to the huge operations we see today, most notably at Aalsmeer, near Schiphol airport. The cost savings on marketing and distribution were huge compared to those faced by the English growers. Deductions to the Dutch grower were about one and a half per cent. Our growers had to face commission charges of ten to fifteen per cent plus the costs of packaging and carriage to market, which were frequently of the same order. By the time our industry woke up to what was happening it was too late; the Dutch had a total stranglehold on the international marketing of flowers and plants, which persists to this day.

Undoubtedly there are successful UK operations still around, but their balance sheets are never public and I remain largely unconvinced.

KSM already had obligations to import significant quantities of part-grown plants from Floreac in Belgium. As these plants were intended for sale in Nine Elms they were of necessity at least three-quarters to fully grown. It was not long before KSM had outgrown their small holding nursery in Kent and the overflow was now coming to us. As my own crops matured and were sold, more and more of the space which had been released was turned over to Floreac's products. The operation opened all our eyes, as none of us had a clue what anything was. The initial influx was all house (green) plants. All we really had to do was keep them fed and watered, keep the foliage clean and pack given quantities to order. Very shortly after the takeover I flew out to Belgium with Colin and Vic to see the Floreac operation. It was so huge that I didn't know what to say. For example they grew five acres of Achmea in a single greenhouse. Achmea Fasciata is a slightly unusual plant which hardly flies off the shelves, and I was intrigued to learn where it all went. Their azalea operation extended as far as the eye could see, and basically it went on in this vein for the whole day. I was presented with very hard evidence indeed just why the UK industry was beginning to struggle as prices went ever lower.

Pot plants had never previously been that easy a product to import, being quite unsuitable for airfreight. However, the roll-on roll-off ferries removed the principal method of market protection in one go. I flew home in the certain knowledge that I had done the right thing, and pitched into the KSM operation with renewed enthusiasm. We used to have a lorry and trailer full from Floreac at least once a fortnight. Unloading these took all day, as each plant was individually hand-wrapped in newspaper and had to be carted into whichever greenhouse they were needed and then unwrapped and respaced. The hardest job was disposing of literally tons of wet newspaper. We used to try to arrange these deliveries for a Friday, which was our only non-packing day of the week. After a couple of years the versatile 'Danish trolley' was to appear, obviating the need to wrap plants at all.

Unloading went from being an all-day operation to one which took an hour at the most.

Pest and disease control became quite a headache, but with my chemical background we were able to rise to the challenge, and KSM were good enough to admit that the quality of plants we were able to turn out was far better than they had been able to achieve on their little nursery in Kent.

The Belgians were the preferred source of green or foliage plants, and of course that country, with its unique soil type, has a virtual monopoly of azalea – and to a lesser extent hydrangea – production. However, the Dutch were the leaders for other flowering plant production, and to this end KSM made an appointment for Cees Eveleens to see me at eleven thirty one morning. I was a bit aggrieved at this as I already had a good network of producers of young flowering plants both in England and Holland. Cees eventually turned up at twelve fifteen, three-quarters of an hour late. I was cross and told him he would have to wait until one o'clock when I came back from lunch. We both laugh about it now, but it was bad behaviour on my part.

After several visits I took to this young man, as did Jacqueline, and we often accommodated and wined and dined him. My brother had given me a couple of cases of very good claret some years earlier, which even I enjoyed, although I am definitely not a wine drinker; Cees couldn't resist it. After he had stayed two or three times, John rang me up to ask what I would like for a Christmas present. I suggested some more of that excellent wine would be most acceptable.

'Goodness, you're not drinking it!'

'Yes, what's wrong? Isn't it ready or something?'

'Yes, it is at its best, but you can't afford to drink it! It's selling at a hundred and fifty pounds a bottle in the auctions, and has turned out to be one of the wines of the century...'

This was a lot of money thirty years ago, and Cees only had one more bottle.

I eventually went out to Holland without Colin and Vic to see the Eveleens' set-up. Cees showed me round several of their nurseries as well as those of some of their contract growers. I liked Cees and all his family members, whom I met on this tour, and decided to throw my hat willingly on their peg. This met with the approval of KSM, and Cees and I have been good friends for over twenty-five years. My old nursery was now run roughly on the basis of one-third Floreac products and two-thirds Eveleens. In monetary terms it was probably the other way round, as Floreac's products were the more valuable, especially considering the huge number of azaleas we had from them. In general terms Colin and Vic were directly responsible for the Belgian purchases and I was responsible for the Dutch business. We continued growing most of the lines we had always had but cut back on the cyclamen dramatically to just a seasonal instead of a year-round crop.

I had always wanted to grow begonias as pot plants and now was my chance. Although the crop had been popular in

Europe for at least ten years, it had yet to make any headway in England. Eveleens were big in the begonia business and I was to meet their propagator, Bert Koppe, on many occasions subsequently. We managed to grow a couple of reasonably good batches but it was always a struggle to sell them. At the end of our first attempt I learned that one of the larger growers of this crop, who had found it a real struggle, had been found dead in his greenhouse. Nothing daunted, I persuaded KSM to stay with it for another year, and Cees managed to persuade Colin and Vic to sell them in full flower instead of in bud. It worked; from then on we never looked back and used to sell up to two and a half thousand begonias a week.

We had one excitement when one of the girls picking up plants for market produced two strange plants, not a variety we had grown, but of quite exquisite colouring. I immediately phoned Cees, as I was well aware that most exciting varieties appear by chance rather than design. Cees said that only five minutes ago he'd had another grower on the phone who had found five 'rogue' plants. He immediately diverted a lorry to this other nursery in Sussex and then on up to Norfolk to collect ours and get them back to Bert Koppe, the propagator, as soon as possible. Bert confirmed that he had not seen anything like it amongst his stock plants.

He took cuttings and surprisingly they bred true, the stock was rapidly built up and this new variety became the number one seller in the market until well after I had turned my back on horticulture. We never found anything like this again, but it was not for want of looking.

Throughout this period I was visiting Eveleens' nursery at least once a month and had many offers of special deals. Some of these, although at first sight opportunistic, frequently turned out better than expected. One which did not involved twelve thousand large azaleas specifically for the Christmas market. As I have said earlier, azaleas tended to be Floreac's preserve, but this was to be a very special deal with Cees. They were all the same variety, all the same size, all in the same size pots, all for delivery in the last week of November. I had drawn up a very tight specification for the condition of the buds as there were only three weeks to get them advanced enough for sale. The last week of November came and went: no azaleas. I chased Cees, who assured me they would be with me the following week. Still no azaleas, and I was getting cross. Two weeks late they finally arrived; we opened the lorry doors and the men started to offload. I just attended to the coal boiler and then went to see what we had got. The men had by then got about a thousand off and they were nowhere near forward enough to make the Christmas market. Skilled as I had become at 'forcing' to a given date, these plants didn't even begin to meet the spec agreed for November delivery. Cees was not contactable (no mobile phones in those days), so I told the driver that I couldn't accept them and he was to take them back. The driver, Pete, who we knew well, said, 'It is not possible, I have no papers.'

Plant health regulations were strict and I knew he was speaking the truth. Whilst we were arguing, Cees's office had managed to get hold of him, and he asked me to take them and do the best I could with them; he would sort it out afterwards. I trusted him absolutely and he in turn trusted me to do the best I could. They were spaced out into houses two and four, and having had a good look at them, I couldn't see any hope for them at all. If I tried to over force them they would be a poor sample; if I applied the normal regime they would be ready in early January, which was not a good selling time.

It was then that I had an inspiration.

Jacqueline had introduced me to 'the box' when Eskimo had arrived crippled with laminitis. The technical term for the procedure was 'radionics'. I still have no idea how it works and writing about it in cold blood it seems totally bizarre. However, we had sent off some hair from Eskimo and put him 'on the box'. Within a few days his lameness started to improve. Subsequently we used the technique several times on the animals with great success. I had always suffered terribly

238

from hay fever. I had had every conceivable allergy test, had all the injections, taken tablet after tablet; nothing had the slightest effect. After our successes with the animals I found a practitioner who specialised in humans, sent her a lock of hair in February, three small monthly payments, and have never had hay fever again. I still have no explanation and don't need one; the facts speak for themselves. I also knew by virtue of our close involvement with 'the box' that plants could also be treated. So I found out the name of a plant practitioner from the Radionics Association who thought she would be able to help. She asked me to draw a site plan, the exact location of the beds in the two houses, and which numbered beds I wanted treated so that we had a control. In fact I elected to treat half the beds in each house. I also sent off a sample of leaves and because time was of the essence, the whole package went 'Special Delivery'.

I myself refrained from doing any watering or having anything to do with the crop; someone else did all that. Eventually, ninety per cent of the treated plants made it for Christmas, but only a few of the untreated were ready on time.

The mid-January market was actually quite good and our 'losses' were minimal, so coming to agreement with Cees was a simple matter. I never told anyone what had happened; it was just too unbelievable. The only conclusion I could come to was that there is a lot we can't explain in the world.

The plant health regulations were strictly enforced by the UK's Ministry of Agriculture, whom we were legally required to inform of every consignment of imports arriving on the nursery. The local inspector, Ron Flowers, was a great enthusiast for his job. Although I found this constant intrusion by a civil servant extremely irritating, he was always polite and diplomatic towards us, so much so that we eventually became quite good friends, frequently picking each other's brains. The better atmosphere between us was, however, severely strained when he came to inspect a consignment of three thousand rubber plant cuttings from the Ivory Coast. We had already potted these when Peter, our foreman, announced that Mr

Flowers was here and looking rather more lugubrious even than usual. With the utmost gravity he asked if I was aware that the Ivory Coast had an outbreak of 'Opogona moth'. I had to confess I had no idea what he was talking about. Having told me that it was potentially as serious as Colorado beetle, he had to quarantine the consignment and install traps to find out if any had come in with the cuttings. He returned the next day with his traps and sure enough, within forty-eight hours he had found what he was looking for and promptly issued a destruction notice. I suggested that as he had only caught one, why didn't we simply kill it?

'Mr de Havilland, I don't think you appreciate the gravity of the situation,' he replied.

There was no appeal, and we had two choices: either burn the crop or bury it. Naively I opted to burn, thinking that the latex in the plants would form an inflammable mixture. It didn't, so a JCB had to be hired to complete the operation.

Not only did the Ministry of Agriculture enforce the plant health regulations but also played the same role with chemical spray materials. Glasshouse red spider was by far the most serious pest in the high heat, high humidity regime which we kept. The available sprays were extremely limited in their effectiveness and an early experiment with biological control was equally useless. However, the Dutch growers had no such problems, being able to use a wonder product called Pentac. This had been used in the Lea Valley for some years with outstanding results. The UK ministry had banned its use in this country, but contraband supplies were relatively easy to come by. Pentac acted as a sterilant and was extremely effective against red spider. Coincidentally, the birth rate amongst the large Italian labour force in the Lea Valley had gone down equally dramatically. I was so desperate to control this pest that I got hold of some for our own nursery. Only Peter and I did the spraying, and truly stunning was its effectiveness. Coincidence or otherwise, but neither he nor I ever had any more children!

It was Cees who had introduced me to Eric Swinkels, and

my association with him was to become a great deal more than just business. His bride-to-be was the daughter of a Sussex nurseryman, and again Cees had good reason to be a frequent visitor to this nursery also. From here on, whenever I went to Holland I would stay with Cees and Barbara. After virtually all the shoots in Holland, which normally took place on Thursday, Friday and Saturday, I would stay Saturday night with them, go to Kempers Roef, our favourite restaurant, on Saturday evening; then on Sunday morning, before flying home in the afternoon, we would visit his cousin who owned a smokehouse on the Aalsmeer lake and buy some little eels straight off the smoke rack. We would take them out to the middle of the lake, stop the boat and eat them. The technique was to snap the heads off, peel them like a banana and eat them two-handed, with the hot grease running down the chin. Sounds disgusting, but oh so delicious!

Cees was very keen for me to try a spring crop of 'calceolarias', abbreviated colloquially to 'calcs'. I was less keen as they were saleable only for Mother's Day, and were very susceptible to the flowers 'damping off' – so susceptible in fact that it was possible to lose a whole crop, literally overnight. Having given in, we went to see the grower who supplied Eveleens with young plants, whose nursery was at Oosterbeek near Arnhem. He gave me some very useful growing advice and we did the deal in the cafe which featured in the film *A Bridge Too Far*. I spent quite a lot of time in the Arnhem/Nijmegen area, on both business and pleasure, and got to know many who were teenagers during the famous military campaign, and I found it quite fascinating to listen to their exploits of that time.

My first crop of 'calcs' were a great success, and they became a regular line just once a year. Interestingly, I have very vivid memories of Thurgood growing these at Horkesley and had recall of his advice even when I was only four years old, especially on the control of humidity. We used to keep the heat on with the ventilation slightly open, just as he did. Not very fuel efficient, but very good for the crop.

I had an initial three-year contract with KSM, at the end of which they asked me to stay on, which I readily agreed to. I was with them for six years which were undoubtedly the best of my entire horticultural career. I gained an enormous amount of experience with many and varied crops, both at Foxley and in Holland. We had deliveries of young plants from Eveleens every two weeks, and I gradually managed to schedule them to arrive the week after I had been shooting. This gave me the opportunity to see what we were getting before it was loaded and make any last-minute adjustments.

More importantly, I had a wonderful home, and a social and sporting life as well. I was able to be with Susan and her mother all the time, and married life truly didn't come better. By the beginning of the '80s, however, this idyllic state had quickly turned to rat shit. Jacqueline had breast cancer.

CHAPTER XXIII

A Second Chance

T he so-called second oil crisis was soon to arrive. Despite rising North Sea production, the world price was also continuing to rise. Whilst the UK horticultural industry had to pay world prices for their oil, the Dutch industry were able to use their gas production at heavily subsidised prices. KSM now decided that they could no longer afford to grow heated crops and wanted to switch to cold-grown crops, importing all the heated crops from Holland and Belgium. I declined to do this, as cold growing was a totally different skill which I did not possess and had no inclination to learn.

Much more importantly, Jacqueline's inoperable cancer was making work more and more difficult and I took this opportunity to leave KSM and to look after her as best I could. Once we had both accepted the inevitability of the outcome she said to me, 'We have had a wonderful twenty three years together. When I've gone, don't sit in a heap of misery, making life hell for Susan as well as yourself. Find someone else and do it all over again.'

'I shall never find anyone like you,' I replied.

'Yes you will, there's always a good woman looking for a good man.'

Jacqueline was able to keep riding until less than three months before her death, but this was a truly ghastly period of my life, the details of which I have no intention of recording. Suffice it to say that my cousin, Felicity, was extraordinarily supportive throughout my ordeal and kindly had Susan to stay immediately after the funeral. This enabled me to go to Holland where I had so many friends of my own. The day after the funeral I turned up at the shooting club in Rotterdam where a couple of friends were practising.

'How are you?' they asked.

'As well as can be expected,' I replied.

I explained the situation and the news quickly spread. During the week I was there, Eric was especially kind and supportive, whilst I spent a few days with him going round the shooting grounds for old times' sake.

It was still, of course, necessary to earn a living, but I had always continued with my commodity trading, although the emphasis had switched from sugar to potatoes. Potatoes were traded in London, but far more important was the exchange in Amsterdam. I was able to keep my eye on these very adequately whilst going about my business in Holland. Most of the trades being profitable, the money kept coming in.

About a month before Jacqueline died, John had requested a meeting with me. At this meeting he explained that he had met up with a Harvard chemistry graduate who had invented a platinum-based additive to improve fuel economy in all fossil fuel-burning appliances, including boilers and internal combustion engines, and what could I tell him about the likelihood of commercial use? Not wishing to appear too negative, I said that I had never heard of one yet which worked. It was not for want of looking, as with an industry such as commercial horticulture, where oil could represent fifty per cent of production costs, if there had been one we would soon have heard of it.

I explained that I was not a fuel technologist and if he could give me a little more detail I could run it past Steve Byrne of the National Coal Board, who had forgotten more about fuel technology than I was ever likely to know. Steve told me that it was always possible that something might one day be produced, but at the moment the physical characteristics of the boiler/burner combination and its influence on the air/fuel ratio were the governing factors rather than some 'snake oil' additive.

Immediately I had returned from my Holland trip, John rang up with a proposition. He said that despite my rather negative reaction at our initial meeting he had checked out that this new platinum-based product really was different and really did work. He produced some very impressive test results and on my return from Holland offerred me a significant batch of shares in this new company, in return for testing it out in the UK and Holland.

I was very appreciative of this offer and saw it as an opportunity to throw myself into something completely different from anything I had done before. John arranged an airfreight delivery of this 'jungle juice' into Norwich Airport. It totally threw the Customs and VAT departments as it didn't belong in any specified category. I was glad that I knew the officials personally or I think it might still have been there. The initial test vehicle was our old horsebox, and after driving round the same hundred-mile route at as constant a speed as possible I could see a very slight benefit, although I had the gravest doubts whether hard-nosed haulage companies would be convinced. It was arranged to try it out in two large articulated vehicles, both of which had fuel consumption records going back two years or more. They achieved much the same results as I had in the old horsebox. 'Jungle juice' mark two, three and four arrived, each with a supposed new formulation, each with broadly similar results.

In the end it was accepted that perhaps its benefits in fuel-efficient modern diesels were too limited to be of commercial benefit, and the company concentrated on large, heavy oil-burning installations where the benefit was more marked. The heavier the oil the cheaper it was, so the fuel economy needed to be that much greater anyway, but the product was still not really commercial. Despite this setback, the company, Fuel Tech, continued to promote the potential reductions of emissions, which did seem more promising. Despite talk of global warming and the need to reduce emissions, there was no commercial benefit to the user to do so unless there was a significant reduction in consumption at the same time, which at that time there wasn't.

In the midst of this work, 'the good woman' to whom Jacqueline had referred on her deathbed, suddenly materialised in the most surprising way.

Towards the end of March, with the new clay pigeon shooting season about to start, I invited Marion Bailey and her son David to lunch and for a shoot afterwards at Deighton Hills, near Norwich. David was working, but Martin was available, his school having broken up for the Easter holidays. I made them a cauliflower cheese to go in the oven later and went to Dereham to get some pony nuts for Susan. With the sack across my shoulders I contrived to slip on the kerb, twisting my ankle violently. Managing somehow to hobble back to my car and get home, I applied generous amounts of horse liniment to it, which killed the pain satisfactorily. After lunch we went to the shooting ground and I felt alright until halfway through the second round. The damaged ankle was swelling up as I looked at it, almost as though it was being blown up with an air hose! Marion rang my doctor, who miraculously was in, and he arranged for her to take me to casualty at Norwich.

We arranged for my next-door neighbour to meet Susan off the school bus and set off for the hospital. It so happened that I knew the casualty officer on duty, and she wanted to keep me in overnight, so severe was the swelling.

I explained as firmly as I could that that would not be possible, as I not only had a motherless daughter to look after but I also had an appointment in Holland the next day. Rosemary Adams knew my personal circumstances, but so awkward had I become that she demanded to see the person who had brought me in. She then announced to Marion that she considered me to be in no fit mental state to look after my daughter, and unless she, Marion, could stay with me overnight, she would arrange for Susan to be taken into care while I was kept in. If on the other hand Marion could stay and bring me back in the morning for outpatient treatment, then she would put the ankle in a soft cast and release me. Marion said of course she would, and I was eventually released. Her husband, John, very kindly brought over some clothes, downed a bottle of my prime claret as though it was a bottle of beer, and took Martin home with him.

Marion took me into the hospital in the morning, where I was fitted up with crutches, my ankle was strapped up and daily appointments made for me at King's Lynn Hospital, where they had supposedly better Outpatient facilities. The treatment was quite painful, consisting of standing in a bucket of ice for what seemed like an eternity, followed by ultrasound. After two or three weeks of this treatment and long periods of sitting with my leg in a sling attached to a hook in one of the beams, I was eventually able to walk reasonably well. Marion now felt she really had to go home, and as my visits for physiotherapy to King's Lynn were down to a couple of days a week only, she invited me to stay with the family at Holbeach until I was finally discharged from the hospital. In any case, Susan was soon to return from Felicity's home, complete with her pony, and shortly to go back to school.

I was with Marion's husband, John, in his pick-up truck, and I made a little speech: 'John, I cannot thank you enough for letting Marion look after me all this time, I really don't know what I would have done without her.'

'That's alright, you can keep her if you like.'

I was astounded and said, 'What do you mean?'

'What I say… I don't need her anymore.'

'Are you serious?' I said.

'Yes, perfectly.'

'All right,' I said. 'I will.'

Fortunately, Marion agreed; she appeared only too pleased to escape from a very alcoholic marriage. The period between being told to take her and her actual coming lasted for about six weeks, during which we conducted an almost surreal courtship. The actual moment of departure was quite unplanned. I simply got a phone call from Marion at nine o'clock in the morning saying, 'I've left and will be with you at about half past ten.'

Mercifully she is still here twenty years later!

Both before and after this coming together, the Fuel Tech saga rumbled on, taking the occasional step forward followed within days by a corresponding step back. Brother John was getting exasperated with my apparently negative attitude, but try as I could I was unable to see any light at the end of the tunnel. Undoubtedly this was the ideal marketing time for a product of this type, but it simply didn't work in terms of fuel economy, although emissions were clearly reduced. The new emissions scare was acid rain, apparently caused by sulphur emissions from the brown coal-fired industrial complexes in Central and Eastern Europe. This was the fashionable explanation for tree death in those areas and beyond.

This was far too fanciful; my extensive experience of sulphuric acid on agricultural crops told me it was nonsense. The wax cuticle of a leaf, especially a conifer, is far tougher than human skin. An acid concentration strong enough to defoliate a tree would totally de-skin the human race. The most likely explanation of those couple of years when Central and Eastern European trees died was a succession of exceptionally mild autumns followed by unprecedentedly sudden and very severe drops in temperature.

The acid rain bandwagon rolled on to the accompaniment of sulphur scrubbers being installed in the offending power stations. A return to more normal autumn temperatures coincided with a reduced tree death, so problem allegedly solved. Central Europe now has a mountain of sulphur it doesn't know what to do with and significantly higher levels of foliar disease on all crops. Any gardener reading this knows, for example, how much more prevalent black spot on roses is nowadays. Sulphur is still the finest fungicide ever made and the minute amounts of sulphur in the atmosphere protected all crops against a wide range of foliar diseases. Has anything actually been achieved? The whole so-called climate change thing has become a political debate, within which rational decisions are difficult to reach. Now that I am working once again with acids, I have done enough practical tests to know that even my skin, acid hardened as it has become over the years, succumbs long before a plant leaf.

I decided to quit my involvement with Fuel Tech, although retaining my shares. However, I was extremely grateful to have been given the opportunity to study the whole phenomenon from close quarters and feel the experience has added to the rich tapestry of my life.

CHAPTER XXIV

A New Beginning

Marion was a wonderful support to Susan, who understandably was feeling embittered and wounded by life, as indeed was I. We had failed to provide mutual support and took our anger out on each other. Without Marion I don't know where we would have ended up. It still took great patience on her part to win Susan's affections, but between them they succeeded. Marion's sons, David and Martin, were equally supportive and eventually a second family unit emerged. It was easier with the boys in many ways because we already knew each other well from our shooting activities. The new family, less David who was working – Marion, Susan, Martin and myself – took our first holiday together in Portugal. We stayed with Cees's father-in-law, who had also sold his nursery in England for much the same reason as I had, and had bought a property in the Algarve.

He lived not far from one of the best shooting ranges in Europe at Villamoura, and both Martin and I took our guns with us in the expectation of enjoying some sport. Martin, despite being a first-class clay target shot, made no secret of the fact that his real passion was live game, especially pigeon shooting. Villamoura shooting ground not only had very good clay target facilities but as we found on arrival, also shooting live pigeons out of traps. This was a 'sport' banned in England in Queen Victoria's reign as one of which HM did not approve. The 'sport' was, and still is, banned in most countries of the world except around the Mediterranean coast. The pigeons are put in traps with collapsible sides set out in a semicircle. The shooter stands in the middle of the semicircle on marks from twenty to twenty-seven metres back from the traps. On the call of 'Pull', one (randomly selected) of the seven traps is electronically collapsed, the pigeon takes off in any direction it chooses and the shooter has to drop it within a circle marked by a white picket fence. A bird dropped within the circle is a 'kill' but outside the circle counts as a 'loss'. The greater the shooter's skill the further back he must stand. However, for the less skilled, having to stand closer has the positive disadvantage of restricted peripheral vision. At the closer ranges it is difficult to see the two end traps simultaneously and it is easy to get caught out. Martin was brilliant at it, and two of the Portuguese shooters tried to persuade him to take it up professionally. Strangely, it is the only shooting sport at which it is possible to earn a living. That year there was a total of £5 million in prize money on the circuit, without the additional betting which is even more important. I was all for becoming Martin's manager, as he was too young to hold a driving licence I could take him to all the venues. His mother protested that he had to go to university after school and my suggestion was totally unacceptable!

I am ashamed to say that we spent almost every afternoon of our holiday at the shooting ground, although we did make an effort to see something else of the district in the mornings. In truth, not being a golfer, there was not much else to see, and my abiding memory of the country is one of dust, flies, heat, mangy dogs and idiots on motor scooters.

On our return we went to see my friend Ingram Capper, the owner of the yacht *Shemaun*, who had been an Olympic rifleman and had himself shot on the live pigeon circuit in the Fifties.

He told us that if you are a really good shot a substantial living can be earned, but we should appreciate that live pigeons whilst not particularly difficult to hit were frighteningly easy to miss and he didn't think that any responsible parent should send their son down that route! My suggestion had not been entirely tongue-in-cheek, but both Martin and I accepted that we had best drop the idea.

Marion was not very impressed with Turnpike Farm,

lacking as it was the creature comforts she had been used to at Holbeach, and indeed had every right to expect from me. She was particularly unimpressed with the comforts provided in the house compared to those outside for the animals! I attempted to justify this shortcoming by explaining that greenhouses and horses had always come first in my previous life. Nothing empties pockets faster than horses and greenhouses; the demands of both are always insatiable so the house always had to take second place.

We set about rectifying the situation, and with the guidance of a very good but eccentric architect, Turnpike Farm was gutted and completely refurbished. In the process we discovered many features from the past which had been hidden. Winnie, the architect, and Tony, the builder, produced a beautiful re-creation of the original house from the middle ages. It was finished just before our wedding day, which was fixed to coincide with my fiftieth birthday. The ceremony took place in Dereham and was a small and private affair. We had a lovely honeymoon in the Yorkshire Dales, staying at Knaresborough. On the morning after our wedding, we woke up to the first snows of winter; the countryside never looked more beautiful than on that sunny morning. A walk along the beach at Whitby, though, proved altogether too bracing for Marion, who had to be revived with copious shots of brandy!

This was all very well but I was now fifty and needed to earn a respectable living. The fuel additive project appeared to be going nowhere and certainly was not in sight of producing any dividend. I had gone back to my beloved commodities but only in a minor way. The risk/reward ratio had shrunk dramatically and with no 'base' income, I could see that life would quickly become financially uncomfortable, for what few money-making skills I possessed lay in activities which were dying out. The only thing I could come up with was to go back to the flower trade, hook into cheaper supplies from Holland, and see if we could make a go of either wholesaling or retailing. The former generated a huge cash flow but it was difficult to make anything stick. A lot of our flowers came from Spain via Holland, and one morning I received a phone call asking if I could undertake seventeen table decorations for the Spanish flower and fruit importers' conference at the Inn on the Park. I had at some stage let someone know that Marion was a very good flower arranger, but I was far from certain whether this type of thing would be within her capabilities. During the conversation I found out a bit more and it seemed fairly straightforward. The colour scheme was orange and yellow carnations combined with oranges, tangerines and lemons.

I said I would ask my wife, and went into the house from my office and enquired, 'Will you do seventeen table decorations in a pub?'

She readily agreed and so I took the job on. After I had put the phone down, she said, 'Where is this pub?'

'The Inn on the Park in Park Lane,' I replied.

Her reply is not printable. However we did the job and it was an outstanding success. The management at the Inn on the Park were really helpful and cooperative; nothing was too much trouble for them. On the back of this successful venture we had the order to do a far larger function for the same organisation in the Savoy Ballroom. This was a tricky one as the Savoy had their own florist. I managed to smooth any ruffled feathers successfully as they had been good customers of mine in the Seventies. We had a long session with the banqueting manager during which we discussed the colour scheme and established they had the correct coloured tablecloths available. He was adamant that we could not start before nine a.m. and we had to be finished by six p.m. the same evening. We were clearly going to be against the clock in a big way. The biggest single task was shaping and decorating forty-two very large melons! They all had to be 'gutted' and stuffed with foam before we could even start. We had enlisted the help of Marion's friend, Penny, who in a previous life as the wife of a turkey producer had prepared the birds for sale at

Christmas. She assured us there was no difference between gutting a turkey and gutting a melon!

With much hilarity we had a practice run at home and got the time for each operation down sufficiently to feel that we could achieve the target.

We got as far ahead as we could the night before; I had conditioned all the flowers so that they were in peak condition and we loaded everything into a large hired van which Marion and I were to travel down to London in, meeting Penny there. We were going to leave at five a.m. to arrive about eight thirty. At about seven o'clock that evening it started to snow; this was all we needed. The forecast was not that bad, but even so I felt we should bring our departure time forward to about three a.m. We went to catch a few hours' sleep and duly left at three a.m. The snow had all gone and we had an excellent run down arriving at The Savoy at seven a.m., only to be told that we still couldn't come in until nine! By a stroke of extreme good fortune the night porter was not only a Norfolk man but like us, from Dereham as well. He pulled the necessary strings and we were in.

We had made a good start and were well on schedule when the staff appeared to start laying up the tables. We were horrified when bright pink linen was produced instead of the promised cream. At the end of a fairly heated discussion when I was told there was no cream linen and we'd have to change the flowers; I 'lost it'. There was clearly no solution so both parties just carried on. We finished at bang on six o'clock, the girls had done a wonderful job, and apart from the clash of colours I was well satisfied. It was amazing what the girls had done with melons, black grapes, orchids, lilac and carnations – to name but a few.

Having loaded all the rubbish and spare materials into the van we went up to the bar to have a much needed drink. I had left my tie in the van so was not allowed in! The organisers were delighted with everything and asked if we would do some more. I think I said at the Inn on the Park yes, but at the Savoy

– never. A pointless gesture, probably, but we have since been to stay at the Inn on the Park and had drinks there on odd occasions, but have never set foot in the Savoy again.

Despite the aggravation at the Savoy, we enjoyed the challenge and did wonder whether retail work might have something to offer. We didn't have long to wait before we heard that the Harrods' flower shop was being franchised out. Harrods had been very good customers of mine over the years, being probably second only to Moyses Stevens in their off take. By now Monica Simonds had sold the Berkeley Square shop and retired. I decided to talk to her about the Harrods franchise and see if she would give me some assistance. She kindly invited Marion and me to her flat; the first thing I noticed was a huge picture of our sweet peas in Buckingham Palace over the mantelpiece in her drawing room.

I had never actually seen the photograph before, even in miniature, and by the time she had told us it was one of the best jobs she had ever done for the Palace I felt very proud and only so sorry that Jacqueline had never seen it. Her advice was to be sure we really wanted to go to Harrods, as all her information was that it could prove to be a bed of nails for whoever took it on. We had a long discussion and eventually arrived at a figure that it might be worth. We made an appointment with the general manager, who outlined his requirements. I think we satisfied him with our hopes, ambitions and ability to carry them out, especially as we would be retaining the existing staff. I put in the bid we had discussed with Monica Simonds but we were not successful.

Penny's husband, Mike, did large and successful business with Debenhams in another field, and told us that they already had a flourishing flower franchise in Ipswich. He had heard on the grapevine that they would be receptive to an approach to open some more in the Midlands. I felt it was worth trying to talk to them, as by now we were both getting to like the idea, and were rather disappointed by the Harrods result.

I met the Debenhams manager responsible for franchises

and was offered a trial site at King's Lynn. I cannot pretend to have been particularly enthused; it was a very small store and having seen the store manager we nearly didn't start. However, I realised that it was probably quite a good opening and elected to give it our best shot.

At the end of the six-week trial we must have done quite well as we were offered additional sites at Nottingham, Bedford, Luton and Harrow, with the promise that if these were successful we could move into their Oxford Street store, when its refurbishment was complete the following spring. I appointed a manager to control this operation who had experience of the general retail scene but who, on his own admission, knew nothing about flowers. He did know about spreadsheets, though, and my ignorance of their limitations combined with his enthusiasm for them was to set us on a very slippery slope. He managed to bring Beatties of Northampton into the fold, which as this was his home town and Beatties were a class operation, put a feather in his cap straight away.

The only two things I was worried about were staffing and the suitability of a department store as an environment for flowers. Graham, our new manager, assumed responsibility for recruiting staff, having decided that retail experience was the first requirement, with some general flower knowledge second. We were tapping into the new marketplace where the bulk sale of product was more important than the art of floristry. After all, the garages and supermarkets were doing it, leaving the artistry to the high street florists, so why shouldn't we? Beatties wanted us to start operations on July 1st and Debenhams a month later.

Both parties were aware that July marked the beginning of the 'kipper' season, but agreed that it would give us all a good run-in before the Christmas and New Year period.

Marion and I borrowed a flat from a friend of Martin's in Verbier in the Swiss Alps for a well-deserved holiday before launching into our new venture. We were going to drive out and take a full two-week break. I had had my Volvo serviced before setting out, only for it to break down with fuel starvation as soon as it came out of the garage. A replacement fuel pump made no difference; a second replacement pump made no difference, and by this time we decided that even if the problem was solved the next day we did not have sufficient time to drive out. We flew out to Geneva and then took the train to Verbier, hoping and praying we could first of all find the flat and secondly that the key would fit. We had not fully grasped the fact that although the winter season was obviously over, the summer season had not begun! The resort was almost totally deserted, with no tourist staff left at all.

Absolutely nobody spoke English, and despite the fact that thirty years had elapsed since I had had to speak French I quickly realised that unless I could reactivate my schoolboy brain we would probably starve. I was surprised how much recall one has when one has to, and actually managed quite well. We had a lovely time in the mountains and returned to England reinvigorated for whatever lay in front of us.

CHAPTER XXV

The Retail Experience

Marion and myself opened the operation at Beatties, generating quite a bit of interest. At the end of the third week we handed over to the staff who had been selected to run it. The logistics of getting Dutch flowers from Aalsmeer to Northampton worked smoothly, and we ourselves moved into the Arndale Centre in Luton. Martin opened up the outlet at Harrow, and I left Graham and his assistant to oversee the opening of Nottingham and Bedford. We were very surprised at the wide variation in the modus operandi of the stores, their facilities and the attitude of the store managers. None of the sites had had any experience at all of perishables, nor indeed understanding of their special needs, especially the need to sell out on Saturday evenings. The stock levels diminished all through the day and this was the first conflict we had, as of course Debenhams' philosophy for all their usual lines was to keep the stands fully stocked. The crunch always came on a Monday when our delivery did not reach us until lunchtime. The only way we could get round this was to keep a small stock of the least perishable items, such as chrysanthemums, in the stockroom, hot as it was over the weekend, to display on Monday morning. The biggest problem, though, was water supply and the presence of water in the selling area.

Luton turned out to be a very successful venture and sales were miles in front of any of the others, in part due to the presence of us two, but equally because we enjoyed a phenomenal 'traffic flow' past the site. The Arndale Centre was the only one of our sites where we had staff capable of running it as a florist's shop as opposed to simply a flower-selling operation. A trained florist, Lisa, applied for a job as soon as we opened and it wasn't long before we realised that the added value of Marion's arrangements, coupled with Lisa's floristry and make-up skills, were the key to prosperity. Straight flower sales were generally, especially in the 'kipper' season, little more than two halfpennies for a penny. After a few weeks it was quite clear that Luton was carrying all the other outlets, and attempts to find a trained florist for each of the others had produced nobody promising. However, when I suggested pulling out of these smaller ones it went down like the proverbial lead balloon. Our presence was clearly far more beneficial to Debenhams than to ourselves, and if we wanted to graduate to Oxford Street, we had to hang in there.

We both found working in such an environment stressful in the extreme. The store management didn't help; they were totally without any sense of humour, and precious little humanity either. An added irritation was that right over the top of our pitch was one of the monitors on which was played, continuously throughout the day, various promotional videos. Almost fifteen years later I can still hear the inane jingle and clearly see the equally inane model. The ultimate frustration, though, was the drawing and disposal of water for the flowers. The only source of water was the staff loos – and female ones at that. Over ninety-five per cent of the staff were female, and I never actually found a men's loo all the time we were there.

I fulfilled the twin roles of 'gaffer' and 'gopher'. The latter consisted almost entirely of chief bucket emptier, washer and refiller. It was awful. I had to be so careful not to drop even the smallest drip of water in the store or the management would have a fit and point out the risk of a customer slipping on it – and this was before the compensation culture had even started! It was always most embarrassing doing this task in the ladies', although the girls themselves were far less embarrassed than I was, and I did my level best to use the off-peak times. After a few days I learned that the girls had a fairly well-defined loo routine and they were on the whole good-natured about it. In the beginning I used to empty the buckets down the pan and flush the whole lot away. However, one day the store manager sent for me as one of the girls had filed a complaint about a pan full of flowers she had to perform on. I then discovered that carnation trimmings wouldn't flush at all, so all carnation detritus had to be picked out first.

In moments of quiet reflection I appreciated that I had come down rather a long way in the world. I used to think quite often about the officers in *Trenchant* and compare them to the management of Debenhams, and the comparison was not favourable. I was determined to see this through as a matter of pride and principle, and contented myself with the thought that this was a situation of my own choosing. It had been my decision alone to leave the Royal Navy and my own pig-headedness to pursue a horticultural career, so it was no good whingeing. Life, after all, is not a dress rehearsal, and who can say whether I would have had as good a life anywhere else? Debenhams was a temporary blip, I assured myself; after all, I didn't imagine there were too many Old Etonians working on the shop floor in the organisation, and no doubt the management found it as difficult to put up with me as I did with them...

There were many consolations, though, and we had our good and humorous times as well. The girls on the shop floor were all lovely and we struck up good friendships while we were there, as indeed we did with our customers. The business was good, and for one week the Arndale management offered us their prime pitch in the epicentre of the complex. I had of course to clear it with Debenhams, and ended up having to pay them a percentage of our take in the podium to make up for any sales they might lose in the main store. That was our best ever week of retailing. It was very hard work, but immensely rewarding. By now the strain was beginning to tell, but we hung in there with the promise of Oxford Street to come soon, and then I felt I could shed the losers if they didn't come good: Oxford Street added to the Luton Arndale Centre should make a nice little business. Valentine's Day was of course a big occasion, and could be very profitable, always provided you judged the red rose market correctly. This actually became harder year-on-year as every conceivable retail outlet sold red roses on this occasion with an opportunist eye on the fast buck.

As demand went up so did the price, not as the popular press put around every year because the growers are greedy, but because there is another far more special day which overlaps it, the Chinese New Year. Marion and I were in Covent Garden (Nine Elms) by two o'clock in the morning and had made arrangements with the night security staff at Debenhams to get into the store at five a.m. to start unpacking, trimming and packaging all the flowers; but especially important were the roses. At eight a.m., while still breakfastless, round the corner comes the store manager – never an easy woman to handle – who made her displeasure at our not consulting her about entry out of hours very clear indeed! At the end of a very successful trading day I was begrudgingly forgiven.

I was getting impatient to get into Oxford Street in time for Mother's Day and was eventually summoned to view the site. I always accepted that we couldn't expect a prime site in such a prestigious place, but was quite unprepared for the abomination of location we had been given and declined to accept it. It could never have worked, for a whole variety of reasons. In the meantime Debenhams undertook to see if they could come up with somewhere more acceptable. I went back to Luton rather confused and disappointed, wondering where we went from there. I didn't have long to wait to find out. For the last few weeks we had endured a number of bomb alerts – all incendiary devices planted in the fur department, which was next to us. The head of maintenance had been complaining for weeks that he couldn't get permission to replace a faulty component in the sprinkler system, which, even knowing retailers' aversion to spending money on maintenance, seemed a bit short-sighted, in view of the activities of the Animal Liberation movement. We only had a very small pitch, and had once or twice been pulled up for having plants overhanging the pathway by a few inches. The assistant manager found our stand one day with the leaves of a spreading plant overhanging the path by six inches and announced he was going to charge us for using 'air space'.

I think I told him to perform an unnatural act upon himself, and we agreed in his office later that we should part company, as soon as a successor was found. We were to be kicked out the week before Mother's Day and the new operators would retain our girls. I was furious on the first count but pleased on the second. We had built up an excellent team of girls and we all worked well together, although Marion and I were only going at weekends by this stage. When I told them the news they all cried and announced they would leave too. I begged them not to, as there was no point in cutting off their noses to spite their faces. Some walked out on the spot, some stayed. A few weeks later I learned from Lisa that someone (not me, I swear!) had firebombed our stand and the next-door fur department. The sprinkler system didn't work, and the whole store was burned to the ground and out of action for a year.

We went back to Norfolk with our tails between our legs. Both Martin and I needed to earn some money, so I started up another wholesale round as I had done some twenty years earlier, while seeing what was to come next. David, meanwhile, in addition to his First Class Honours degree in law at Oxford, had won a scholarship to UCLA in Los Angeles. He was to take Joanne, his bride-to-be, with him, not only as company but to earn some money to support them with. Seven weeks before departure Joanne had had her visa application turned down. The only way she could get one was for her and David to get married. We were given six weeks by David to organise his 'shotgun' wedding from Turnpike Farm, complete with marquee on the lawn. We did all the catering ourselves, with considerable help from our neighbours, especially Maisie Parfitt. Our ex-florist from Luton, Lisa (in a heavily pregnant state), did all the floristry, including the bride's bouquet, whilst Marion did the floral arrangements in the church and the marquee. Martin arranged for one of George Cushing's mobile fairground organs to be in attendance. All was set fair and Foxley Church was full. As many of the guests were shooting friends, four of them were instructed to bring their guns so that with me and Martin, and Henry and John from the village, we could form a guard of honour with crossed shotguns. The vicar thought it a bit unusual but raised no objection. In preparation I had had our septic tank pumped out, and I removed all valuables from the house, as a large percentage of the guests were unknown to me.

Marion thought I was being provocative but I convinced her it was a sensible precaution. I made one mistake in that I retrieved our camera from its hiding place for a quick batch of photographs in the marquee. Instinctively, I put it back on the corner of the sideboard where it always lived and it was never seen again.

Real disaster was soon to strike; I had totally underestimated how quickly the septic tank was going to fill up, and less than an hour into the reception the loos were all overflowing. John Parfitt kindly went to get a submersible pump, I found a suitable length of hose and there we both were in our morning dress suits pumping the overflow into the storm water drains, about which there had been so much controversy a few years before. That problem having been sorted, I went up to our bedroom for something and found one of the guests going through my clothes. He said he was looking for an earring which he had lost. Now, young men with earrings were not to my taste so I threw him out. It transpired he was one of the bride's relatives and I was not the flavour of the night, especially when on going to bed I found the missing earring on the chair!

Apart from these minor mishaps we all survived and the day was pronounced a success. Lisa stayed the night with us, giving us a blow-by-blow account of the Debenhams fire, which we both assured each other we had nothing to do with. We took her round the sights of Norfolk in the morning and she decided to stay another night and have supper with us. By late afternoon she was complaining of back pains, and although only seven months pregnant she gave Marion sufficient concern for her to take her to our doctor in Fakenham. He thought it was the first signs of labour and booked her into the maternity wing of the Norfolk & Norwich Hospital.

On her return to Foxley, Marion made me take Lisa in as I knew the way far better than she did, and she would wait for Susan to come in from work. I am pleased there were no speed cameras in those days. I really did think she was going to have her baby car in the car by the time we actually reached Norwich! She was whisked straight off to the ward while I had to fill in the papers. This was a huge embarrassment, as I didn't know her precise address and I didn't even know her mother's or father's name. I didn't know who the father of the child was – in fact I didn't know anything. By this time some more nurses had appeared at the desk and I felt I was rapidly being branded as some kind of pervert. However, this feeling was nothing compared to that with which I was greeted on the ward.

Nobody would tell me anything, as they couldn't work out my connection with Lisa, although they had their suspicions. I had a horrid feeling that something was badly wrong. A little while later it transpired that the baby had died. Nothing in life had prepared me for this. The nurses clearly regarded me as a suspicious character. Lisa wouldn't let me tell her parents, and she wanted me to stay with her and not leave her alone in this strange place. In those days there were no mobile phones, just one public call box, which I had to queue for to ring Marion. I eventually escaped at three a.m. I decided I couldn't *not* tell Lisa's parents, and they collected her from hospital the next day. She decided to name the baby after Marion, so at least the poor little thing had a name to be buried with.

David and Joanne arrived safely in the States and we were to join them a year later for a two-week holiday.

Unusually for me, battle hardened as I was to everything going wrong, I suffered a bout of depression after this incident and just wanted to get the hell out of anything and everything remotely agricultural.

I plodded on with our van sales, wondering how much lower I could go. The only glimmer of hope on the horizon was the planning application I had put in to develop our substantial garden for housing. I didn't like the idea, but then as now, the only realistic chance of putting serious money into one's pocket was windfall planning consent or winning (in those days) the 'pools'. The application was submitted in the Autumn of 1987 and the indications were that it would be successful. I sold off the van round for a nominal sum and headed off for a two-week holiday with David and Joanne in Los Angeles.

I had a vague expectation that this nation of free enterprise might give us some ideas of where to go next.

CHAPTER XXVI

Chasing the Dream

California exceeded all our expectations; we loved it, all of it, all of the time. We were very fortunate to have not only David and Joanne to guide us but also Olivia de Havilland's husband, Pierre, who was staying at the Beverley Hills Hotel. Olivia is a distant cousin of mine and she had very kindly arranged for Pierre and us to meet. He filled in the gaps that David hadn't and we were able to avoid the hiatus of where to go and what to do, which helped us to fill our time to the full. Pierre introduced us to Gladstone's Restaurant and the joys of Southern Fried Catfish as well as Hollywood Studios, Malibu Beach, Santa Barbara and the Pacific Highway. The studio was a slight disappointment, as the sets were all much smaller than I had imagined. On the other hand window-shopping in Rodeo Drive was an unbelievable experience. We spent several days amongst the yachts belonging to the 'beautiful people' at Marina del Rey. The Californian girls who were in abundance at the yacht club more than lived up to my expectations; even if they were all silicone they were still lovely. By the time we had been to Palm Springs, Disney Land and so on, our two weeks had gone all too quickly. Before we finally left Marina del Rey I picked up a leaflet on sharing a yacht. I had nothing specific in mind but felt it might be useful.

On our last night David and Joanne took us to Monty's, a very agreeable restaurant overlooking LA. Two events there left their mark. First, the flow of traffic generated smog lying like a thick blanket over the whole town. Secondly, the black rock singer in the restaurant was wonderful, particularly in his rendition of 'Rocking all over the World'.

We returned home in time for Christmas and very early in the New Year got the formal approval of our planning application. This was excellent news as the financial pot was now to be topped up again. Pulling out the leaflet from America on sharing a yacht, I felt the need to investigate. I didn't have any clear idea of what I was looking for except that I wanted to go 'boating' again. I put an advert in *Motor Boat & Yachting* and received an answer from a Greek gentleman, living in England, with two yachts he wanted to sell in Piraeus.

Eventually we were on a plane to Athens where we were met by Andreas and driven to Piraeus, where we would spend three nights on another of his yachts while he entertained us royally and made every effort to sell *Princess Krita.*

The first morning we saw *Krita,* Andreas left us on board to have a thorough look around. We took a few hours and were a little disappointed by her slightly shabby interior but felt this could soon be rectified. The important thing was the state of the hull and the engines. We go to sea the next morning for a short cruise round the Greek islands to prove everything was in working order. The smell of the sea, the teak decks underfoot, a glorious spring day with warm sun and a gentle breeze... and I was losing my soul to *Krita.*

I took the wheel for a time and was able to confirm that steering a ship is a skill that once learned is never forgotten.

In the evening I floated my ideas for yacht-share over him and found he was quite supportive. I gained the distinct impression, though, that his only real enthusiasm was for selling his yacht. I was not sufficiently impressed with *Krita* to pursue her any further. Even so, I still felt there might be something in the yacht-share idea, although I wasn't sure quite what. Further research was needed, so we chartered *Circus,* an eighty-three foot Italian built motor yacht for three weeks in Puerto Banus, on the Costa del Sol, partly for our own enjoyment and partly to see if there were any commercial possibilities. *Circus* came with a crew of four: Manuel, the captain; his wife, the cook; Jacques the steward; and a deckhand. Our party was Marion and myself, Martin, our youngest, and two friends. Our brokers, Brett and Angela, gave us a royal welcome and had also arranged temporary accommodation, as *Circus* was not due to arrive until the next day. The arrival in harbour of 'our very own' yacht was a momentous occasion marred only by the Captain's refusal to allow us on board until exactly noon when the charter officially started. Brett had arranged a berth on 'Millionaires' Row' exactly opposite Christian's restaurant. Christian's was to become a regular haunt where we indulged in their fish soup and profiteroles. Returning fifteen years later, Christian's was still there, serving the best fish soup and profiteroles in the world. But that morning, knowing that we had never actually seen *Circus,* we couldn't wait to get on board.

Walking over the stern gangway we entered a really luxurious saloon, with the 'owner's' stateroom immediately below, the galley for'ard and access to the number two stateroom and two twin-berth cabins below that, with crew accommodation in the bows. This latter was in total contrast to ours and we all felt immediately guilty. Marion and I took the main stateroom as we were to be on board the whole three weeks. Our friends took the smaller stateroom as they were only there for the first week. Ours was luxury to a standard I had never even dreamed about, with a huge double bed and 'his' and 'hers' separate bathrooms. On the upper deck was an open wheelhouse with a deck below and behind it for sunbathing and/or posing, from which the whole port area was clearly visible. The local press turned up in the form of Cheryl, the very young owner of the local paper.

Cheryl owned a fast 'Cigarette' speedboat and invited Marion and me and two friends, Peter and Judy, who had joined us from England for their birthday celebrations, for a trip along the coast. We found her and her craft at the jetty on the appointed hour and I was somewhat surprised to find her clad in nothing but a G-string – and then only just. She had been a gymnast with the GB team some years earlier and had developed that figure which appears to be specific to female gymnasts. Cheryl drove, I was secured in the bucket seat next to her, while Marion, Peter and Judy sat behind. We had a most exhilarating trip and after half an hour she asked if I would like to change places with her. This would have entailed squeezing past that deliciously naked posterior, which left absolutely nothing to the imagination, and I really felt I couldn't handle that, so reluctantly declined the invitation.

Puerto Banus is a totally unreal world, but enormous fun with a never ending social scene. The port was full of yachts, varying from unbelievable luxury down to quite ordinary 'fun' boats.

Bars and restaurants, fashion and jewellery boutiques were in abundance. We made many short-term friends and took some of them for trips along the coast and out to sea to see the dolphins on several occasions; always with an eye on yacht-share possibilities. One day Brett asked us if we would like to make *Circus* available to the *Wish You Were Here* team to do some filming from. If we were agreeable, I was to contact Judith Chalmers to tie up the operation. I met her in her hotel over breakfast, a meal we both agreed was the most important of the day. The next day Judith, Anneka Rice, John Carter and a camera crew arrived on board to do their stuff. What a delightful trio they turned out to be.

One day in Brett's office I was introduced to Captain Stewart, an old friend of his who was skippering a yacht for Sheik Jebere, also on Millionaires' Row a few boats away from us. Apparently there was a small cocktail party on board two or three nights each week, which we were invited to join the following evening at eight thirty. Marion and I turned up and were met at the gangway by a delightfully eccentric man who could only be described as the Prince of Ruritania! I introduced us both and the conversation flowed freely. When he heard my name he immediately asked whether I had any connection with the aircraft company, as he apparently used to race in the Mille Miglia, which older readers will remember as a murderous road race, with 'Cat's Eyes' Cunningham, de Havilland's chief test pilot, as co-driver. John Cunningham himself never confirmed this story but on this particular occasion it made for good conversation. We quickly established that we had both been to Eton and he was the brother of the current Queen of Belgium. We were both getting on like a house on fire when the Sheik arrived. Captain Stewart made the introductions, and we must have given a reasonable account of ourselves as we were invited back to his palace in the hills behind Marbella for supper the following evening; he would send a car for us at eight o'clock.

Captain Stewart briefed us as best he could but nothing could have prepared me for what was to come. At eight o'clock sharp, an enormous stretched Mercedes with blacked-out windows arrived. The driver got out, and a more sinister gentleman I have yet to meet. He *was* 'Oddjob', he *was* Korean, and he *was* wearing a bowler hat! He didn't speak but made an unmistakable gesture to get in. Marion was convinced we would never be seen again, and I was none too sure either. Up into the hills we went, and on approaching the palace we were surrounded by security guards, all carrying AK47s, and eventually ushered into the 'presence'.

The Sheik was the perfect host; there were only the three of us for supper, apart from the girl whose sole job was to change the tapes in his music centre, and his pilot, who arrived after we had eaten. We sat down to enough food for at least forty people. We had a fresh lobster each, with all the trimmings, and goodness knows what all the rest was. We ate our fill but had made no impression at all on the table. He must have noticed our concern at the apparent waste but assured us it would go to the household staff and guards. We had an interesting conversation, and he volunteered to talk about his family, his wives, his houses and palaces and his friends. He pointed to a photograph of Adnan Kashoggi, the international arms dealer, whom he described as his greatest friend. He was not a royal Sheik but was very friendly with

King Fahd; in fact they had adjacent palaces in Morocco. He had two children, both of whom were a disappointment to him; a staff of seventy, including forty whom he described as his travelling staff; five wives and was about to marry a sixth, whom he had unexpectedly got pregnant.

All this was supported by a personal disposable income of three and a half million $US a *month*. He was finding it difficult to manage on this and had had to reduce his travelling staff.

He had also temporarily evicted his daughter with only limited pocket money of $18,000 a month – to try to teach her financial responsibility!

The Sheik had recently acquired Katherine Hepburn's villa on the beach at Marbella and would be pleased if we – quite clearly meaning Marion – would care to join him for a swim in the morning, in the pool. We would be collected at eleven o'clock.

It was getting late by now and 'Oddjob' returned us to *Circus*. We were both speechless; there seemed nothing to say.

In the morning I reminded Marion that it was her he was leching after, and was she sure she wanted me to come? Oddjob collected us as planned and we were greeted warmly by the Sheik. The pool was surrounded by parrots and hawks, each on a stand, as we see so often in films. Marion and I swam around, although I felt more like a chaperone than a husband, whilst under the continuous eye of our host. It was on this occasion that he announced he would be going to his palace in Tangiers in ten days' time, and would we like to come for a few days? I said that much as we would like to we were due to go back to England by then. He was most disappointed and said that he would be happy to fly us back to Marbella in his private plane if it would save time. I thanked him for the offer and said we would be pleased to accept it, as in any case, having already had a peep into Aladdin's cave, I felt we might as well go right inside and might even meet King Fahd, who by then was in residence next door.

We enjoyed and reciprocated hospitality from and with other owners on Millionaires' Row. Two berths away was the massive *Galaxy Star* with a young potential owner, who like us had hired it for a while until he made up his mind whether to purchase or not. It transpired he had a chemical spraying business in Scotland so we had quite a lot in common. Being fairly conversant with agricultural economics, something did not ring true, and he eventually disclosed that land he also farmed had very rich seams of exceptionally high grade silica sand, the sale of which was to fund the purchase of *Galaxy*. He eventually decided to go ahead, and I said a few days later to Bill Thiem, Brett's assistant broker, 'Well, *Galaxy* is sold, then.'

'Not yet,' said Bill. This healthy degree of cynicism turned out to be justified, as the whole project eventually collapsed.

An antique but very beautiful yacht berthed alongside us and we were soon chatting to the owner, a well-tanned man of late middle age with a stunningly attractive lady of what appeared to be South American extraction. I invited him and his wife on board the next evening, which he accepted for himself only, as his companion was leaving in the morning to go back to London. I asked him if he was joining her later. He said, 'Oh no, she is not my wife – just an escort girl I hired to come around the world with me for six months!'

It was now time for our trip to Tangiers to stay with Sheik Jebere. On the morning of departure we were driven to Gibraltar where we caught the ferry to Tangiers. As soon as we arrived in Tangiers harbour I realised I had made a most basic error, having only bought one-way tickets.

Sure enough, immigration wanted to see the return half and then followed an unpleasant few minutes. 'Why are you here?' they asked. When I explained that we had come to see Sheik Jebere I got the Arabic version of 'pull the other one, sunshine'. I explained he was a friend of ours and pointed out his yacht on the other side of the harbour.

'Oh yes, *we* know it's his yacht... let's see if *he* knows you,' was the reply.

We were then frogmarched with all our luggage in stifling heat around the harbour, knowing that the Sheik was almost certainly in his palace, and entirely reliant for identification on Captain Stewart being on board. I prayed and prayed, *Please God, may Captain Stewart be on board.* For what seemed like an eternity, during which I tried to visualise the inside of an Arab jail, no one appeared. Just as I had almost given up hope the Captain appeared. 'Oh yes, these are friends of Sheik Jebere,' he said.

What a change of attitude! Bowings, scrapings, apologies... *Bastards*, I thought.

A call was put through to the palace and about fifteen minutes later a brand new black turbo Bentley arrived for us. The Sheik had a fetish for cars, owning more than two hundred; they were all used on a rota so that each one was out at least once a month. We were driven first of all to our hotel, where we left our luggage. The Sheik had paid for everything we were assured, and we were to enjoy our stay.

The driver – not Oddjob – waited for us to freshen up and then drove us to the Sheik's palace. We passed an old man with his worldly possessions on a donkey, and Marion said, 'Don't you feel guilty?' I could only reply, 'All I feel is relief that we are not in jail!'

We were greeted by the Sheik in the warmest possible manner. After coffee he asked if we would like to meet his new wife, whom he had married the day before. He apologised for her being ill, and asked if we minded meeting her in bed. She was an absolutely charming lady who made us feel so welcome. She had a long conversation with us in so easy a manner that we felt we had known her forever. The poor girl in fact had a miscarriage a few days later.

Later we had a small private lunch and learned that the Sheik's business colleagues were arriving that afternoon. We learned a bit more about him, and how his father had been a small trader supplying bits and pieces to the early oilmen, and from that had grown the current oil trading company. He did an enormous amount of business with Shell, and the visitors would be a mixture of his own and Shell employees.

After lunch, whilst drinking coffee, I was aware of some commotion in the trees and sure enough there was a sheep being killed, later strung up to be skinned. I suggested to Marion that this was probably tomorrow's lunch. Indeed it was. The Sheik asked us if we would like to see round his extensive refurbishment works, explaining at the same time that this was why we were all in hotels rather than living in. We naturally concurred, whereupon he summoned a French Moroccan serving girl, wrapped in what I can only describe as a brown blanket, to show us round. There were lots of mini-palaces for various family and wives, and when we got to one particular one she said, 'This is my sister's palace.'

I was cheeky enough to enquire why her sister qualified for a palace, 'She is the Sheik's new wife,' came the reply. So much for the Moroccan serving girl! Allowing for the fact that French Moroccan girls are amongst the most beautiful in the world, this one was, despite the blanket, something very special indeed. The major part of the works, apart from the mini-palaces, involved a mosaic archway costing four million US dollars. It was all quite bizarre but promised to be an interesting couple of days.

We were taken back to our hotel, where a taxi was organised to take us to the cocktail party on the yacht, where we were to meet the Sheik's visitors.

There were twenty-three of us on board and conversation flowed freely and easily, although the Sheik himself was not a great conversationalist. The party broke up at eleven o'clock and when we emerged onto the dockside there was a fleet of twelve turbo Bentleys to take us all back to our hotels and the Sheik himself to his palace.

He confirmed that we were expected for lunch the next day and would be collected at midday. We were to check out and take our bags to another hotel en route to the palace.

We were duly dropped off at our hotel, but were absolutely

starving, having had nothing to eat on board, only canapés, drink and tobacco. The hotel had stopped serving food, so we trudged the back streets of Tangiers looking for the Moroccan equivalent of fish and chips and ended up with curried chicken and rice in a paper bag, which we ate on the end of the bed.

We went to sleep that night wondering whether we were dreaming and trying to guess what tomorrow had in store. All the transport arrangements worked and we arrived at the palace for lunch. The business meeting was still in progress, so we were given pre-lunch drinks by the Sheik's secretary, and she entertained us until the meeting was over. After a short interval for some more pre-prandial drinks we went in to lunch.

The Sheik escorted Marion in to sit between him and his brother at the head of the table. I was right, yesterday's sheep was on the menu; the head, boiled, complete with orange in its mouth, eyeballs intact and surrounded by boiled rice, fixed Marion with its sightless eyes. The rest of the sheep had been roasted over a spit and was at our end of the table. The same people who had been at the party the night before were at the lunch, and except for Marion, the Sheik and his brother, we could all look forward to a good meal of roast lamb. Each guest had a personal waiter to keep the glasses and the plates full. The Sheik kept offering Marion various delicacies which she refused, but eventually realising she had to eat something, said 'yes' to one proffered dish.

'A very good choice, my dear, they were flown in specially from Jeddah this morning.'

To give her credit she was managing to get it down, although not enjoying it. 'They' turned out to have been camel's testicles! After that she settled for a little boiled meat and rice, whilst the two brothers extracted the eyeballs, ate them, and then tackled the eye sockets and rest of the face with two-pronged forks. From my end of the table they reminded me of a pair of carrion crows on a moor pecking at a sheep's carcase. We fed very well at our end of the table, but every one of the men felt sorry for Marion, and greatly admired her courage.

After lunch the Sheik presented the women – there were two others there – with a kaftan apiece. Marion naturally had first choice and chose a pale blue and gold one, saying, 'Thank you so much, Sheik Jebere, I will wear it for the farewell banquet tonight.'

At this his eyes came out on stalks and he said, 'Thank you very much, I look forward to seeing you in it.'

Back we went to the new hotel where we had a quick forty winks to get our strength up for the finale. I was having a shave when I heard a shout from Marion. 'I'm not wearing this – it's see-through!'

By this time I had got fully on board that the Sheik was an extremely heavy guy in Tangiers. Whilst he undoubtedly leched after Marion, he was always the perfect gentleman and I certainly did not want to offend him.

I asked the hotel manager for advice with our problem. He said, 'We Arabs like to see Westerners in Arab dress, but more importantly if your wife promised Sheik Jebere she would wear it, it would be best if she did.'

Marion was defiant and said, 'Okay, but I will wear it totally see-through', which she did! On arrival at the restaurant which the Sheik had taken over for the night she was whisked away by him and introduced to the Ambassador of somewhere and the Prince of somewhere else, and spent the rest of the night with the great and the good. I spent the evening with some Australians, who were most amusing company. The tables were laid out with gigantic portions of langoustines, lobster and caviar. The latter was the genuine article; I can't imagine the cost of this lavishness. We were halfway through our first course when there was a commotion at the entrance and what appeared to be two gatecrashers charged in carrying Adidas sports bags, out of which they tipped a quantity of cobras down the central isle. This was a snake-charming act, apparently, and these snakes were everywhere. I tucked my feet under the bench, being terrified of them. I was reassured by my Australian neighbour that we should be alright. After the act was over and the snakes had all done their stuff the performers brought them round to show us. One handler was pouring blood out of a bite as he held them to our respective chins for inspection.

Next came the acrobats and tumblers, who, in a very confined space, gave an amazing and fascinating display. They were followed by the belly dancers, which again for me were fascinating, as I had never seen them performing live before, only ever on the silver screen. The final act was singing by our hostess, who was none other than the girl who had shown us round the palace. She was standing in for her sister and was the most stunningly beautiful girl, certainly, that I have ever seen. Dripping in emeralds and diamonds, she really was the million-dollar girl. I do not find oriental music remotely enjoyable, and performed by anyone else it would have been awful.

The party was over by one o'clock and we all went back to our hotels in the turbo Bentleys. The high spot of the night was the farewell kiss from our hostess, and the expression of hope that we would meet again. Sadly we never did.

After about three hours' sleep we assembled in the foyer of the hotel with the other two people travelling back to Malaga. Outside was a huge stretched Lincoln with four armchairs, one in each corner of the 'lounge', and a white Rolls-Royce. We all piled into the Lincoln and the Rolls brought our luggage. We swept through the desert in the small hours to a small airport where, after minimal customs formality, we boarded the Sheik's private aircraft for the flight to Malaga. Both the pilot and stewardess had been part of the social gatherings we had enjoyed. We landed at the Sheik's private end of the airport, said goodbye to the others, and were driven in another stretched Lincoln back to the main arrivals area.

It was altogether a quite extraordinary insight into how the other half live. Sheikh Jebere was a wealthy man by any standards, but incredibly lonely with apparently few real friends, other than Adnan Kashoggi, who regrettably we did not get to meet, as he was out of the country while we were there. A founder shareholder of BCCI bank, his business empire appeared to have a mix of what may be euphemistically described as kosher and non-kosher activities. Also he was unquestionably a man of generous disposition and doer of good works. In this respect he matched the profile of most of the owners of yachts tied up on Millionaires' Row.

We did not find any serious commercial interest in yacht-sharing, but the trip had been immense fun and I was sure that some of the seeds we had sown would germinate. Everything was alright at home, Susan had enjoyed her freedom, chaperoned from a distance by our neighbours, Jim and Jane.

I didn't have to wait long for something to turn up when suddenly out of the blue came a telephone call from an old friend who had quite recently retired from the Navy, asking if I would like to join a small party of five civilians for a day trip on an 'O' class submarine. He said it was going to do some deep diving trials in the Channel before proceeding on patrol in the North Atlantic. I leapt at the opportunity, and Marion could not contain my excitement for the few days I had to wait. Joining instructions were to report to the guardroom at HMS *Dolphin* at 0630 to sail at 0730.

I arrived at least an hour early to avoid any chance of missing the boat. Going down the forehatch and smelling the old familiar smells of thirty-five years ago was pure magic. I stayed in the control room while we got under way on the main motors, heard the changeover to main engines as we proceeded to the exercise area and then while soaking up the atmosphere came the call for Diving Stations, immediately followed by the klaxon. Whereupon the main vents were opened, the diesels fell silent and all that could be heard was the rush of air out of the ballast tanks as the seawater came in to take us down to periscope depth. The hairs on my neck stood up just as they had on my first ever trip. Once we 'fell out' after diving stations I could wander about and felt just as at home as ever. Very little had really changed at all. The most noticeable was the wearing of radio headsets combined with ear defenders for engine and motor room staff, which made communication so much easier above the deafening din of the diesels. Also the switch gear in the motor room was all enclosed instead of fully exposed as in *Trenchant*, for example. Otherwise almost nothing had changed at all. A truly magical day, and for the umpteenth time since I left the service I wondered why on earth I had. I was invited to the party that night as this was the last night in harbour for the crew, but remembering what they entailed I thought I had better not.

Sure enough some seeds sown at Puerto Banus started to germinate, but again, not at all as I had expected. I received a call from a softly spoken and obviously quite well-educated man who introduced himself as Roger. He said he had an unusual request in that he had been given my name as one who might be able to supply him with craft for special purposes. I enquired where he had got my name from, but all he would say was I clearly had some powerful friends. He declined to say any more over the phone including what these special purposes might be, but suggested we might meet in the Charing Cross Hotel in London. With my curiosity aroused, but with no little trepidation, I set off for the meeting. He told me he was representing an Australian company with interests in the Middle East who wanted to purchase up to ten craft with a capacity to carry four to five men and their equipment at a speed of at least sixty knots. This was clearly a very serious 'piece of kit' they were looking for, and I quickly came to the conclusion that the use was indeed 'special'. Over lunch he explained that he was an ex-Army man himself and specialised in sourcing various items of military hardware that fell outside the normal realms of government-to-government deals, either because of size, speciality and sometimes legality. He explained that he was not an expert in naval or air equipment but wanted to be able fill the naval part of this particular contract as it included many items which were in his field.

I knew that Tiger Marine built craft for our own Special

Forces so I said I would refer to them for guidance. He refused to give me his telephone number but said he would ring me to fix another meeting in ten days' time. I fixed up a meeting with Tiger and went with rather mixed feelings, but they were quite unfazed and calmly announced that these were for the Iranian National Guard as an upgrade for the Norwegian 'Boghammers' which had proved too slow and unmanoeuvrable against the Iraqis, and although the official war was over, the Iranians did not want to get caught again. Tiger would not be able to supply themselves as they were too involved with our MOD. This all sounded highly dodgy, but when I mentioned it to Brett, our broken from Puerto Banus, in one of our frequent conversations he was highly excited and thought he knew someone in France who would be seriously interested.

Roger did ring again and I had another meeting with him and a colleague, again at the Charing Cross Hotel. I told them about Brett's French contact. They were very interested in this as the French were much easier to deal with having few, if any, moral principles. An 'interesting' two weeks in Marseilles and Paris ensued, during which time I became sucked into the vortex of illegal arms sales to a 'proscribed' country. I encountered a mountain of plausible bullshit, parted with considerable upfront fees, always with the promise that 'we were getting there'. We never did, of course; my nerve eventually failing me when I realised that these vessels could have been used against the Royal Navy. I bailed out of the whole business and went to ground where I couldn't be found. Some years later I learned from one of my very close friends, whose phone number I had once given Roger as a contact, that these villains kept trying to find me. My friend quite truthfully told them I had disappeared.

Suffice it to say that I had gambled away my recent planning windfall. I was so cross with myself for my stupidity and betrayal of Marion, that I went into a very sorry state of mind, which culminated in my suffering a stroke a few days later.

CHAPTER XXVII

Reprieved

It was a beautiful sunny July morning, and I was in Marion's father's bungalow; he was in hospital for removal of a cancerous section of bowel, the knife being due to fall at ten thirty. At eleven I sat down to have a cup of coffee but my right arm wouldn't move. At the same time I felt as though I had been chopped in half lengthways, as I could feel everything on one side go numb, even down to having feeling on one side of my nose and not the other. I was terrified, as I knew exactly what was happening. I managed to make enough noise to attract Marion, and within two minutes the doctor was with me. While I was waiting I could do nothing except wonder how much longer I had left to look at the blue sky... and would I end up in a wheelchair or a wooden suit...

I was very lucky as there was only a doctor on duty every other day, this particular Monday being one of them, and the surgery was less than a hundred yards from the house. My blood pressure was 250/150, at which the doctor announced I was very lucky to still be here at all and luckier still – as he thought – I had only had a TIA and should regain feeling in forty-eight hours. Forty-eight hours can seem like an eternity in those conditions, but after twenty-four hours I convinced myself I could feel something in my arm and, as the doctor had said, after forty-eight hours most of the feeling had returned. I don't know to this day how Marion coped that July morning when it must have looked as though the Grim Reaper was going to harvest both her husband and her father on the same day. However, we all survived, father-in-law for another ten years before finally giving in a few months short of ninety-four; and I am still alive and typing!

This is, however, meant to be a salutary warning for any reader: don't ignore high blood pressure! Mine was first detected when I was twenty-three at the Fleet Air Arm medical referred to earlier, and for over thirty years I ignored it, with near fatal results. For years I had every insurance policy I ever took out heavily 'loaded' and still did nothing. However, I was one of the lucky ones, and although chasing a dream had cost us all our money, I escaped with my health more or less intact, and above all I'm still here. However, at the time I had to face the likelihood of never working again. A fifty-five-year-old male, self-employed for most of his life, never having had a CV, recovering from a stroke, was not a very employable proposition in the middle of a particularly deep economic depression.

Having paid a self-employed National Insurance stamp all my life, I was aware of the fact that this was primarily an additional tax on the self-employed rather than the purchasing of some future benefit in hard times. This indeed it turned out to be, as our entitlement was £123 every two weeks – or just over £30 a week each for everything! The fortnightly 'signing on' was the most humiliating thing I have ever had to do, and I understood the rage so many of my 'brother signers-on' felt against the system. The whole Jobcentre environment is designed to intimidate and belittle. What job adverts there are are for crap jobs at crap wages. The staff do their best but they too are subject to intimidation; all in all it's a degrading and humiliating experience for everybody.

It probably did *me* more good than most, as up until then I had tended to side with 'on your bike' Tebbit and believe that everyone there was there by choice and were simply work-shy. Unquestionably, a proportion were in that category, but they were a very small minority.

On balance, though, it is probably as good a system as can be devised, and it certainly persuaded me to leave it at the earliest opportunity. The manner of my leaving the dole some two years later was pure chance, in that Peter Underwood who, with his wife Judy, were the proprietors of Bawdeswell Garden Centre, sought my advice on bringing his irrigation system up to scratch. We had been friends for quite a long time, and indeed they had come to stay on *Circus* with us some three years earlier. I still think this gesture of Peter's was primarily an act of great kindness to get me rehabilitated after my stroke. Marion was already working there assisting with the Christmas displays and gift departments. In fact she still works there but now has sole responsibility for the truly magical displays the Garden Centre puts on every Christmas. I must have been some help to him, as he recommended me to one of his friends, also with a garden centre business, who in turn recommended me to his former plant manager who was by then working for Hilliers, the world-famous nurserymen and owners of a chain of garden centres.

Before I knew what had happened I had become a part of one of the real success stories of the horticultural industry. Over the last ten years or so the garden centre industry has boomed with continuous year-on-year growth. Not only have plant sales expanded at a phenomenal rate but even greater has been the expansion of non-plant sales.

Most garden centres had antiquated and largely inadequate watering systems which required updating, but for me, more significant was a requirement for water treatment to remove the lime deposits from plant foliage. In the same way that customers no longer want vegetables covered in mud, neither do they want plants which look as though they are covered in mildew. There was only one cure for this in hard water areas and that was treatment with nitric acid. The equipment for acid injection had become marginally more sophisticated than was available to me on my nursery, but even so was still very crude, inaccurate and dangerous. A chance meeting with two electronics engineers who were developing a new generation of dosing equipment enabled me to carve myself a useful niche in the marketplace installing, advising on, and servicing these units. I was soon to earn the nickname of 'the acid man', and I am still known by this rather ambiguous title. This work steadily grew and grew until it took me all over Southern England, from Bath in the west to Canterbury in the east. Whilst Marion still had her father at home it suited us both for me to be away for three or four nights a week, but after his demise in 2001 it became an increasingly unsatisfactory arrangement. I liked the work, I liked the people and above all I could choose my customers, but even so, the attractions of life on the M25 were beginning to wane and I wound down the general irrigation work, whilst retaining the specialist acid and pump-house work.

In the autumn of 1995, as I was coming up to my sixtieth birthday, my brother John very kindly asked Marion and myself, with David and his new wife, Catherine, to dinner with him at Guildford. John had by now retired from Schroder's Bank and was Chairman of the National Rifle Association at nearby Bisley. His family had emigrated to South Africa so he was effectively commuting between England and that country. I knew they all loved South Africa and had holidayed there for many years; even so, it seemed an elaborate way of enjoying the best of both worlds. Marion had always wanted to see elephants and other large animals and John had also tried to persuade me to visit 'the Dark Continent'. I am ashamed to say that neither appealed to me at all and I never got beyond offering to take her to the zoo.

At this birthday party John and Marion hatched a plot to get me to South Africa. He had acquired something like sixteen square miles of wild flowers and scrubland on the southernmost tip of the country at Cape Aghulas where the Atlantic and Indian Oceans meet. So as to limit resistance from me, he gave us two return tickets to Cape Town, and offered to meet us at the airport, drive us to his home where we would stay for one week, hire us a car and turn us loose for the second week. How could even an old curmudgeon like me refuse? We went in October – which was supposed to be like our spring, but wasn't. Unbeknown to any of us at the time, for Marion and me this was to be the start of our love affair with Africa.

The only health hazard John and Hilly warned us about were snakes, especially puff adders. If there is one thing I really do not like it is snakes, so to everyone's amusement I kitted myself out with a pair of leather gaiters. Needless to say this was total overreaction, although we did come across a few. In fact, by far the greatest hazards were John's chocolate Labradors, which made rather too effective guard dogs. The weather was absolutely vile, quite typical of a bad English spring, although with enough fine breaks to make it tolerable.

John's property was forty miles from the nearest town of Hermanus, approached by a dead straight road for the last twenty miles. All supplies both in and out had to undertake this journey, but the sheer beauty of the place made it all worth while. The harsh cry of the Hadeda ibis, the gentle cooing of the Cape turtle doves, the vivid blues and orange of the jacaranda and flame trees, the cry of the fish eagle and so many, many other sights and sounds are all part of the fascination of Africa, which we now return to again and again.

Primarily their farm consisted of uncultivated *feynbos* – as the indigenous flora of the Cape tends to be called – but also included some cultivated proteas and sugar bush. These South African flowers are part of the country's huge horticultural export trade, and the farm was busy most days cutting, drying, dyeing and delivering to a central packhouse. Hilly was breeding bontebok, a type of South African antelope threatened with extinction, and was about to do the same with hartebeest; but apart from the ostriches this was all the wild game life there was on the farm. Wherever we went we saw acres and acres of what we call 'exotica' growing wild by the roadside: arum lilies, clivia and agapanthus to name but a few. Many believe that Africa is the birthplace of mankind, but what is not disputed is that almost all our more colourful flora originate from the Cape.

For the second week we just drove where the spirit moved us, but predominantly 'did' the Garden Route. We saw the ostriches in the Karoo, the Kango Caves, whales at Hermanus and all kinds of flora and fauna on the way, but the high spot of the trip was born whilst staying at a farmhouse bed and breakfast near Plettenberg Bay, when our hosts suggested we might go to Ado Elephant Park near Port Elizabeth. At the word 'elephant' Marion's eyes lit up and our hosts made the booking for us from noon to noon the following day. They showed us on the map how to get there and we set off on the two hundred-kilometre drive to PE. They forgot to tell us that although it was a main highway there were no petrol stations along it.

I think we saw five other vehicles the entire way, and it was getting hairier and hairier as the fuel gauge nudged the red, but just before we spluttered to a halt we were in the suburbs of PE and a gas station hove into view. We filled up and checked the route to Ado which took us through the middle of one of the 'townships'.

This was not an enjoyable experience, although in truth it was no more threatening than driving through London. We did lock the doors, but so does one in London. By now the weather had changed from the predominantly grey, cool weather we had endured so far, with a maximum of about fifty fahrenheit to bright sunny weather with a maximum in the camp that midday of exactly one hundred degrees, all this in the space of an hour. We checked in, found our little rondavel, had lunch and collected a map of the Park. We were told we could go where we liked as long as we stuck to the tracks and didn't get out of the car.

We collected a disc which had to be handed in when we returned, so that all the guests could be accounted for before nightfall, and had the car checked for oranges. It seemed that the Ado elephants had a predilection for even the smell of an orange.

We drove for what seemed an eternity before we saw our

first wild animal, a little meerkat standing sentry by its burrow. On and on we drove but saw nothing, until rounding a corner we came across a solitary elephant drinking at a waterhole. Out came David's camcorder, and when I got to within thirty yards I stopped the car but didn't dare turn off the engine in case it wouldn't start in an emergency. The elephant was taking no notice of us at all when Marion spotted another one coming out of the bush and then another and another... until a herd of thirty-two were enjoying a bath.

I wasn't an accomplished sexer of elephant at that stage so couldn't tell what gender they all were; there were lots of little baby ones as well, all being looked after in an almost humanoid way by those that were obviously their mothers. We used up a whole tape and were just thinking of moving when the whole herd moved back into the bush whence they had come.

We were completely on our own for the whole period, and the thrill of it entirely negated any concern for our safety. It was apparently the best sighting of the day. We ate a hearty supper in anticipation of a 'night drive' in a Land Rover accompanied by a game ranger. Our guide was a little South African girl who told us, as they all do, that we might see nothing at all. As it turned out we saw a myriad of small ground game plus some elephant and impala. Our little guide said we must be her lucky star as that was the best night drive she had ever had. I now know this was no exaggeration and it is certainly the best night drive we have ever had; in fact, most of them are such a waste of time that we rarely go on them nowadays. The real shock was to come when we got home and collected the bill from Barclaycard. For twenty-four hours' full board, plus game viewing, it came to £28.50 total! We had already learned how cheap SA was, but this was ridiculous!

That was the end of our trip away from John's home and we drove back to his farm in a state of great elation. Having been out in the country for so long they of course knew where to go and we were steered in the direction of Kruger National Park for our next African trip. We both knew that Africa had got its hooks into us before we had been home very long.

CHAPTER XXVIII

Kruger National Park

David and his new wife, Catherine, had engaged a South African nanny, also a Catherine, whom we referred to as 'Kate' for identification purposes. Kate was a lovely lass with whom I got on really well. She had left a boyfriend, Gino, behind in SA, who just happened to have done a catering course in Cape Town with the son of the owner of Casa do Sol, a lovely hotel not far from the Kruger Park. Suffice it to say that with Gino's help I eventually made contact with South African tour organisers MFAFA in Hazyview, and booked a fourteen-day holiday with them, again for October. They sent us what seemed an ideal itinerary, and off we went from London to Johannesburg to be met by their rep at the airport.

As we got off the plane and into the immigration hall I was concerned to find the contents of a 747 in the shape of Japanese tourists in front of us. Two windows for foreign passport holders, six for SA passport holders. By the time we were through immigration I realised there was no hope of MFAFA's rep still being there, and I decided I would just have to find a phone and ring them. To my utter surprise we were met by a man holding up our names who answered to the name of Harry. He told us we had a four-hour drive to the hotel (Casa do Sol) and suggested we stop for a break on the road.

He gave us a running commentary all the way. We went past the gold mines, which of course we had never seen before but looked much the same as English coal mines except for different coloured slag heaps. Sugar cane was another new crop, which despite my antics in the sugar market I had also never seen before. Huge areas of forests – all commercial, apparently – stretched as far as the eye could see. We established that Harry had served with the Parachute Regiment in Northern Ireland, so what on earth he was doing in the Transvaal we never established. He duly delivered us to the hotel and asked what time we wanted to be picked up in the morning. It was then we discovered he was our personal guide for the full two weeks. We had no idea that we'd bought this level of service, assuming we would be just two of a party. Anyway, it was a pleasant surprise to go to bed with. Casa was wonderful, with superb food – common throughout South Africa, as we now knew – and all the facilities which go with five-star hotels, although I think Casa in fact only had three.

The first few days we did the sightseeing bit, including the classic Pilgrim's Rest, Blyde River Canyon, God's Window, Bourke's Potholes, and so on.

One evening included a visit to a private game reserve, Bongani, and a night drive. The setting was truly breathtaking, but we saw little game apart from giraffe and a very distant elephant. The next couple of days were spent visiting Harry's friends, and took in growers of mini-bananas, avocados, macadamia nuts, lychees and many other exotic fruits such as we had only ever seen in supermarkets before. The last day before going into the Kruger Park proper was spent with another of Harry's friends who was a taxidermist. Up until then my knowledge of taxidermy was confined to stuffed birds and small animals, but here was the most amazing workshop with stuffed elephants, buffalo and even a lion. The latter was in fact two halves of different lions 'welded' together.

The story was that the trophy lion was late being collected and the vultures had got at the rear part of it, so the rear end of a non-trophy lion had to be stuck on instead. He'd made a wonderful job of it and it was impossible to see the join. All species of big game were in his workshop, except on this occasion there were no rhino.

Living in the politically correct UK, with all its attendant nonsense, I never expected to see such a sight and was intrigued to know where it all went and who his customers were. The reply was, 'Every country in the world except yours.'

Those who live amongst animals all the time have a much less squeamish and more realistic attitude to nature than our urban man with his 'cuddle a fox' mentality. Overprotection invariably leads to overpopulation, which in turn leads to more disease and more destruction of the habitat. By the same token, indiscriminate killing as carried out by the Edwardians in the old days, and the poachers of today, eventually leads to extinction of certain species. In all my trips to Africa I have been impressed with how delicate is this balance of nature and how skillfully those in charge of Africa's wildlife heritage are maintaining it. In a continent as poor as Africa, money is always a limiting factor; so yes, in the bush there is trophy hunting. Americans especially, but also many Europeans, are prepared to pay enormous sums of money to kill big game, and this is a valuable source of income, which nowadays appears to go straight into the various game departments' coffers rather than into the general government maw. Those in charge of granting licences would seem to prefer to put the price up as high as the market will stand rather than increase the number of licences. This was the basic message given by Harry's friend, and which all our subsequent visits have borne out.

We then went into the Kruger National Park, where there is a network of tarmac roads which visitors are not allowed to leave. We saw a great deal of large game, and four out of the 'Big Five', missing only the leopard. Although we were confined to Harry's people carrier, we had an excellent view of everything, accompanied by a stream of amusing little anecdotes mixed with the dissemination of information on all that we'd seen. We spent one night at Lower Sabie and two nights at Pretoriuskop, both within the Park. Harry cooked all meals for us on a barbecue, including breakfast out in the Park where we had to vie with the monkeys to keep our food on the plate. My abiding memory of this trip was disturbing an elephant having a mudbath. He took the most violent exception to us, filled his trunk with liquid mud and hosed down the VW with it! Both Marion and I had our windows open. I was filming and got completely covered; Marion made a frantic effort to close her window, tearing her thumbnail in the process. This has never healed and she carries it as a memento of a wonderful experience to this day. From here Harry took us to 'Honeyguide', a private tented camp, where we were to spend two days and two nights.

We now said goodbye to Harry for a couple of days as he handed us over to Matthew for safe keeping. Matthew, like all his ilk, was charming and polite, and despite his tender years, a very knowledgeable young man. He took us to our tent, albeit a fairly luxurious one but still a tent, and explained that under no circumstances at all were we to come out of it after dark. For dinner we would be fetched and escorted back afterwards, but by daylight we could proceed unaccompanied. Somehow the tent didn't seem much protection against a lion or an elephant, let alone a rhino.

We were regaled with a story of an American lady who, feeling cold after supper, returned to her tent for a sweater, never to be seen again, having fallen victim to a lion. We had to not only zip up the tent but secure the zip with a safety chain, or the baboons would help themselves.

We and two other couples set off into the bush in an open Land-Rover, with Matthew driving and his African tracker riding on the catcher's seat à la John Wayne on the front, armed with an ancient .480 rifle. We had hardly got off the road before we had a puncture. It didn't need Matt to tell us we were vulnerable whilst the wheel change went on. Our next excitement was a very close-range encounter with an elephant. We were stationary as he walked very slowly towards us to investigate; once he was within ten feet we moved slowly out of his way. He was not aggressive but they do look huge at close quarters.

Our slow meander through the bush in the Land-Rover continued, and whilst we were not seeing perhaps the variety of wildlife that we had in the Kruger we were seeing greater concentrations of buffalo and wildebeest especially. The amusing little warthogs (leopard fodder), scampering about with their tails erect, were a constant source of pleasure; then suddenly the vehicle came to a halt.

Matt explained that the tracker had seen some fresh lion spoor and they were going to follow it on foot. We were to stay where we were, Matt took the rifle and left us marooned in an open Land-Rover in the full sun, with no means of self-protection. They were only gone for twenty minutes but it might have been twenty hours. No one spoke, not a word. Matt had identified what looked like quite a large pride of lions of about twelve to fourteen, and said he would try to find them. Arriving at a waterhole we found the remains of a dead giraffe – not that old, because it was still smelling quite strongly. We were made to dismount and examine the work of the various predators, how the vultures and hyenas have the rest of the meat after the lions have had their fill, and the jackals eat the bones. Nature may be red in tooth and claw but it's mightily efficient. Not long after we found the pride probably responsible and counted fourteen of them.

There were, as always, huge quantities of impala. Although they are as common as rabbits and the basic food for many predators, they are probably the most graceful animals of all, and to me are sheer poetry in motion. The visit to Honeyguide peaked on the last morning. I sensed excitement in the air as soon as Matt appeared. He drove us to a very large termite mound at the base of which was a dead full-grown giraffe, with the pride of lions we had seen the day before still feeding off it. It seemed they had digested the giraffe of a few days earlier at the waterhole and decided on an even larger one this time… Matt explained that to be able to pull down such a tall animal the giraffe had probably been ambushed by a lion on top of the termite mound mounting the attack, while the rest of the

292

pride, acting as beaters, drove it into position. He told us that a full-grown giraffe is too big for a single lion to tackle, and also more often than not they can outrun their attackers. There had not been a pride in that area for some time and the giraffes had become complacent. They were expected to buck their ideas up now that this large pride had suddenly appeared. We sat and watched nervously from very close quarters, but Matt assured us that now they were fed they were too lazy to be interested in us.

After breakfast Harry arrived to collect us and take us to our chosen venue for end of holiday rest and relaxation, an essential ingredient of a safari holiday.

Safaris are not a relaxation. The mixture of early starts, high temperatures, travelling over rough terrain and above all the sheer excitement and anticipation of what is round the corner are quite tiring; in any case it is pleasant to wind down before the hassle of going home. Our chosen venue was a cottage in Swaziland where we were to be for four days before returning to Casa for the last two nights. Swaziland was totally undeveloped and existed on a primitive agricultural industry, including a large amount of commercial forestry. Where we were was an oasis of primeval scenery. Wherever we looked it had obviously been that way for millions of years and we spent our time just walking and exploring. There was a hotel some ten minutes' Jeep ride away where we commissioned the carving of an elephant out of a log of jacaranda wood. The carver used only a small and primitive adze but the end result, which we collected on our last day, exceeded all our expectations. Harry again collected us, and after a final wind-down at Casa we were taken back to Johannesburg for the journey home.

By now the African flame had been truly lit and we vowed to save up for another trip as soon as possible.

CHAPTER XXIX

Zimbabwe

We left planning the next African adventure until the size of the holiday pot was able to be calculated. It wasn't very large that year but enough to have a ten-day 'cheapie'.

We elected to fly Air Zimbabwe from Gatwick to Harare out, Victoria Falls to Nelspruit for access to the Kruger, and Nelspruit to Johannesburg for the journey home. All went well until we had been sitting on the tarmac at Gatwick for over an hour, during which time the Captain had made a series of unconvincing announcements as to why we were still not airborne. I detest air travel anyway and Marion always finds me a handful on these occasions, none more so than when at eleven p.m. – the plane should have left at nine thirty – the Captain announced that he was waiting for a fax from Harare before he was able to take off. I said to Marion, 'This is Afrospeak for, "My C of A (certificate of airworthiness) has run out and I'm trying to sort it out."'

'Don't be so ridiculous, sit down and shut up,' she replied.

Within five minutes he announced just that, and everyone was to get off, return any duty-free goods and collect their baggage from the arrival carousel. We would all be accommodated at the Europa Hotel until the problem was sorted. We were also to collect meal vouchers so that we could use the airport facilities until transport had been arranged. We duly collected our vouchers, but it being a Sunday night everywhere was now closed. Fortunately we had no duty-frees to return, and our luggage all turned up on the carousel. However, three couples were not so lucky. Their luggage was lost and the plane hadn't even taken off! The Europa coped well with the sudden influx, but the next morning was utter chaos, as nobody knew what was happening and it seemed we might not get away until that night. However, having got five minutes' notice to be on the coach, we eventually took off just after midday.

Travelling privately as we were, there was no tour guide to ask at either end and I had already calculated that we would arrive in Harare at one o'clock in the morning. As we had connecting flights to Kariba and then light aircraft to Tiger Bay in the middle of Lake Kariba, it didn't require much imagination to guess what was going to happen next. Air Zimbabwe's staff at Harare were first class, finding us all hotel accommodation in the middle of the night, as well as refreshment. They assured us there was plenty of room on all the transfer flights – which of course there wasn't – and we were to stop worrying. It actually took us all day to get to Kariba, finally arriving about four o'clock. To our amazement the light aircraft pilot was still there waiting for us. He told us this sort of thing was absolutely normal for Air Zimbabwe, and he thought we'd turn up in the end! As soon as we got to Tiger Bay we were to jump in a boat for a river safari. Although we had only been delayed by eighteen hours or so in London, it was actually two whole days of daylight we had missed, so we jumped in straight away, travel weary as we were.

We were later shown our accommodation, a delightful open-fronted bungalow with a stunning view across the lake. We were warned about the resident hippo, nicknamed Pavarotti, and to be careful as we made our way across to the restaurant. There we met up with our pilot, whom we had asked to have supper with us, so relieved were we to have been picked up by him. He held a dual passport – UK and Zimbabwean – but had lived in Zim all his life. We got on well from the start and established that we were both the black sheep of our respective families.

He told us internal flights in Zim were totally unreliable and suggested if we ever came again we should fly from camp to camp. I told him we were not in that financial bracket, but he replied that if we could find two friends to come with us he would take two weeks' holiday and we could have him for free and his plane at cost which would make an attractive deal. It seemed like a good idea and we expressed our gratitude.

When the time came to say goodnight he asked me to countersign a chit confirming he had delivered us. He had already signed, and recognising the unusual name I asked him if he had a brother called Nick, to which he replied that he had. I told him that his brother had been my brother's assistant at Schroders in the Sixties and that whilst I didn't know his brother well we had worked together on sugar expeditions to Europe. This seemed to cement an already good relationship and we agreed to meet up when he came to England in a couple of months' time.

The following day we enjoyed very different safaris, compared with what had gone before, all from a boat. We were seeing much the same animals but from a totally different perspective. There was an abundance of aquatic flora and fauna, especially fish eagles, herons, hippos and crocodiles, river bank birds like the gloriously coloured carmine bee-eaters and kingfishers, to name but a few. The atrophied trees remaining after the Kariba Dam had been constructed made ideal lookout posts for the eagles and cormorants. Lake Kariba was also home to the exciting tiger fish which make such wonderful sport fishing.

On our last morning we opted for a walking safari, which I frankly found almost too exciting, armed as our guide was. We came into very close contact with elephants, which proved considerably more scary on foot than close contact in a Land-Rover had been. However, we survived, and safely back at base we were able to reflect on the excitement of it all. Our time at Tiger Bay came all too quickly to an end, and Paul flew us back to the airport at Kariba for our onward flight to Victoria Falls, where we were to stay at Illala Lodge for two nights.

Having checked into the hotel, we found various tours

were on offer in addition to the obligatory viewing of the Falls themselves. The amount of water coming over the Falls had been drastically reduced by the long dry spell, but even so they were truly awesome. We booked up for a night game drive which proved very disappointing, in that we saw very little game beyond various eyes which were identified as something special, but we could never see what. The high spot of the Vic Falls visit was the early morning canoe trip down the Zambezi. We were collected from the hotel at the appointed hour by our guide for the trip. He then dropped us off at a crossroads while he went off to collect the canoes and his mate, telling us to wait for him. Waiting at the base of a giant baobab tree we were suddenly aware of movement in the bush, and eventually a rather large elephant emerged. We had been taught to stand still, and knowing that they were very short-sighted animals we hoped we were invisible against the tree. He showed no interest in us and walked straight past, continuing on his way. It wasn't long before our guide returned, apologised if we were scared, but intimated that we had a more scary time to come – and so it proved!

We set off with him in the lead canoe, the rear being brought up by his armed colleague in the other canoe. We spent the next two hours amongst large pods of hippos and an abundance of crocodiles, which were almost impossible to see or distinguish from logs or general vegetation. After an hour of this I decided that at my age going down a crocodile's throat would at least be quicker than dying in an NHS bed so I gave up worrying. After two hours of unbelievable experiences we went onto the river bank for breakfast, our guide having satisfied himself there were no crocs in the vicinity. He was obviously very well educated and had a great knowledge of world affairs. He had a degree in computer studies, and when I asked him what on earth he was doing canoeing up the Zambezi for a living he replied, 'Which would you rather do?' His father was equally critical of his choice of career, but he said, 'We have almost everything we want here except the two priceless advantages you have in England: democracy; and a guaranteed meal on the plate.' How those words stick in my memory, knowing what has now happened to this once beautiful and prosperous country...

Our flight to Nelspruit was uneventful and we were met by one of the owners of MFAFA and taken to Casa, where we were welcomed like long lost friends. We had a trip to Kruger organised for the morning, leaving at five thirty. We had a wonderful dinner yet again, but just before the end of the meal we were hit by a violent thunderstorm which knocked all the power out, so went to bed by candlelight and with assurances from the management that these storms never last long and all would be well by morning. It wasn't. When we got up it was still pouring with rain and bitterly cold. We had to pick up other guests and it was over an hour before we were actually en route for Kruger. It was an awful journey, we shipped nearly as much water as if the Land-Rover had been open-topped. Our Afrikaner guide apologised for the weather but said, 'If it's any consolation, it is ideal weather to see leopard.'

Marion had actually turned blue by the time we got to the Park and we all felt that seeing to her survival was the priority. A good breakfast and some hot drinks did the job, not just for her but for all of us. By the time breakfast was over it had stopped raining and was beginning to warm up a bit.

As we were driving and looking, one of our party called out to stop and was pointing and exclaiming, 'There! There!' None of us could see anything, but he was insistent that there was a leopard in the bushes. Sure enough, he was right. She suddenly got up and paraded herself round and round our vehicle like a mannequin on the catwalk. It was the most incredible ten minutes so far. Even our Afrikaner guide admitted that it was the best sighting he had ever experienced. In the process of congratulating our fellow guest it transpired that he was a photo-reconnaissance pilot with the RAF; he truly had eyes like the proverbial hawk.

Our guide at one stage thought there were lions in the area, although he couldn't see them, and began to utter the most lifelike call. After about five minutes one came out of the bush right up to us and again a great photo opportunity presented itself. What started as a most unpromising trip turned out to be one of our most spectacular. This, of course, is the fun of safaris: you never know what is round the corner.

The flight back from Johannesburg via Nelspruit was uneventful, but we were already planning next year's adventure.

CHAPTER XXX

The Best of the Best

When we came home, we found that our friends Peter and Barbara, who had also had various South African adventures, would like to join with us on what was intended to be my sixty-fifth birthday treat of a lifetime. We spent a long time planning exactly what we were going to do, and so excited were we with the itinerary that we decided we couldn't wait and should go that coming autumn. I was quite happy to do this, partly as a safeguard in case I didn't make it to official retirement age, and also because Paul, who was the essential ingredient to make the whole escapade feasible, advised us that Zimbabwe was now unravelling rapidly and in another year's time the option might not be available to us. Peter booked the flights for us (via BA this time) to Harare and back. I booked all the Africa bit with friends of Paul who had a travel agency in Harare. Although we specified the itinerary, it was important to have a local source through which we could communicate and who would liase with the various camps and lodges.

We didn't know Peter and Barbara well; in fact our acquaintanceship so far was confined to the bridge table, and they placed an enormous amount of trust in us to even be part of the scheme. Their friends all told them they were mad to entrust such huge sums of money to an unknown agent in a country like Zim. We were told we were equally mad, but I trusted Paul totally. One thing we did know about each other was that Barbara and myself were the mercurial halves of each marriage and both Peter and Marion, as the placid halves, vowed to keep their respective spouses under control! We'd be travelling all the time in a light aircraft, so we were severely limited as to the amount of baggage we could take with us. An essential part of any safari, for it to be enjoyable, is to allow adequate rest and relaxation at either end of the trip. On Paul's recommendation we arranged to stay two nights at each end of the trip where we could leave the excess baggage and retrieve it on return. Wild Geese Lodge was chosen for this particular function. It was so named, I believe, as much of the film bearing that name was shot on location at this particular site.

Finally the great day arrived and we all met up at Gatwick ready for departure. Despite the trust which Peter and Barbara had placed in us, they couldn't help being slightly apprehensive, not least on account of the considerable sums of money which had been telegraphed, as far as they were aware, into the middle of the African bush...

The flight was uneventful, especially compared to that with Air Zimbabwe a year earlier. We arrived at Harare on time, and the relief at finding Paul waiting for us was etched all over Peter and Barbara's faces. The hotel transport took us the short distance to Wild Geese Lodge and we were all thrilled with what we found. We each had our own little cottage in the garden surrounded by indigenous flowers and plants, looking over their small private game reserve stocked with giraffe, zebra and various antelope. There were no predators that anyone was aware of so we were encouraged to go and explore anywhere, provided we kept our eyes open. On our first expedition we encountered a lone giraffe who insisted on following us wherever we went.

Barbara was slightly apprehensive, and when Peter uttered reassurance that giraffes were not vicious, the reply of, 'What do you know, you are only an accountant from Norwich,' collapsed us into laughter, after which we all relaxed and made it back to base unscathed.

While we were having drinks in the piano bar before dinner, Mike the pianist came up to us and asked, 'Which of you is de Havilland?' When I put my hand up he asked me, 'Does the name Butler mean anything to you?'

I said, 'In connection with de Havillands, of course it does, he was one of the principal backers of Sir Geoffrey when the aircraft company was expanding, and later became Chairman of the board. Why do you ask?'

What I did not know was that A S Butler, when he retired from de Havillands, emigrated to Southern Rhodesia – as Zimbabwe was called in those days. Mike told me of his family circumstances, which so nearly changed my life yet again. A S Butler's son was apparently an Olympic yachtsman due to compete in the infamous games at Munich in 1972. On his way to Munich he was killed in an accident on the autobahn leaving two sons, Anthony and Rhett. The latter was so named after Rhett Butler of *Gone with the Wind* fame, in which Olivia de Havilland had played a leading role.

Anthony had a large rose farm just outside Harare and had been murdered a few weeks before we arrived. Rhett, who had a travel and hotel business in Zimbabwe, suddenly found himself running a large rose farm about which he knew little. Mike asked whether I would like to meet Rhett when we returned at the end of our safari, to which of course I gave a positive reply. The others had all gone into dinner by now and I was beginning to have silly thoughts about growing roses in Zimbabwe. After being forced out of rose growing in England I had made two other attempts to get back into the industry, one in Holland which was vetoed by Marion on family grounds, quite rightly too, and the other was when I was tempted to apply for a job to set up a rose-growing venture in Kenya. I never got round to applying, as I felt I was too old in the first place, and secondly, if family considerations scuppered the Holland idea, Kenya had no chance. I was also conscious of the fact that some of my mother's family used to farm in Kenya before having their land taken by none other than the recently retired President of Kenya, Arap Moi; and also that however beautiful Africa may be, the fact remained that the whole continent was a 'basket case' – politically and economically – from one end to the other. These were my thoughts twenty years ago, so what on earth was I thinking about – especially as the 'basket case' mentality had spread ever southwards in the ensuing years! I put these thoughts out of my mind and we went to bed full of anticipation for the morning. The Wild Geese courtesy truck delivered us to Paul's plane at the small aircraft section of Harare International. Here we were introduced to his boss, who had so kindly made the plane available for the next ten days.

Our first stop was at Chikwenya, an eight-tented camp on the eastern boundary of the Mana Pools National Park. It was stunningly beautiful, with the Zambezi River, its backwaters and flood plains and the mountains of the Rift Valley providing the backdrop. The area was home to large numbers of elephant, buffalo, hippo, crocodile and eland antelope. There were also lion and leopard in abundance, but our experience so far suggested they would not be easily found. The flight took just over an hour; such a journey by road would have taken a minimum of eight hours, we were told.

Quite apart from the time saving there was an added advantage of having your own plane; everything looks quite different from the air. This is especially striking when viewing herds of plains game such as wildebeest, buffalo, all the antelopes and to a lesser extent the elephants. We could not help feeling a little like Robert Redford in *Out of Africa* as we swooped low over these herds and saw the full beauty of their movement over the ground.

Having checked in, we were introduced to our guide for our two-day stay, a very attractive young lady called Jo, who had only recently achieved her life's ambition of qualification as a fully trained game ranger. She was delightful company and was, as all rangers are, extremely knowledgeable. She only had the five of us to look after. Indeed, this was the case for the whole holiday at all the sites, and fraternisation with other guests was limited to mealtimes.

At all the camps the routine was fairly standard: reveille at five a.m.; coffee and biscuits to wake us up; a morning game drive; returning for breakfast at about ten thirty; rest and relaxation or a visit to a hide or waterhole; lunch; siesta; and an afternoon game drive from about three thirty until six thirty or seven. Supper followed and then rest and relaxation around the campfire and sometimes a short night drive. One of the major benefits of having our own plane was the ability to leave after the morning game drive, having had breakfast, and arrive at the next destination in time for the afternoon game drive. Relying on road transit or internal flights, the whole day is lost each time you move camp.

For our first afternoon drive Jo took us in search of the elephants, for which Mana Pools is so famous. We found them – hundreds of them; big ones, huge ones, medium-sized ones and babies of all ages. They are *so* human in their behaviour, especially in their care of their babies. If one of the herd dies or gets killed the whole family turn up to mourn. Above all, elephants are a matriarchal society, which presumably is why women find them so appealing, especially the way they turn surplus males out of the herd! They are also appallingly destructive, not only devouring enormous quantities of vegetation, but they also have the charming habit whereby if there is something they want which is out of reach they will simply push the tree right over to get it.

After a most enjoyable dinner when we met up with the other guests at the camp we turned in in reasonable time ready for the morning trip, which was to be a walk. I remembered our walk the previous year at Tiger Bay and was slightly apprehensive of what was in store, the more so because there was a much greater density of game here than we had seen at Tiger Bay. I had not been asleep long when I was woken up by a crashing of undergrowth; needless to say, Marion was still asleep. I crept out of bed, and looking out of the perspex window, was face to face – certainly no more than ten feet away – with a full-grown elephant pulling down a tree right outside our tent! Marion was now awake, and as we were speculating on its chances of coming into our tent it moved on to do the same outside Peter and Barbara's tent some twenty yards away. Exciting stuff.

Jo came to get us at five o'clock, and we then learned that we had a new guide, another Paul, for our walk that morning, as she was to take his party on a drive. She explained that as she was only recently qualified she had not got the necessary time in yet to do walking tours as they were inherently much higher risk. However, she was to take us over again for the afternoon trip.

Under Paul's guidance we learned the basics of tracking, and identified the various 'spoor'. On this outing the main presence were elephants and buffalo. Buffalo are referred to locally as 'Dagga Boys', quite why, we never established. However, Paul emphasised that they were extremely aggressive animals, of which one must be eternally wary. I again found this walking trip slightly spooky, and we were all a trifle jumpy every time we heard the branches snapping.

Back we went for breakfast, which is always something special in these camps. I personally have had a cooked breakfast every day of my life, it being far and away the best meal of the day; but the others did not share my tastes, until they were persuaded to try. I don't know what the Africans do to their bacon but it is like no other bacon money can buy. We all pigged out on breakfast every day; perhaps we were just extra hungry. Another drive in the afternoon, again amongst the elephants, when we saw one standing on his back legs, reaching into the top of a tree with his trunk to what seemed an unbelievable height. Baboons were everywhere and most amusing were their antics. We also saw a leopard curled up in a tree, but too far away to photograph, and by the time the Land-Rover had got within range she had gone.

Dinner on the last evening was, as dinners all are on the final night, a slightly sad event. This is one of the downsides of this type of excursion, both for guests and staff; just as we were getting to know each other it was time to move on. Jo was looking most attractive in a long dress – not at all the little game ranger in her shorts. I sat next to her that night and heard all about her childhood, growing up during the civil war, and her ambition to spend her life amongst the animals. Now that Zimbabwe has completely disintegrated I often wonder what has become of her in particular, and all the other wonderful and dedicated trackers and rangers we have met who have had their whole lives destroyed.

After a morning game drive and another super breakfast the next day, we loaded up our minimal baggage and Jo took us out to the airstrip. The road was blocked by two elephants who refused for several minutes to let us by, almost as though they didn't want us to leave.

We took off for our flight to Tiger Bay, passing over the Kariba Dam at low level, and were able to appreciate the enormity of this hydroelectric project, which had been responsible for the creation of this vast artificial lake. We landed on the familiar strip where we had been a year before. The camp staff had changed in the previous few months but we were still made more than welcome. We were in chalet number three, as before, and it was all delightfully familiar. One sad piece of news we were greeted with was the demise of Pavarotti, the resident hippo, who had had to be put down as he was proving a danger to the residents and camp staff.

As Barbara and Marion had never caught a fish in their lives, we decided to go fishing on our first afternoon. We all had a go and everyone caught at least one fish, except me. However, the others shared their catch and the chef cooked them for us that evening. I have no idea what they were but they made excellent eating.

Most of our time here was spent on the lake, with the emphasis this time on the bird life. Peter and Barbara were the bird experts amongst us and I think they got more out of it than perhaps we did. The high spot of Tiger Bay's entertainment for us was a visit to the rhino sanctuary. It is a sobering thought that in the mid-1880s, black rhino were the commonest species of wild game in Africa. As recently as the 1960s there were estimated to be a million of them, but by now there are a couple of thousand at the most.

They were all black rhino (hook-lipped) at the sanctuary, which are now much rarer than the white rhinos. This distinction is in fact nothing to do with colour, for they are both broadly similar. The distinction is wide-lipped, as compared with hook-lipped, the 'wide' becoming *wit* in Afrikaans, which through the ages has become 'white' in English, the commonest language in the game areas.

The young here are bred in captivity and shipped into this reserve as soon as the calves are self-sufficient. Here they are allowed to grow until trans-shipment into the wild. They were well used to human company, and we were allowed to walk amongst them.

Close to, they are truly formidable prehistoric animals. One of the downsides of rearing like this is of course they lose their inherent fear of man and become easy prey for the poachers when they are released. We spent all day amongst these rhinos and were sad to say goodbye to such magnificent creatures. In fact 'the wild' means National Parks in this part of Africa, and they are heavily policed against poachers. National Park staff in many areas are authorised to shoot to kill poachers on sight without having to get prior permission, and whilst poaching of both rhino and elephant will continue for as long as there is a ready market for horn and tusks in the world, at least the tide was beginning to turn. Even so, there is a far more insidious force than poaching working against the wild game of Africa; government-sponsored tsetse fly eradication programmes. My ex-RAC friend Peter Aitchison, referred to earlier, was one of Africa's leading experts on tsetse fly and devoted most of his life to its eradication. It was very sad to know that he had very mixed feelings about what he had done, for as he acknowledged at the end of his life, in the final analysis the tsetse fly is the guardian of African wildlife. When the fly is finally eradicated to the unquestioned benefit of the domestic livestock farmer, so too, in all probability, will the last wild game animal have gone.

After the morning boat trip we flew into Hwange National

Park to stay at Little Linkwasha Camp. The landing strip was about half an hour's journey by Land-Rover from the camp itself, and we were surprised to see, on making our approach, just how many light aircraft there were there, the reason being that this landing strip served all the game lodges in the Park. We were met by Orbert, a large native game ranger, who coincidentally also held a commercial hunting licence and would sometimes escort licensed trophy hunters. On this occasion he just had us on a photographic hunt. The journey to camp was a game drive in its own right, and during it we had our first sighting ever of cheetah – although, it must be said, at extreme range.

Little Linkwasha was a small and very private camp with just three accommodation units, so we were the only occupants. Orbert was probably the most skilled tracker and bush specialist we had met so far, and as well as the game drives he took us on a mini survival course in the bush, showing us how everything we needed was to hand. The plants necessary to cope with mishaps, how to make a toothbrush and even the home-made toothpaste to go with it. All the usual animals were there, and also large numbers of eland and – most beautiful of all – sable. The latter we had never seen before, and neither were we to see again, so this was indeed a bonus.

The next morning's diversion was a cricket match in the bush. The bat was formed from the dried leaf of the illala palm and the ball from its fruit. It was all great fun with the added excitement of the wild animals all around us. There was an enormous variety of bird life, of which the most interesting to me were the secretary birds and the different varieties of vulture. The latter are not very attractive creatures but are very good for leading one to a kill, as we were eventually to use for our benefit.

The last evening was spent around an open campfire while Orbert regaled us with his tales and folklore of the bush. After the morning game drive and the magnificent breakfast which went with it, Orbert took us back to the aircraft; again, the trip was a mini game drive in its own right.

From here we made the short journey to Victoria Falls. We took a taxi for the journey from the airport to Illala Lodge, where Marion and I had stayed the previous year. The staff had not changed here and allocated us to Room 31, which we had had before. We were only here for one night; the sole purpose of the visit was to see the Falls, which neither Peter or Barbara had seen before. Paul had flown low over them on his approach to the airport to further whet our appetites for the adventure to come. After lunch we walked to the entrance gate for the Falls. Vic Falls is, unfortunately, synonymous with tacky tourism, filth, dirt, hassling street sellers and grinding poverty, although the Falls themselves are relatively civilised. In fact they are awesome, although as in the previous year, the amount of water coming over them was by their standards at a relatively low level. We of course were viewing them from the Zimbabwean side, and on our way out Barbara decided she wanted to see them from the Zambian side, which entailed a route march over the Vic Falls Bridge. It also meant having to go through Zambian customs with the knowledge that a temporary visa was also likely to be required. I was less than enthusiastic and refused to go on foot, suggesting we take a taxi. The local bystanders all speak and understand perfect English and – hey presto – as Barbara and I were arguing, a man with a taxi offered his services, which we accepted. He took us to his car, which from a distance looked reasonable. However, when he opened the door to the back seat, it promptly fell off; there was no back seat, just the framework where it should have been. Nothing ventured, nothing gained... so we all got in. I got into the front seat, and was surprised to find no dashboard! The driver hot-wired it to start it but nothing happened. His mate arrived alongside with some jump leads and away we went across the bridge to the customs post. As we had negotiated a return fare we made him wait but suggested as tactfully as we could that he didn't turn the engine off. However, he assured us it would start alright now it had had a run! He came with us to the customs post, where it was established there was a two-hour wait for visas.

I said something like, 'Stuff this for a laugh, what is so different about a waterfall from the other side?' The rest agreed, and they suggested we walk back about halfway and get the taxi to pick us up. This was agreed, so having communicated this to the driver we set off, pursued by a pack of human hyenas trying to sell us anything and everything. I succumbed to a pair of wooden elephants, only to be ridiculed by the others. I then 'lost it' and to my eternal shame reminded Barbara that it was her stupid idea anyway, and if I wanted to donate a fiver to underprivileged African youth then I would! I am ashamed to say all this altercation was conducted in lower deck invective, but dear Barbara just laughed and said I had improved her knowledge of the English language!

I was mortified, as this was precisely the moment our two spouses had been afraid of. She was so sweet to me afterwards that I felt even more ashamed!

We decided perhaps it would be best to abandon our walk, as it was proving rather stressful. We signalled to the taxi to come and get us, and yes, it did start this time; but when it drew up beside us, petrol was leaking out of the petrol tank and it really did look a bit lethal. As one does on these occasions, we took a fatalistic view of the situation, and after assuring Peter that I wouldn't be tempted to smoke, we arrived back at the hotel in one piece.

When we met up over dinner Paul advised us of a change of plan. We were due to refuel at Vic Falls airport for our final destination in Botswana but he had learned there was no fuel available. He had suspected this might be a problem, for as I have already remarked, Zim was beginning to fall apart; he assured us we had enough to get to Kasane in Botswana to refuel, but it would add time to our journey.

We had to spend a couple of hours at Kasane and took the opportunity to draw some Botswana currency for out-of-pocket expenses whilst we were at our final safari destination, Duma Tau. This camp was Peter's special choice. We had originally intended to stay for three nights, but as the cost of a tent here was the same as a suite at the Ritz in London we reduced it to the standard two nights.

The bush below us during the flight looked so dry and burnt up it was difficult to imagine anything living in it, but as we approached Duma Tau things began to green up a little. We were met at the airstrip by two guides this time, Kenneth and the unusually named Prayer. The camp itself was quite similar in many ways to Chikwenya, but with even more elephants everywhere. Again we were not allowed out of our tents at night under any circumstances but it seemed likely, with all the elephants around, to be just as hazardous by day. However, Kenneth assured us that we *ought* to be alright as long as we remembered not to take the animals by surprise. To this end he advised us to carry a stick or something similar to tap the fence or trees so that they were aware of our presence; but we were told not to shout at them and not to run away. I was reminded of our gamekeeper's admonition when I went on my first day's beating at a shoot at Horkesley, 'Rattle your stick and beat the bushes, but above all don't make noise or you'll frighten the birds!'

Our first afternoon game drive blended into an early night drive, the high spot of which was watching some lions stalking a herd of buffalo in a dried-up river bed. Our inexperience led us to believe we might see a kill, but as though at a given signal the buffalo turned head on to the lions. There followed a stand-off lasting about five minutes which the buffalo won, the lions slinking away.

The morning game drive introduced us to the African wild dog, which was another first for us. They were all different colours, slightly larger than hyenas, and not at all worried by our presence. Their behaviour, surprisingly, was almost doglike! This pack of about thirty were usually resident somewhere in the area. Kenneth explained that there were only about six hundred left in the whole of Africa, and now of course with the disease outbreak a couple of years ago they are rarer still. Kenneth was the only guide we ever had in the bush who never carried a rifle. When we asked why not, he said, 'My gun is in my head. I never stop watching so I don't get caught by surprise.'

After our usual wonderful brunch we went back to our tent for a freshen up before going to the bookshop at the lodge. I went out before Marion and had only just got onto the walkway when an elephant stepped over the fence and blocked my way. Remembering the advice never to turn your back but let them know you are around, as on account of their extreme short-sightedness they might not have seen you, I did as I had been told and rattled my stick on the fence, whereupon he unhurriedly stepped back over it again.

For our afternoon game drive we were to go on a river trip, primarily to see hippos and crocodiles. On our way to embark we were aware of some lions in the long grass alongside the river, but quite some distance from the embarkation point. The boat was relatively substantial compared to the canoe we had been in on our previous year's trip up the Zambezi, but still well capable of being overturned by an angry hippo. We did indeed see large pods of hippo, but as usual only their heads were visible, it being quite rare to see 'hippos with legs' on dry land, but only then can you fully appreciate their enormous bulk. We also came across an army river patrol. Kenneth told us that the Botswana Army are the primary anti-poaching enforcers in the country, and ruthless and effective they are too.

By the end of the trip it was getting dusk, and as we drew alongside the jetty, there, right beside our Land-Rover, was a lion lying down on the driver's side. This did cause the hairs on our necks to rise with anxiety, especially when Kenneth announced, 'Gentlemen, we have a problem. Do exactly as I say and keep quiet.'

After much discussion in the native language, which we

could not understand, a diversion was created, the lion got up and ambled off into the long grass, and Prayer was put ashore to get into the Land-Rover. This operation was successful, and mercifully the engine started straight away. The Land-Rover backed right up to the boat's gangplank and we crept ashore and into the vehicle. The lion followed us all the way back to the camp but posed no danger. Game are not concerned at all with vehicles, they apparently are mere inanimate objects to them; it is only when the occupants get excited and stand up in full view that trouble occurs. For all that, it was exciting, to say the least.

On this last evening of our stay Kenneth decided to give us a talk on the stars. It was a particularly bright sky that night and it was fascinating to identify some of the stars which we can also see on the other side of the world. We all felt slightly flat on the final evening, having had such a marvellous time at all the camps we had been to, all differing in landscape and game variety, all worth every penny of the considerable cost… but we could never have guessed what the morning had in store for us.

We set out for the final game drive of our holiday with Kenneth at the wheel. As was his usual practice, he just drove in no particular direction to see whatever appeared. After about twenty minutes I spotted a lion about four hundred yards away walking as though with some particular objective in mind. Kenneth thought it could be the same one that had met us off the boat the previous night and decided to follow her on a parallel path some four or five hundred yards away and see where she took us. She was quite definitely headed somewhere specific, and after about ten minutes we saw some vultures milling around and assumed there was a kill of some sort beneath them. With both the lion and ourselves heading towards this spot I suddenly smelt the unmistakeable smell of rotting flesh – although no one else could until later. Quite why I have such a very strong sense of smell, especially having been a smoker all my life, I have never discovered, but this was quite overpowering, as even the others admitted in the end.

Round the corner and behind a bush was a three-quarter

grown elephant which had been killed, providing a meal for sixteen lions, all bigger than any we had seen before. Kenneth identified these as the Savuti Pride, which were known for their size, and no others were considered large enough to tackle a fifteen-year-old elephant. We stayed upwind of them to avoid the appalling smell whilst they fed, paying no attention to us at all.

We were also treated to a ringside view of the mating game, the actual act of which occurs several times, in very quick succession, before the male is worn out. Whilst we were absorbed with this, another huge male got up and walked slowly and very deliberately towards us. I was sitting in the front passenger seat and Marion was in the seat directly behind Kenneth. I froze as he came right up to Marion with nothing between her and him, and it seemed all he had to do was put a paw up and pull her straight out. She started to edge her way inboard and I heard Kenneth whisper, 'Don't move, keep absolutely still.'

He came within two feet of her and lay down in the shade beside her. After a decent interval Kenneth gently drove off, having ascertained that his body was not actually touching the Land Rover and he was still asleep. Probably our hairiest moment ever – and certainly Marion's. A good topic of conversation at our farewell brunch, and a great note to leave Duma Tau on.

We now had a long flight back to Harare, having exited the country at Kasane, and arrived just as it was getting dusk.

Mike, the pianist at Wild Geese Lodge, was there to greet us, and said he had arranged for Rhett Butler to visit at teatime the following day. I had made Mike aware of my previous life as a rose grower when we first arrived, and he introduced me to a man I used to know in England who had pursued his love of roses by becoming Rose Adviser to the growers in Zimbabwe and Kenya. During our safari I had managed to get any ideas of growing roses in Africa out of my head, so the meeting was a straightforward social event, as was our meeting with Rhett the following day. In the light of subsequent events, how right that decision was! Paul came to see us the following day to debrief and say his farewells with expressions of hope that we would all do it again some other time.

CHAPTER XXXI

Pension Time

I had cheated slightly by having my last great African adventure a year early, but now that I had actually survived to my sixty-fifth birthday I felt I couldn't let the occasion go without some recognition. My love of pyrotechnics gave me the clue: a fireworks party – 'Bill's Big Bang'. My original intention was a small dinner party for close friends in the house followed by a firework display in the garden. I was fortunate that my birthday (November 8th) was always near to Guy Fawkes night, so holding this event in the middle of a town would not land us in trouble with the noise abatement society or any similarly politically correct organisation at that time of the year. Wrong again!

I wanted to send out forty invitations hoping to get acceptances from thirty or so of my close friends and colleagues. I allowed myself to be convinced that I was too curmudgeonly to have that number of friends who would come, so sent out seventy-two invitations and received sixty-nine acceptances! This was far more than we could accommodate in comfort so we had to hire a marquee, with an open viewing area on one end. My request to the fireworks contractor was for a 'miniature battle of Alamein with assorted star shells for good measure'. As this was quite a serious pyrotechnic display I arranged with the Cricket Club, whose ground adjoined ours, to have them all going off there, to comply with the safety regulations. The contractor was as excited as I was and his programme included rockets to fifteen hundred feet.

The marquee was erected the day before in beautiful

November sunshine and I set out all the tables and tablecloths that evening. We were going to have a hog-roast and were preparing all the rest of the food ourselves with an army of friends and helpers.

During the early hours of Saturday morning we were subjected to torrential rain and strong winds; I looked out of my bedroom window and saw the marquee had gone and all that was left was the tablecloths hanging in the trees. I remember thinking, That's enough then, and I opened the window and jumped out. As I hit the ground I woke up! Everything was in fact alright, it was all just a bad dream. Even so, heavy driving rain kept up all day. The weather was so bad that I couldn't have blamed anyone for chickening out; however not one person failed to turn up. It was lovely to see old friends and colleagues again; some of us hadn't met for over forty years.

Halfway through our dinner I had a call from the fireworks man to say that he couldn't set up anything, as the rain was just too heavy. He was, however, prepared to set all the primers in the dry and bring the cargo, fully primed at the last minute, provided my nerves would hold!

I replied, 'It's not my nerves but yours, you are driving it!'

'I'm game to risk it. If you see a gigantic explosion in the town you will know what has happened!' He also said, 'The moment I am ready we shall have to start.'

David gave a very humorous speech in which he likened me to Eeyore, which name has stuck ever since.

The fireworks were spectacular, so much so that in the twenty minutes it took to let them off we had two hostile visits from members of the public, and the police, who were present here, received eight calls asking if war had broken out! Once it was all over an air of anticlimax prevailed, and I couldn't help feeling, That's it, then.

Marion's father was still living with us and celebrated his ninety-third birthday. Marion was committed to full-time caring 24/7, although Social Services were as helpful as the law and circumstances allowed them to be. Quite soon after my birthday he had a spell in hospital during which he contracted MRSA; this eventually killed him some six months later. We were finally on our own now, but the loss of father-in-law's tax-free pension meant I still had to keep working in the south of England and Marion converted her very part-time job at the local garden centre to nearly full-time.

This living apart was not what we had planned for our old age but was the price to pay for my misdeeds in the past. It has also provided ample time for reflection and I am reminded of the sandwich-board evangelists of my youth proclaiming, 'Be sure your sins will find you out!' As it is, I have had a wonderfully interesting life and feel that I and all my generation have been lucky to be born when we were. We have all lived our adult lives in a war-free environment, thanks I am sure primarily to the invention of nuclear weapons and the doctrine of mutual deterrence. Not only have we lived free of major wars but also through a period of unprecedented change and economic stability. We came into a world of horses, steam and railways; lived most of our working lives with the benefits of the motor car and the aeroplane; and now we are witnessing the greatest change of all with the arrival and consolidation of the computer and the mobile phone.

However, for every plus there is a minus and whilst we may have seen the abolition of fascism and communism we now have an equally virulent form of evil dressed up as religious fanaticism.

England is still the finest country in the world to live in; why else does the whole world want to come here? Our public services may not live up to our expectations; the criminal justice system is virtually useless; rights may take precedence over responsibilities; but otherwise life has never been better.

We are far more racially tolerant than we were, and sexually far more liberal than certainly I was ever brought up to be; I feel I have missed out badly! Of all the insidious imports from abroad, the blame and compensation culture from America has been the most harmful, with the idea that nobody is responsible for their own actions. The flood of directives from Brussels mostly beggar belief, but it is our overzealous bureaucrats and lawyers who insist on following every detail who are the real villains. After all, the French don't seem to have too much of a problem ignoring what they don't like.

My task for the future is not to become a Victor Meldrew but to enjoy the company of my friends and family, and to count my many blessings in my beloved Norfolk.

Printed in the United Kingdom
by Lightning Source UK Ltd.
104034UKS00001B/65